Effective Writing
in Psychology

Effective Writing in Psychology

Papers, Posters, and Presentations

Bernard C. Beins and
Agatha M. Beins

Blackwell
Publishing

© 2008 by Bernard C. Beins and Agatha M. Beins

BLACKWELL PUBLISHING
350 Main Street, Malden, MA 02148-5020, USA
9600 Garsington Road, Oxford OX4 2DQ, UK
550 Swanston Street, Carlton, Victoria 3053, Australia

The right of Bernard C. Beins and Agatha M. Beins to be identified as the authors of this
work has been asserted in accordance with the UK Copyright, Designs, and Patents Act
1988.

First published 2008 by Blackwell Publishing Ltd

1   2008

Library of Congress Cataloging-in-Publication Data

Beins, Bernard.
 Effective writing in psychology : papers, posters, and presentations / Bernard C. Beins and
Agatha M. Beins.
     p. cm.
   Includes bibliographical references and index.
   ISBN 978-1-4051-5878-7 (hardcover : alk. paper) — ISBN 978-1-4051-5879-4 (pbk. :
alk. paper) 1. Psychology—Authorship. I. Beins, Agatha, 1976– II. Title.

   BF76.7.B45 2008
   808'.06615—dc22
                  2007030477

A catalogue record for this title is available from the British Library.

Set in 10.5/12.5pt Galliard
by Prepress Projects Ltd, Perth, UK
Printed and bound in Singapore
by Markono Print Media Pte Ltd

The publisher's policy is to use permanent paper from mills that operate a sustainable
forestry policy, and which has been manufactured from pulp processed using acid-free
and elementary chlorine-free practices. Furthermore, the publisher ensures that the
text paper and cover board used have met acceptable environmental accreditation
standards.

For further information on
Blackwell Publishing, visit our website at
www.blackwellpublishing.com

Contents

Preface

Mark Twain recognized the importance of effective writing skills when he said, "The difference between the right word and the nearly right word is the same as that between lightning and the lightning bug." We wrote this book to help writers generate their own version of lightning when they write papers, create posters, or develop presentations in psychology.

As we have taught courses in writing and in psychology (one of us for over a third of a century), we have become very aware how important it is for students and researchers to develop solid communication skills. No matter what type of professional work you undertake, it will be critical for you to convey your ideas well.

As you write and communicate in psychology, you will face challenges that some other types of writers do not. Writing in psychology involves two separate components. One concerns the ability to create clear and crisp prose that people want to read. The second relates to the ability to convey a compelling message in technical and scientific language. All too often, scientific writers understand their concepts exceedingly well, but they fail to present a message that readers can understand, appreciate, or even want to read. Here this book enters the picture. We present suggestions and guidelines that will help you create interesting papers and cogently delivered oral presentations that will capture the attention of others.

This book will help writers at all levels of experience and skill. Some components of the book are oriented toward effective writing and give tips that are relevant for communicating with many different readerships. Other components provide direction for successful use of writing in American Psychological Association (APA) style. By using both of these aspects of the book, first-time and experienced writers can be comfortable knowing that their words will have an impact and that their work will be recognized as of professional quality.

We have worked to make this book both accessible and useful. At the same time, we have made it rigorous because writing should be as clear and precise as it is interesting.

ORGANIZATION OF THE BOOK

The book begins with an overview of different kinds of writing and what makes writing for psychology different. In addition, we introduce some of the principles for developing credible arguments and effective communication, whether you are writing or speaking, or creating graphic presentations. We also introduce APA style, which is common in many of the behavioral and social sciences.

The book details guidelines on developing your own ideas and conducting Internet and library research to integrate them with issues that others have already addressed. The next focus of the book involves organizing your thoughts and beginning the process of writing and revising.

Following the chapters on effective communication strategies, we offer guidance on the technical aspects of writing a paper in APA style. In chapters 10 through 15, you will learn how to use APA style accurately and effectively. If you have not already discovered that APA style involves detail after detail, you will learn it here. But we explain those details in ways that will permit you to follow them as you need to.

We also recognize that not all scientific communication occurs through papers. Consequently, in the last section of this book, we offer strategies for creating poster presentations, giving oral presentations, developing Internet presentations and writing proposals for institutional review boards.

Finally, we have included a sample APA-style paper to help you write and format your own work. One of the unique features of the sample paper is that it contains annotated errors that writers frequently make. Seeing a paper that illustrates errors that you might make often helps your writing more than seeing flawless papers. If you don't know that you made a mistake, it is hard to know that you need to correct it.

FEATURES

We provide features in this book that we hope will make the process of writing more effective and efficient. First, we tell you not only what constitutes good writing, but why. As a result, you should be able to generalize the points beyond the specific examples we use. Furthermore, the examples in the book come from published research, which gives you a good sense of how effective writers convey their ideas.

Second, we use many tables and figures that illustrate specific guidance in many areas that pose problems for writers. Rather than simply listing formatting details, we have tried to bring them to life in ways that you will be using them.

Finally, as we noted above, we include examples of the types of errors students and researchers actually make. You can learn from the mistakes of others. The sample paper in the appendix includes stylistic and formatting errors that commonly occur so that you can see what to avoid.

Acknowledgments

A book is the product of its authors, but it also takes its final shape because of the contributions of others. For this book, we have benefited from the help of Linda Beins, a librarian extraordinaire with extensive insights into finding and developing information. We were also fortunate to have the keen eyes and intellect of Stephen F. Davis, Kenneth D. Keith, and Suzanne Baker, who provided us with feedback on early versions of the chapters. Finally, we are grateful for the consistent help of Chris Cardone, Executive Editor, and Sarah Coleman, Development Project Manager, two of Wiley-Blackwell's astute staff who have made this project as seamless as it could have possibly been.

Writing in Psychology

Write what matters. If you don't care about what you're writing, neither will your readers.

Judy Reeves

I'm not a very good writer, but I'm an excellent rewriter.

James Michener

When you write about psychology or any of the other sciences, you are telling a story about people. Scientists are people, complete with individual personalities, likes and dislikes and ordinary human qualities. The way they are affects what they do and how they do it. As such, "science writing is not so much about science, but about people—human problems and their solutions, curiosity and discovery" (Holland, 2007). In this book, you will learn how to convey your thoughts on the important problems and solutions in psychology.

It would be hard to overstate how important it is to write effectively. Writing constitutes one of the "3 Rs" of a basic education: reading, writing and 'rithmetic. In the world of business, success is dependent, in part, on effective writing. For high-level positions, "writing is a 'threshold skill' for both employment and promotion" (College Board, 2004, p. 3). In one survey, many companies noted that writing was important in hiring. One respondent asserted that, "in most cases, writing ability could be your ticket in . . . or it could be your ticket out" (College Board, 2004, p. 3). Potential employees who do not write well are unlikely to be hired and, if they are, are unlikely to be promoted.

Graduate school admission may also depend on writing effectiveness. Graduate programs routinely request essays as part of the application process. This writing is "often used to make final selections of students with similar GPAs and standardized test scores. If you are on the borderline of being accepted and the admissions committee could go either way, a sterling essay can increase your chances of success considerably" (American Psychological Association, 1997).

The type of writing that you learn in psychology provides the same skills that will help advance your career. You develop clarity and logic in your ideas, along with a style that will engage the reader. If you create such prose, you will attract the attention of possible employers and graduate school admissions committees, and you will effectively present your ideas in psychology.

WRITING IN PSYCHOLOGY

Most people find psychology interesting and are eager to learn more about it. But they do not want to fight through dull and meaningless writing. As writers, the biggest hurdle that we face involves turning complex, technical concepts into prose that others can appreciate.

Writing successfully is not easy. It requires knowledge of the topic we are addressing; judicious selection of the best words, phrases, and sentences; and editing and revising what we have composed. If there were a magical formula that we could use to generate good prose, everybody would succeed in communicating even complex and hard-to-understand ideas. If you have read the work of scientists, though, you will have discovered that, much of the time, scientific writing is dense and impenetrable. Many writers hide interesting concepts inside packages of dull prose.

On the other hand, people sometimes produce lively prose that may not convey the message accurately. Engaging, but deceptive, prose is no better than accurate, incomprehensible writing.

Fortunately, there is the desirable middle ground that Sigmund Freud and Williams James occupied, where prose was stimulating, not sleep inducing. Those of us who do not initially fall into this category can learn to communicate effectively. The purpose of this book is to help you find the path to better communication. If you are motivated, you can work on the skills you need to get your point across meaningfully and accurately.

HOW DOES PSYCHOLOGICAL WRITING DIFFER FROM OTHER KINDS OF WRITING?

If you are trying to write like a psychologist, your style will be unlike much of the writing that you have done in the past. When psychologists write professionally, they usually attempt to convey specific information with a great deal of precision, minimizing ambiguity and the possibility of misunderstanding. The adage to say what you mean and mean what you say is highly appropriate for technical writing. You want your reader to understand the points you believe are important, and you want the reader to know exactly what you intend to say.

In other forms of writing, the emphasis may be on crafting artistic prose. The writer attempts to impress the reader with both content and style. The words that Shakespeare wrote for Macbeth illustrate the point. Macbeth lamented that life "is a tale told by an idiot, full of sound and fury, signifying nothing." These poetic words convey Macbeth's despair. However, Shakespeare's style would not be appropriate for a scientist because the style of science is to be straightforward and unambiguous so the reader does not have to puzzle through the words to find meaning in them.

Psychologists often receive training in how to write objective, scientific papers. Unfortunately, the writing style is often "bloodless" (Josselson & Lieblich, 1996, p. 651), meaning that it is not particularly engaging. Sommer (2006) has encouraged psychologists to learn to write with color and style for lay audiences without sacrificing accuracy. But he also implied that the writing style in academic journals need not be dreary.

In scientific writing, we focus on the content of the message. The point is not to impress the reader with the prose, but to render the prose invisible while making the content foremost. This type of writing can be as difficult to do well as literary writing because you need to be concise without omitting important information; you need to choose your words carefully so they engage the reader without obscuring your point; you need to say enough to let your reader understand your message without being repetitive.

Another difference among the various types of writing is that, when we write scientifically or technically, we generally rely on a vocabulary specific to the topic at hand. Professionals understand this wording, but others are not likely to be as conversant with the terminology. This is one of the reasons that scientific writing has the reputation of being incomprehensible—you need to know the jargon. (The concepts are also complex and may be hard to understand, which does not help.) Actually, technical terms are helpful because they let us communicate complex ideas clearly in a few words, although if you do not know the meanings of the words, the prose is meaningless or, at best, difficult.

USING APA STYLE

A further difference between scientific or technical writing and less formal writing is that, in science, authors typically follow a specific format in preparing reports. In psychology, for instance, authors use guidelines that appear in the *Publication Manual of the American Psychological Association* (American Psychological Association, 2001), commonly just called APA Style. (Some other disciplines, such as sociology, education, and nursing, may also use APA style.) Research reports usually include six sections, as described in Table 1.1.

Most of the time, if a writer submits to a journal editor a manuscript that deviates from an expected style, the editor is not likely to reject the manuscript as unsuitable for publication. Instead, editors work with authors so that the final version of the manuscript is consistent with APA style (Brewer, Scherzer, Van Raalte, Petitpas, & Anderson, 2001). However, editors have commented that deviations from APA style often accompany problems with the content of a manuscript. So if you create a manuscript that fails to follow appropriate style, a reader who is familiar with (and used to) APA style may assume that you paid as little attention to your ideas as you did to the way you expressed them. In the workplace, employers have expressed similar sentiments, that poor writing reflects poor thought (College Board, 2004).

According to the research of Brewer et al. (2001) on the use and the importance of APA style, when writers depart from APA style, it is

Table 1.1
Typical Sections in an APA-Style Research Report

Section of the report	What the section contains
Title page	The title of the paper, the names of authors, and the affiliations of the authors
Abstract	A brief overview of the entire project of about 120 words
Introduction	The background and logic of the study, including previous research that led to this project
Method	Minute details of how the study proceeded, including descriptions of participants, apparatus, and materials, and what researchers and participants actually did during the study
Results	A detailed statement of the statistics and other results of the study
Discussion	What the results tell us about thought and behavior
Reference	Where to find the work cited in the paper that relates to the present study

likely to involve presentation of research results and references. So you should pay particular attention to these facets of your writing. If you write a paper in APA style that does not involve empirical research and data analysis, APA style can still apply. The structure of your paper is likely to have elements in common with the Introduction, Discussion, and Reference sections of a research paper, which we discuss in later chapters. Once you learn the basics of APA style, writing an effective paper might be easier than you anticipated because you will have a good sense of what belongs in a paper and where it goes.

As you write for a professional audience, keep in mind that readers are willing to be convinced with persuasive arguments, but you have to convince them. The approach to scientific writing is to present a series of logical arguments that follow from one another. At the end, your good logic is going to make a believer out of your reader. If we are going to accept the process of science, it means that when a writer offers a logical argument that is supported by good data, we should be willing to accept that argument.

MAKING A CREDIBLE ARGUMENT

The difference between scientific writing and other writing has to do with the nature of how psychologists attempt to persuade readers. In everyday life, if you want you to change somebody's mind about something, there are several ways of doing it. One is to appeal to authority. That is, by quoting an expert (i.e., an authority), you can often convince people to believe you. After all, experts know more than others in their field of expertise. Unfortunately, experts can be wrong.

You can also appeal to what "everybody" knows is true; some things are so obvious, they must be true. Unfortunately (again), there are some things that everybody knows to be true that simply aren't true.

You can also appeal to others' emotions. Politicians and advertisers do this all the time. Unfortunately (again), conclusions based on emotional appeals can make a person feel good about a decision that, ultimately, proves to be troublesome. Furthermore, such conclusions are often not very stable (Petty & Cacioppo, 1986).

We should not simply believe the experts (even though they are probably right more than they are wrong in their areas of expertise); they should have to convince us with logical arguments. We should not simply trust our senses (even though a lot of what we feel to be true has validity). We should not simply believe in what makes us feel good or reject what makes us feel bad; it should have logical validity.

When trying to convince your reader of your arguments, you should engage the reader in critical evaluation of your ideas. Research has revealed that persuasion based on logic and on attention to important details leads to greater and longer-term acceptance of an argument. This is the type of persuasion that you should strive for in your writing.

DIFFERENT TYPES OF COMMUNICATION

If you want to communicate with your audience, you need to know what your audience expects. Depending on whether you are writing, speaking, or presenting visually, your approach will differ somewhat, even if the underlying message is the same.

Written Communication

If you are writing a formal, APA-style research report, as you would for publication in a journal, your reader will expect a structured presentation with considerable detail. The advantage of such a written presentation is that your reader can go back and review the background you cite, review your methodology to make sure it is sound, evaluate your results to judge if they are appropriate, and see if your conclusions are justified from your results and if they relate to the ideas you presented in your introduction. A written document is a permanent document that the reader can go back to at will.

Professionals (including professors) expect the writing to be free from colloquial or informal expressions and to be entirely grammatical. You should choose your words carefully because they are lasting expressions of your ideas.

Oral Communication

In contrast, if you are delivering that same research in an oral presentation, you cannot possibly pack the same level of detail and expect your audience to understand your ideas. Working memory is limited to between three and seven chunks of information. So if you are talking to people in an audience, it does not make sense to introduce as many ideas as you would in writing; your audience cannot go back to review what you have already said. They are forced to listen to your ideas in the present.

In an oral presentation, you should limit yourself to three or four main points you want your listeners to remember. You can introduce minor points to help reinforce the major ideas, but your audience will have a hard time keeping the details in memory. Professional speakers suggest that you tell your audience what you are going to say, then say it, and finally tell them what you just told them. There is something to this philosophy, although in a research presentation, you should not be quite so simplistic. You should establish the framework of your presentation and repeat critical points when appropriate. Still, in the short period of time allotted to oral presentations, usually 10 to 15 min, you are limited in the amount of information you can convey, just as the audience is limited in its ability to comprehend your ideas.

Poster Presentations

Yet another medium of expression is visual. Increasingly, research conferences are relying on poster presentations for reporting research findings. In this form of communication, you present all your information in a small display that might be about 4 feet by 6 feet (i.e., 1.3 meters by 2 meters) in size. The dimensions vary from one conference to another, but the amount of space always seems to be smaller than you would want.

One of the worst things you can do is to fill the poster with text. Nobody wants to fight through a poster with endless strings of sentences. The viewer is typically interested in your main points. The use of tables, figures, bulleted points, and other eye-catching features is a good idea in a poster. During such a presentation, the author of the poster is typically present, so if viewers want to know more details than are available on the poster, they can simply ask.

So, for a poster, you should present the main points with as little text as you can get away with. Visual elements are often a more meaningful way to make your points accessible. The result is often more information than in an oral presentation, but less than in a complete APA-style research report. It helps that the researcher is present to clear up any misconceptions that arise because not all the information is available on the poster. Furthermore, if you are presenting a poster, you can create a handout that resembles an APA-style manuscript. In this way, interested people can get the gist of your research and can ask you any questions that come to mind right away. Then they can take your written handout and attend later to the level of detail they desire.

Internet Publishing

A relatively new option for communicating your ideas is through the Internet. Web presentations combine various features of traditional manuscripts and of visual displays, but there are some additional elements that foster effective communication. A web-based presentation allows easy use of visual elements that are often too costly to include in printed manuscripts. In addition, you can use hyperlinks with your text to refer the reader to related web material or to references.

A simple web page is fairly easy to create if all you need is to present text, figures or pictures, and hyperlinked text. It is helpful to know the code for the language of the web, HTML (HyperText Markup Language), but with the authoring software on the market, knowing HTML is not absolutely necessary. Fortunately, it is fairly easy to learn. You can even save word-processed documents in HTML format, although generating a well-formatted web page from a word processor can be tricky.

EFFECTIVE COMMUNICATION

A professor named Denis Dutton held a bad writing contest for a few years. The sentence that motivated him to begin the contest appears below; it was about an attempt at educational reform. The prose, which was not intended to be bad, was absolutely incomprehensible. (You should not feel bad if you don't understand it.)

> [It] would delegitimate the decisive, if spontaneous, disclosure of the complicity of liberal American institutions of higher learning with the state's brutal conduct of the war in Vietnam and the consequent call for opening the university to meet the demands by hitherto marginalized constituencies of American society for enfranchisement. (Dutton, 1999)

This book is an attempt to prevent you from writing such incomprehensible prose.

No matter what you choose as your medium of presentation, there are some characteristics of good communication to remember. First, you should establish your theme and organize your thoughts around it. Developing an outline or an idea map (as illustrated in chapter 2) can be very helpful. To create either requires that you know what you want to say. It is tempting sometimes to start writing without a coherent idea of your message. If you operate this way, your writing may meander toward irrelevant topics.

Second, if you want to communicate effectively, you should make sure that your grammar is flawless and that your selection of words is judicious. When your writing is technically competent, your reader will not be distracted from your message by having to figure out what you mean. You also need to go back to your work to edit and revise it.

It helps to re-read your work when it is not fresh in your own mind; sometimes you can spot problems that are not initially apparent. In addition, your writing may benefit if you ask somebody to read your work and explain to you what is unclear. Mark Twain recognized the importance of revising one's work: "The time to begin writing an article is when you have finished it to your satisfaction. By that time you begin to clearly and logically perceive what it is you really want to say."

Finally, it is important to remember that even lengthy manuscripts begin with a single sentence. In order to maximize the effectiveness of your writing, you should set up a schedule and a process. B. F. Skinner is a good example; he was an early bird, so he arose and did his writing for a few hours in the morning, a practice that he continued right up until his death.

HOW TO BEGIN

Find a place where you can concentrate free of distraction, at a time when you are clear-headed. If you are a night owl, that may be the best time for you to write; if you are an early-morning lark, that would be a good time. In either case, you should establish a routine. Writing does not happen until you do it. And when you develop your routine, remember to positively reinforce yourself. Identify a goal for your writing session and reward yourself when you reach it. So you might decide to explore and write about a given topic for 30 min. After 30 min, you should reward yourself with a break.

You may need to shape your behavior first, though, so you might need to start with a shorter work period, gradually extending it until you identify the longest period of time during which you can write effectively. Psychologists have identified a phenomenon called *post-reinforcement pause*. It refers to a period of time after a reinforcement when the animal (including the human animal) stops working toward another reinforcement (Felton & Lyon, 1966). You should make sure that your post-reinforcement pauses are not too lengthy.

By developing good writing habits, you will have taken the first step toward successful communicating. The task is often not easy, but the results are eminently satisfying.

In the next chapters, we will explore how you can develop your ideas, connect them to what others have already written, and express them in a style that reflects a sophisticated knowledge of psychology. In the end, you will have an impact on your audience when you write and when you speak about psychology.

Part I

Organizing and Developing Your Ideas and Writing

2

Formulating Your Ideas

It is not the answer that enlightens, but the question.

Eugene Ionesco

Somewhere, something incredible is waiting to be known.

Carl Sagan

IDENTIFYING YOUR FOCAL QUESTION

You have a paper due in two weeks. You have not started doing research. You do not even have a topic yet. What do you do? The purpose of this chapter is to offer guidelines for developing a research paper topic and thesis. We offer suggestions to help you identify a topic, use sources to narrow the topic, and develop your thesis in a way that meets academic standards.

When you start a psychology writing assignment, you might already have a specific question you want to answer or a specific set of studies to evaluate. However, if you need to generate your own idea and you're not sure what interests you, how do you choose an appropriate topic with an appropriate focus? First, examine the writing project parameters closely. What is the purpose of the project? What objectives do you need to achieve? Who is your audience? After reflecting on these questions, there are several ways you can go about narrowing your focus and developing a question through *pre-research* and *preliminary research*.

Pre-research refers to research you do before you have a focal question or even a general topic for your writing project. Preliminary research is the research that helps you narrow your focus once you have a general idea and gives you background information on your topic. Once you identify a viable focus for your writing project through pre-research and preliminary research, the next step is *focused research*. In focused research, you read and evaluate sources that you plan to incorporate into your paper. Although these three types of research seem distinct, the differences blur during the research and writing process. You will probably move back and forth between pre-research and preliminary research as you identify and narrow your focus. Furthermore, you may not use all the sources you find through focused research in developing your argument. Table 2.1 outlines distinctions between these three kinds of research.

In the preliminary research stage you should start establishing your *focus* and considering the *academic value* of your research questions and claims. The focus is the scope of your paper and is shaped by the assignment guidelines, how broadly can you explore the topic, and your intended audience. Each of these aspects will affect how you approach your writing. For example, the focus of a paper about communication between identical twins will be different for a 10-page and a 20-page paper; if you are writing about the topic for an encyclopedia, a class project, or *The American Journal of Psychology*; and if you are reporting your own original research or analyzing others' research.

Furthermore, you want to pick research questions that are not so broad that you end up with too much information to sort through, and you do not want your topic to be so narrow that you cannot find enough information. Think about the difference between the following two focal questions: (a) What is the best strategy for students who are trying to learn material for a test? and (b) Do students learn more by studying in a single, long session or in a series of shorter sessions? The first question might be useful when you are starting your pre-research because it is broad; however, because it is so broad it will be very difficult for you to answer thoroughly and meaningfully. Instead, you could use a question (a) to guide your pre-research to form a question more similar to question (b).

The academic value of a research topic is related to the kind of focus you frame, specifically regarding your audience: who are your paper's potential readers, why would or should they be interested in your topic, and is there any room for you to contribute something new or original to the topic. When you write an academic paper, you are taking part in an ongoing conversation among psychologists. Therefore, whether you are writing about your own original research or building on others' research, if you are able to approach your topic in a new way or to offer a thoughtful critique of existing scholarship, you can strengthen the academic value of your writing.

Table 2.1
Different Kinds of Research

Kind of research	Purpose	Activities
Pre-research	• To help choose a paper topic • To give you general information about potential topics	• Brainstorming lists of possible topics • Skimming through popular and scholarly sources to determine if there has been enough research related to a potential research topic • Slowly narrowing your focus to one or a few research questions about one topic
Preliminary research	• To gather a broad range of information about a particular topic • To determine what research questions have and have not been asked • To narrow your focus and start formulating a thesis	• Choosing the questions that seem the most viable as research topics • Reading through more scholarly sources to familiarize yourself with other research related to these topics • A combination of skimming sources and reading them more closely • Taking notes as you read sources
Focused research	• To give you in-depth knowledge about a particular research topic • To help you develop your thesis statement • To find sources that offer a variety of perspectives on your topic	• Reading scholarly sources that you plan on using in your paper • Reading sources closely and taking notes on the ideas in that source • Keeping track of citation information for each source

You never know when an interesting and meaningful idea will strike. Perhaps you will be watching the evening news on TV, sitting in class, reading a billboard sign, or overhearing a conversation. An idea that initially does not seem feasible might end up being the subject of an innovative thesis statement. Consequently, we suggest that you initially cast as broad a net as possible and that you start researching before you commit to or discard a topic.

LOCATING RELEVANT SOURCES

During your pre-research phase two sources that may be useful are the texts you have read in a class and the instructor teaching the class. Look through the class's assigned readings for a topic that interests you. Unless the instructor has specifically identified a source as unreliable or a topic as off-limits, these articles and textbooks could offer a number of possible paper topics. Additionally, your instructor is presumably knowledgeable about the topics covered in the class, so she or he can help you brainstorm research topics or questions. Although these sources—your textbooks and instructors—probably will not end up being references you cite in your paper, both can be useful in the pre-research stage, when you are still deciding which topic to explore.

During the process of choosing a topic, you might rely on both scholarly and popular sources. Popular sources, such as newspapers and magazines, will be useful because they provide brief overviews of scientific research. Journalists are writing for a lay audience, so they will present information in a way that is easy to understand, and you can probably identify the article's main idea easily. Remember, though, that popular sources tend to focus on controversy and may ignore important information if it is not sensational, so you need to verify through scholarly sources any ideas or topics you find in popular sources. This verification will also help you weed out studies that are pseudoscience or that fail to meet the standards of academic scholarship. (See chapter 3 for more information about finding and evaluating sources.)

Newspapers and general-interest magazines often have sections on science and health, so you can skim through several different issues to find out what research is newsworthy. Browsing through popular magazines that focus primarily on psychology, such as *Psychology Today*, might make your pre-research more efficient. If you do not subscribe to these publications, you will find that public and university libraries usually have a range of such newspapers and magazines. In many libraries you can also access Internet databases such as LexisNexis and Academic Search Premier. Through these databases you can plug in keywords (such as "abnormal psychology" or "subliminal advertising") or names of researchers and then skim through the results to see if any articles interest you.

Popular sources frequently relay very current information. Occasionally journalists will report on scientific work before the researchers have published an article in an academic journal. Even though you might not be able to find an academic study referred to in a newspaper or magazine article, one characteristic of academic scholarship is that it builds on previous research and writing. Consequently, if you come across a research topic in a popular source, you will most likely be able to find other research on this topic in academic journals.

If you are having trouble thinking of topics or finding resources on a specific topic, libraries can offer additional assistance in two ways. First, most libraries have one or more reference librarians; and some libraries make it possible for you to call or email questions to their librarians. Librarians are there for your benefit, so don't hesitate to contact one for help with your research.

Additionally, university libraries generally have links to Internet resources by topic or subject. For example, within the Rutgers University Library Web site, there is a subject research guide at the following URL: http://www.libraries.rutgers.edu/rul/rr_gateway/research_guides/research_guides.shtml. If you click on the topic "Psychology," you will be led to a series of links for resources such as citation indexes, electronic journals, psychology organizations, and career and professional resources. For some of the links, only Rutgers students have access; however, other links are open to the general public. If you are affiliated with a university, that university's library resources should be available to you.

Other Internet sources that might offer topic ideas are:

- http://www.lib.odu.edu/libassist/idea/ideas.php?s_id=7

This is a link to the Old Dominion University library. On this page there is a list of possible psychology topics that might be useful as key words when you search article databases and your library's book collection.

- http://library.sau.edu/bestinfo/alpha.htm

This link, from St. Ambrose University, connects you to series of Internet sites related to psychology and behavioral disorders, psychological effects of the Internet, psychology, psychology and multimedia issues, and psychology of sport.

- http://dmoz.org/

This third link, the Open Directory Project, leads you to an array of resources on a variety of topics, including psychology (listed under the

"Science" heading). Many of the links in the Open Directory Project will take you to professional, scholarly sources.

Preliminary research also entails locating scholarly sources. Because you need to use scholarly sources in an academic research paper, preliminary research is ideal for identifying a number of potentially relevant scholarly texts. Scholarly texts are those written by academics for other academics in that field. Thus, an encyclopedia entry on schizophrenia, because it is written for a general audience, is not a scholarly source, even though it may contain accurate information about schizophrenia. The scholarly sources you want to find are those that either report the results of original research or that develop an argument based on others' academic research. Generally, you will find these sources in academic, or peer-reviewed, journals.

We recommend library catalogs and article databases such as PsycINFO when you start searching for scholarly sources. The library catalog will offer results in print form: books located in the stacks, reference books, and occasionally government publications. To find journal articles about your topic, do not use the library catalog. There are too many journals for the library to enter all the citation information for each article in each journal issue. Besides, companies now offer article databases to which libraries purchase access. These companies catalog articles, and through the databases they create, you can search for articles based upon a variety of parameters: keywords, subject headings or descriptors, author's name, article title, and journal title. (See chapter 4 for more information about research techniques.)

As you search, you can develop a list of sources that might become part of your own research paper. As you transition from preliminary research (the research to help you develop a research question or hypothesis) to focused research (research for sources you will likely use as support), you will add to and revise this list. In the next two chapters we offer more detailed information about library and Internet research, so please consult those chapters as you look for credible sources.

RECOGNIZING MULTIPLE VIEWPOINTS

As you start a writing project, your attention will probably be divided between doing research, writing, adjusting your focus, and developing a thesis statement. In the writing process, each part is important and is integrated with the other parts. That is, your thesis statement will reflect your focus; your thesis statement and focus should be informed by the work other psychologists have conducted, which you find through research; and, of course, what you end up writing is shaped by research, your focus, and your thesis. Furthermore, as we have been emphasizing, this process is not linear. Rarely will scholars move from research to writing and then not conduct any more research, and rarely will the first version of a thesis statement be identical to the thesis statement in a final draft. The convolution of this process is due, partly, to the complexity of academic research topics.

Academic research topics are complex on several levels, and this complexity will shape how you write your paper as well as how you evaluate your sources. Because almost any focal question you pose will have more than one answer, you need to navigate those different responses and evaluate their strengths and limitations. Part of this evaluation involves analyzing the author's hypothesis, data, conclusions, and discussion sections because differences in the interpretation of results and the development of experiments can produce multiple perspectives about the same focal question. For example, although statistics might appear to represent research results in a straightforward manner, numbers can be manipulated or incorrectly interpreted, as chapter 8 shows. Furthermore, two scholars might interpret the same statistics in different ways, and both interpretations could appear to be logically sound. As writers have noted (e.g., Best, 2001, 2004), statistics are not simply objective facts; they are the results of decisions authors have made about how to generate them.

Rather than interpreting results differently, some psychologists might start their research with fundamentally different assumptions about an issue. For example, clinical psychologists have different perspectives about how to treat people with attention deficit hyperactivity disorder (ADHD). Although there is a general consensus that a combination of pharmaceuticals and therapy is most effective, there are different kinds of pharmaceuticals and different kinds of therapy, as well as different combinations of the two. The different assumptions that inform an experiment about treating ADHD will affect the kind of results a researcher obtains. Thus, as you read sources, pay attention to the way the authors set up their research as well as to how they interpret their results.

Despite the professional disagreements that psychologists (and scholars in all disciplines) might have, most professionals realize that a variety of perspectives is what allows scholarship to thrive. This dialogue is one that scholars engage each time they present a paper or poster at a conference, publish an article or book, or write a paper. They are taking part in a larger conversation about an issue, using disciplinary conventions to produce a credible argument that might help others who are researching the same topic.

Another layer of complexity in research relates to psychology as a discipline. Human beings are complicated animals. Thus, psychologists who try to explain human behavior rarely find that there is one simple cause of a behavior or that every instance of that behavior has the same cause. That is, behaviors have multiple causes, and what causes a behavior in one circumstance might not have that same effect in another.

To prevent oversimplifying human behavior, psychologists place quite narrow parameters around their conclusions, emphasizing that the results apply only to a specific population or that the results are valid only under certain conditions. Through these qualifications, psychologists are recognizing the difficulties of developing and supporting an argument. Consequently, when you read sources pay attention to the boundaries of the research and the researcher's conclusions. Slight variations in the constraints of different experiments can produce different results and conclusions.

The complexity of human behavior and the various possibilities for developing experiments and interpreting results produces a research situation in which you must combine your own background knowledge with other scholarly arguments to develop a thesis for your own writing. As you narrow your focus and choose a specific research question, evaluate different perspectives in the material you read.

ETHICAL WRITING

We begin this section with an excerpt from a scholarly source and a paragraph that attempts to paraphrase the scholarly source (this example is inspired by a University of Kent's psychology department Web page at http://www.kent.ac.uk/psychology/studying/studyskills/plagiarism.htm). In Figure 2.1 we will outline the mistakes in the paraphrased version and then offer a way to rewrite it, which is described in Figure 2.2.

Scholarly Excerpt

According to self-determination theory (Deci & Ryan, 1985, 1991) individuals who perform an activity out of choice and pleasure regulate their behavior in a self-determined manner. In contrast, individuals who participate in different activities out of internal and/or external pressures regulate their behavior in a non-self-determined fashion. Throughout the past two decades, much research has shown that self-determined motivation is a useful concept to understand human behavior (Senecal, Vallerand, & Guay, 2001, p. 177).

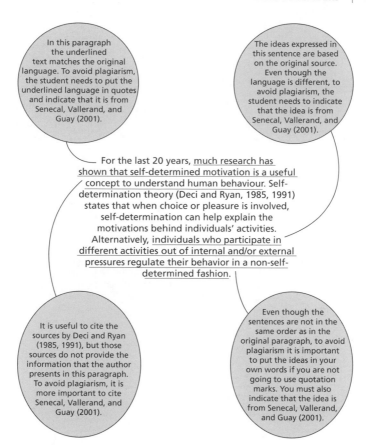

Figure 2.1 Avoiding plagiarism.

Attempted Paraphrase

For the last 20 years, much research has shown that self-determined motivation is a useful concept to understand human behavior. Self-determination theory (Deci & Ryan, 1985, 1991) states that, when choice or pleasure is involved, self-determination can help explain the motivations behind individuals' activities. Alternatively, individuals who participate in different activities out of internal and/or external pressures regulate their behavior in a non-self-determined fashion.

Paraphrase Rewrite

Senecal, Vallerand, & Guay (2001) draw from research done by Deci & Ryan (1985, 1991) for their own work on self-determination theory, which offers insight into the relationship between human activities and motivation. According to Senecal et al., when choice or pleasure is

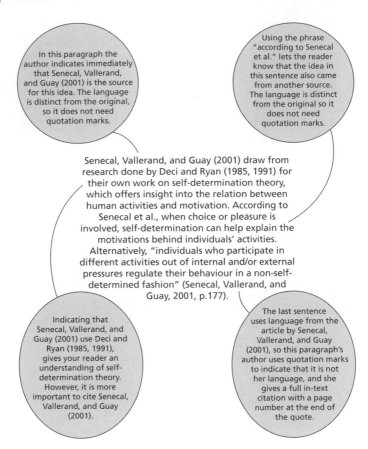

In this paragraph the author indicates immediately that Senecal, Vallerand, and Guay (2001) is the source for this idea. The language is distinct from the original, so it does not need quotation marks.

Using the phrase "according to Senecal et al." lets the reader know that the idea in this sentence also came from another source. The language is distinct from the original so it does not need quotation marks.

Senecal, Vallerand, and Guay (2001) draw from research done by Deci and Ryan (1985, 1991) for their own work on self-determination theory, which offers insight into the relation between human activities and motivation. According to Senecal et al., when choice or pleasure is involved, self-determination can help explain the motivations behind individuals' activities. Alternatively, "individuals who participate in different activities out of internal and/or external pressures regulate their behaviour in a non-self-determined fashion" (Senecal, Vallerand, and Guay, 2001, p.177).

Indicating that Senecal, Vallerand, and Guay (2001) use Deci and Ryan (1985, 1991), gives your reader an understanding of self-determination theory. However, it is more important to cite Senecal, Vallerand, and Guay (2001).

The last sentence uses language from the article by Senecal, Vallerand, and Guay (2001), so this paragraph's author uses quotation marks to indicate that it is not her language, and she gives a full in-text citation with a page number at the end of the quote.

Figure 2.2 Why plagiarism has been avoided.

involved, self-determination can help explain the motivations behind individuals' activities. Alternatively, "individuals who participate in different activities out of internal and/or external pressures regulate their behaviour in a non-self-determined fashion" (Senecal, Vallerand, & Guay, 2001, p. 177).

Whether intentional or unintentional, plagiarism is a very serious infraction. By *plagiarism*, we mean the use or representation of someone else's idea or information as your own. This can include

- summarizing someone else's idea without giving that person credit;
- using someone else's language without giving that person credit;

- using someone else's language without quotation marks, even if you give that person credit for the idea;
- taking work that someone else wrote for you and presenting it as your own.

However, scholars do not consider it plagiarism if you present information that is *common knowledge* without a citation. That is, if you offer information that you expect an average person would know, such as the temperature at which water freezes or who the fifth United States President was, then you can include that information without needing to cite any sources. However, the margins of common knowledge are not always clear. For example, if your audience is other psychologists, what is considered common knowledge might be different than if your audience is a group of sociologists. Whereas psychologists tend to know that John Watson was central in explaining human behavior through conditioning, sociologists might be less familiar with that knowledge, so you could include a specific reference to Watson's work if your readers are not psychologists.

We encourage you to become familiar with what is and isn't plagiarism not only because you may face severe consequences for plagiarizing, but also because including citations and references in your academic scholarship can strengthen your work. For example, if you are proposing that people who were spanked as children are more likely to spank their own children, drawing from other psychologists' credible, scholarly research that points to the same conclusion will increase the validity of your stance.

Referencing perspectives that might contradict your stance can benefit your work, too. Showing your audience that you are aware of and have evaluated research that presents different arguments or conclusions than yours indicates that you have explored multiple perspectives and still consider yours to be the strongest. So, revisiting the spanking example from the previous paragraph, if you were to make an argument about spanking, you could reference studies that do not find a connection between being spanked as a child and then spanking one's own children. Through this strategy, you might convince more readers of the credibility of your argument, and it is possible that addressing counterarguments may persuade someone who previously disagreed with your stance to reconsider its validity.

Here we hope to offer strategies for eliminating the chance that you might unintentionally plagiarize, and we hope this book provides you with resources and tools so that you do not even consider plagiarizing intentionally. You might unintentionally forget to cite a source when you are writing your paper, or you might have taken notes but forgotten to write down which source those notes are from. Regardless of your intentions, the first example is plagiarism and the second could become plagiarism. Consequently, preventing plagiarism starts when you are in the preliminary research phase and continues through the research and writing process.

Each time you take notes, you want to be able to connect those notes to a specific source. There are different systems you can use to do this, and through your own research and writing you can develop a system that works best for you. For some people, recording a source's complete citation information and then writing notes keeps everything in one place and makes it less likely that either the citation or the notes will be lost or separated. Almost all library catalogs and search engines allow you to email or print citations, and through some article databases you can email or print out entire articles. However, should you email or print citations, you then need to figure out how to connect the citations with your notes about that source. If you will be using a number of sources, programs such as EndNote (a computer program that helps a writer keep track of research and sources) can help you record your sources and connect them to your notes.

What we want to emphasize, though, is the importance of keeping track of your sources at the initial research phases and throughout your writing project. Not only can this strategy prevent plagiarism—intentional or unintentional—it can also be more efficient in the long run. There are few things as frustrating as knowing you've summarized, paraphrased, or quoted a source but not knowing which source it is, which causes you to spend time reading through sources or even revisiting the library to get a source you had already returned.

3

Assessing Your Sources

In all affairs it's a healthy thing now and then to hang a question mark on the things you have long taken for granted.

Bertrand Arthur William Russell

The most erroneous stories are those we think we know best—and therefore never scrutinize or question.

Stephen Jay Gould

Imagine that you have been diagnosed with an illness and need treatment. How do you find out what treatment is the best for your condition? Would you be more likely to trust a doctor or medical student? Or would you trust advice from someone who was diagnosed with and recovered from the same illness? Would you choose a drug regimen based on a television advertisement or an Internet pop-up ad?

Although writing a paper generally is not a matter of health or sickness, there may be some parallels between your decision about treating an illness and using a source in your paper. Consider the following questions: Where does the information come from? What kind of credibility does the person presenting the information have? Are there ways that you can find out more about this information? Who is telling you the information and what kind of credibility does the source have? Credibility, the central concept of this chapter, can be a useful yardstick for evaluating sources, for the greater your sources' credibility, the more confident you can be in the information they contain. In an academic paper, credible sources also strengthen your own credibility as a writer.

There is a variety of different kinds of sources, and they can shape your research and writing in various ways. We hope that this chapter will give you some tools for evaluating the sources you encounter. This process involves determining not only the credibility of the source but also what biases or assumptions shape the information in a credible source.

THE DIFFERENCE BETWEEN PRIMARY AND SECONDARY LITERATURE

Before going into the specificities of popular and scholarly sources, we think it important first to distinguish between primary and secondary literature. Primary literature is the publication of an investigator's own research. That is, when a researcher works with human participants through experiments or interviews or directly with archival material (e.g., letters, films, literature, popular cultural artifacts), the publication will constitute primary literature. These kinds of publications will introduce the research, describe the methodologies used, present the research results, analyze and interpret the results, and include references to the sources that shaped the research.

Secondary sources, however, are those that are based upon primary publications. Scholars often write articles that are based upon experiments and research that they themselves have not conducted. Although it is a secondary publication, these authors still may be making original contributions to their field. By putting a set of sources or studies in conversation with each other, authors of scholarly secondary sources are offering an analysis of other authors' analyses, which can help readers understand primary literature in a new way.

THE DIFFERENCE BETWEEN POPULAR AND SCHOLARLY SOURCES

When researching for psychology papers, regardless of your topic, you must use scholarly sources to support your argument. Popular sources address a general audience, so they present fewer details and less technical material about the research. As such, they provide a less thorough picture of the research than a scholarly article does. As a result, for professionals, popular articles are less credible than scholarly ones. Because it is important that you draw upon credible and rigorous—and thus scholarly—sources in academic writing, we offer the following criteria to distinguish between popular and scholarly sources. Each subsection starts with questions that you can ask when evaluating a source.

Who is the Author? Is the Author an Academic or Professional who is Writing about Research that He or She Conducted? How Many Authors are Listed?

For scholarly sources, the authors are usually academic researchers. If the text is a primary scholarly source, the authors are also the researchers who are reporting the results of their original experiments. In scientific disciplines, because several researchers may work on an experiment, scholarly articles often have more than one author. Popular sources occasionally have more than one author listed, although it is more common for popular articles to have one author, and for some articles no author is listed. Consequently, the absence of an author's name is a good sign that you have a popular source. When a popular source does list an author, the author's academic and professional background is frequently in journalism. That is, the person who writes an article in *Newsweek* about sibling rivalry will most likely be a journalist, not a psychologist who does behavioral research. However, the authors of an article about sibling rivalry in *The British Journal of Developmental Psychology* will be the people who actually conducted the research.

Who is the Audience? Does the Reader Require Technical Knowledge to Understand the Information in the Source?

The authors and readers of scholarly sources tend to be academics, therefore, authors whose publications are scholarly expect that their peers will read the publications. Thus, the authors construct a well-supported and logical argument, and they write so that a professional audience will understand their ideas.

An article about the same topic that appears in a popular source will be written differently because it is aiming at a different audience. A lay audience—or an amateur audience—composes the readership of popular sources, so, although popular publications may be about a specific subject (such as psychology, economics, movie stars, sports, computing, and technology), these publications will not assume that their readers have a highly technical knowledge of the subject. For this reason, authors of popular sources use language that makes the research methods and results accessible to those who are not experts in the field. Of course, people who are academics or professionals might read popular sources, but the reverse is improbable: those untrained in a specific field are unlikely to read that field's scholarly sources.

In what Kind of Journal did your Source Appear? What Kind of Editorial Process did the Source go Through Before Being Published?

Many scholarly journals use a system of peer review. In this system, journal editors rely upon reviewers who are knowledgeable in the journal's academic area to assess the merit of articles that are submitted for publication. Peer reviewers will read the submissions at various stages in the publication process, often offering comments, asking questions, and making suggestions to ensure that the journal publishes sound and accurate research results. Sometimes reviewers even recommend that the investigators conduct more research to strengthen their conclusions. Some databases, such as PsycINFO, are devoted largely to cataloging scholarly publications, and PsycINFO, like some other databases (e.g., Academic Search Premier), allows you to limit your search results to peer-reviewed publications.

In contrast, editors of popular publications want a general audience to be able to understand the content of an article, so they will make sure that jargon is omitted or carefully explained. Although they also go through fact-checking procedures, they will most likely not be able to evaluate the researchers' accuracy or credibility because they are not familiar with the conventions of the field. Therefore, using popular sources to support your thesis may actually weaken the credibility of your paper, rather than strengthen it.

What Additional Features Does the Source Have?

Some features of scholarly publications are an abstract, tables and/or charts that display research results, sections dividing the article (such as "Method" and "Results"), and a listing of works cited. Articles organized as described are likely to be scholarly.

Some scholars in the humanities rely heavily on popular sources for their scholarly work; however, they usually use popular sources as texts to be analyzed critically rather than as authoritative voices that lend credibility to their arguments. Thus, you do not want popular sources to be the only or the primary support for your thesis.

EVALUATING SOURCES

Whether a source is popular, scholarly, or in the gray area between the two categories, it is vital that you consider the credibility of the information presented, specifically in relation to your research project. Many popular sources report scientific studies and, although their reporting might be factually accurate, it might not be complete. Additionally, all scientific studies will have some biases and will be based upon certain assumptions. Thus, we encourage you to read all sources critically, even those that appear in academic journals and books. In the following sections, we will outline some guidelines for evaluating a variety of sources you might encounter.

Much of the popular press is a for-profit industry. Magazines and newspapers exist to make money. To a great extent, this objective shapes editors' decisions about what to include, what to exclude, and how to present what is included. For this reason, there are popular print publications that focus on specific issues (such as *Sports Illustrated* and

Rolling Stone) to increase sales. Additionally, publications target specific audiences. So, although *Time* and *Newsweek* cover similar issues, *Time* generally targets a more conservative audience and *Newsweek* a more liberal one. Because of differing audiences, then, articles about the same topic might offer slightly different information or reveal different biases.

A for-profit status also affects the way authors present information in an article. Editors want to catch the attention of readers, so they will place the most sensational or provocative information in the headline or first paragraph. This structure of writing is called pyramid writing, and journalists use it because they know that most people won't read to the end of the article. If 100% of readers read the headline, only 70% will read the introductory paragraph, and only 50% will read through to the fourth paragraph (O'Connor, 2002, p. 117). In popular sources, journalists frequently place the most titillating information at very beginning of the article. The qualifications that some results do not reinforce a certain conclusion, or that more research is needed to confirm a hypothesis, are often brief and appear only at the end of the article.

Because of the desire to provoke readers and sell more issues, popular sources can sometimes publish pseudoscience. What is pseudoscience? Literally, the word means "fake science"; however, it is not subject to a simple or easy definition, and there are some guidelines you can use to determine whether or not a study is pseudoscience. You cannot merely state that real science is neutral and objective whereas pseudoscience is biased and subjective. Nor can you always argue that real science follows the scientific method, but pseudoscience is sloppy. And you also cannot argue that pseudoscience results from a specific political agenda, and real science is separate from politics. So, what makes some areas "fake" and others "real"?

In pseudoscience, as with science, you want to evaluate the content of a study and the publication in which the study appears. If you can determine that the study is published in a scholarly source, this is one indication that it is less likely to be pseudoscience.

Additionally, a working knowledge of logical fallacies can be useful for separating science from pseudoscience. The phrase *logical fallacy* refers to a position that is logically untenable. In other words, the writer uses unsound thinking to support a hypothesis, which can lead to an invalid conclusion. There are a number of different logical fallacies, but we will describe only those more relevant to identifying pseudoscience in Table 3.1. You can find a more detailed exploration of logical fallacies at: http://www.fallacyfiles.org/.

Table 3.1
Logical Fallacies

Fallacy	How it works	Example
Emotionally loaded terms	Appeals to a reader's emotions without using logic or other support to back up the argument	If you really cared about children, you would vote for the pro-life candidate
Bandwagon fallacy	Argues that, because everyone else thinks or acts a certain way, the reader should as well	The candidate won with a huge majority of votes, so she must be very qualified
Faulty cause and effect	Sets up a cause–effect relation without support that the two events are causally related	As more homes have televisions, literacy rates have decreased; therefore, an increase in televisions causes a decrease in literacy rates
Either/or reasoning (also a black and white fallacy or false dichotomy)	Presents a situation as having only two alternatives	Either aggression levels are biologically determined or they are caused by environmental factors
Hasty generalization	Develops a conclusion or rule based on only an individual case or a few cases	This study shows that college students scored well on the test; therefore all 18- to 21-year-olds would score well

The presence of a logical fallacy does not necessarily invalidate all the work a scientist has done in a study; however, fallacies should be warning signs that there might be other weaknesses in the research. Other items to look for when evaluating a source's credibility are unexplained or unacknowledged contradictions, persuasion with creative language rather than valid evidence, the presence of jargon that other scientists do not use, and the lack of reliable sources that support the hypothesis and conclusion.

There are numerous web sites that explore various kinds of pseudoscience. Some examples are:

- http://physics.syr.edu/courses/modules/PSEUDO/moller.html
- http://www.quackwatch.org/01QuackeryRelatedTopics/pseudo.html
- http://www.softpanorama.org/Skeptics/index.shtml
- http://www.lhup.edu/~dsimanek/philosop/creation.htm

EVALUATING INTERNET SOURCES

For a paper about serial killers, the following four sources are relevant:

1. Wikipedia has an entry on serial killing at http://en.wikipedia. org/wiki/Serial_killer.
2. Through Google Scholar you found an article titled "Predicting serial killers' home base using a decision support system" by David Canter, Toby Coffey, Malcolm Huntley and Christopher Missen in *Journal of Quantitative Criminology*.
3. Through PsycINFO you found "Critical characteristics of male serial murderers" by William B. Arndt, Tammy Hietpas, and Juhu Kim in *American Journal of Criminal Justice*.
4. A Yahoo search with the key words "serial killer psychology" connected you to a page on the Crime Library's web site: http:// www.crimelibrary.com/serial_killers/index.html.

Which source(s) will be useful and credible? Which source(s) would increase your reader's confidence in your ideas? Use the following points to assess the sources according to how useful they would be for an academic paper on serial killers.

- Using sources written by psychologists for psychologists may strengthen the credibility of your paper.
- Using sources that are NOT written by psychologists for psychologists may indicate to your reader that you were too lazy to look for scholarly sources.
- Using sources whose content is not peer reviewed and that do not cite references may weaken the credibility of your paper.
- Using a source that is not peer reviewed and does not have references may contain accurate information and still not meet the standards of academic credibility.

Anyone with access to a computer, time, and the ability to make a Web page can place information on a personal Web site. Because of this, you want to be particularly alert when you encounter a Web site that is not part of an already established academic journal. However, do keep in mind that many academic journals make their content available through article databases such as PsycINFO.

In general, the five areas you want to explore when getting

information from Web pages are accuracy, authority, objectivity/advocacy, currency, and coverage. We briefly explain these categories in Table 3.2 and illustrate how they can be used to determine the validity of online information.

For some Web sites an organization or sponsor claims authorship, rather than a single author. In this case, you want to ask the same questions you would of a single author. If it is not possible to determine who sponsors the site, you can try truncating the URL (the Web page address) by deleting the part of the address to the right of the leftmost single backslash and then hit "enter." This should take you to

Table 3.2
Evaluating Internet Sources

Evaluation category	Questions to ask
Accuracy	Can you verify any of the information from your own experience and does the information seem consistent with other sources you have found? Are there references or links indicating the source(s) of the information? Are you able to access the references cited, either through the library or through the Internet, and do those sources seem credible? Does the site conform to standards of academic English and grammar?
Authority	Who is taking credit for the information on the site? Is there an author listed on the site? If an author is not listed, why? What kinds of credentials does the author have that makes him or her qualified to write about this topic? Are you able to contact the author or find out other background information?
Objectivity or Advocacy	What kind of site is this (e.g., entertainment, business, reference, news, advocacy, or personal), or what is the site's purpose? What is the site's domain (e.g., .com, .gov, .edu, .org, .net, .mil, or a country code such as .uk)? How might the site's purpose affect the kind of information it includes or excludes? Does the site present different perspectives?
Currency	When was the information put on the site and when was it originally written? What is the copyright date and when was the page was last updated? Are the links from the page still current?
Coverage	Does the author present information in a fair and comprehensive manner? Are perspectives other than the author's acknowledged and addressed? What kind of tone does the author use? How does the author treat ideas that conform to or differ from the author's perspective? Whose perspectives and voices are included and excluded? What kinds of outside support does the author use?

the home page and give you more information about the sponsoring organization.

For example, take the following address, which leads you to a site with information about evaluating web sites: http://www.vuw.ac.nz/staff/alastair_smith/evaln/evaln.htm. Truncating it to the left-most single backslash will give you the URL http://www.vuw.ac.nz, which is the home page for Victoria University of Wellington, New Zealand. Knowing that this is an educational site, rather than a commercial or personal one, gives you information that can help determine the purpose of the information on the page.

Determining the source and purpose of the information on the site can highlight some of the possible biases or assumptions that shape the information on the site. Each of the following pages contains information about ADHD, but each has a different purpose, as Table 3.3 indicates. To practice evaluating Web sites, apply the criteria outlined in Table 3.2 to the following links:

- http://www.weitzlux.com/adhd/adderall/ritalin/sideeffectsresearch_156855.html is a page for a law firm;
- http://www.pbs.org/wgbh/pages/frontline/shows/medicating/drugs/ is part of a public television series about medicating children;
- http://www.adhdinfo.com/info/parents/about/par_understanding_adhd.jsp?from=adhd&checked=y is part of the web site for a pharmaceutical company Novartis;
- http://www.nimh.nih.gov/studies/studies_ct.cfm?id=2 is part of the National Institute of Mental Health's Web site.

Knowing the purpose of a site's existence can point to the possible biases or assumptions that shape the site's content. For example, although the third URL does not contain a company's name, a pharmaceutical corporation called Novartis sponsors the site. Although Novartis ultimately wants to sell pharmaceuticals, the information is not necessarily inaccurate; however, it could mean that some facts are highlighted whereas others are deemphasized. Knowing this will help you ascertain the credibility and accuracy of the information on the site.

Asking the questions we have offered in this chapter—both for popular and scholarly sources and for Web sites—will help you identify some biases or assumptions. You might also find some ideas or perspectives that have been left out or with which you disagree. Noting these limitations will not only help you determine the kind of source

Table 3.3
Web Pages, Advocacy, and Coverage for ADHD

URL	http://www.weitzlux.com/adhd/adderall/ritalin/sideeffectsresearch_156855.html
Host/author	Weitz & Luxenberg, PC, a personal injury law firm
Site's purpose	To find potential clients for the law firm, which is a for-profit business
Possible limitations of the site	This site offers information about attention deficit hyperactivity disorder (ADHD), specifically about the dangerous side-effects of drugs used to treat ADHD. Although the medical information on this site might be accurate, because the site does not provide information about the benefits of pharmaceuticals used to treat ADHD, the coverage is weakened. Therefore, any arguments you make about treating ADHD should draw information from sources that are independent of this Web site
URL	http://www.pbs.org/wgbh/pages/frontline/shows/medicating/drugs/
Host/author	The Public Broadcasting Service (PBS), a non-profit media project
Site's purpose	PBS is an educational resource without corporate affiliations. It advertises itself as a resource that "uses the power of noncommercial television, the Internet, and other media to enrich the lives of all Americans through quality programs and education services that inform, inspire and delight" (PBS, 1995–2007)
Possible limitations of the site	The information on this specific page has been put together through *Frontline*, a public affairs series that PBS sponsors. This site is an informative one, and because it is not affiliated with an organization that has a specific political or business agenda it should offer a variety of information, representing different perspectives about treating ADHD. However, PBS is a popular source with a lay audience. Although it references scientific studies and interviews scientists, it does not present the studies themselves. Furthermore, PBS relies on monetary support from viewers, so, like a newspaper or magazine, it may foreground more sensational or controversial information. Therefore, any arguments you make about treating ADHD should draw from scholarly sources as well, and you want to make sure you read any articles mentioned on this site in their entirety
URL	http://www.adhdinfo.com/info/parents/about/par_understanding_adhd.jsp?from=adhd&checked=y
Host/author	Novartis Pharmaceuticals Corporation

Table 3.3
Continued.

Site's purpose	The purpose of this site is to inform care-givers about their options for treating a child with ADHD. Because Novartis is a for-profit company that manufactures and sells pharmaceuticals, one purpose of this site is to present pharmaceuticals as an attractive option for treating ADHD
Possible limitations of the site	Because Novartis ultimately wants to sell pharmaceuticals, they are more likely to include information that shows the benefits of drugs like Ritalin for children diagnosed with ADHD. This site also offers information about therapy and behavioral management as treatment options; and it has links to a number of non-profit and scientific organizations (such as the American Psychological Association), which increases the strength of its coverage. However, because it is a popular source that targets lay people, any arguments you make about treating ADHD should draw from scholarly sources as well
URL	http://www.nimh.nih.gov/studies/studies_ct.cfm?id=2
Host/author	The National Institute of Mental Health (NIMH), which is a part of the National Institutes of Health (NIH)
Site's purpose	The NIMH Web site states that "The NIMH mission is to reduce the burden of mental illness and behavioral disorders through research on mind, brain, and behavior" (NIMH, 2005). The purpose of the NIMH Web site is to provide information related to mental health issues
Possible limitations of the site	This site has links to a wide variety of information, and its informative purpose indicates that, like the PBS site, you would find useful coverage of different perspectives about ADHD. Additionally, the site links to resources such as scholarly publications—although the publications are not part of the NIMH site—which strengthens the site's credibility. Nevertheless, the information is directed to a lay audience, so this site alone would not provide sufficient evidence to support a scholarly argument

you have found, it will also give you insight into the credibility and validity of the author's (or authors') argument. However, remember that all research is based on biases and assumptions and that almost any area of psychology will have reputable scholars who disagree about the best methodology or hypothesis, or how to interpret results. Thus, identifying limitations does not necessarily mean that the source is invalid. Rather, it may have strengths you can draw on and weaknesses that you should spot.

4

How to Conduct a Literature Search

A library, to modify the famous metaphor of Socrates, should be the delivery room for the birth of ideas—a place where history comes to life.

Norman Cousins

Learn from the mistakes of others—you can never live long enough to make them all yourself.

John Luther

Consider the argument that "The female brain is a machine built for connection" because "of eons of evolution that allowed women to tell what their pre-verbal infants needed and predict what bigger, more aggressive males were going to do" (Weise, 2006 p. 9d). Do you believe that women and men have different kinds of brains or that giving birth and nursing produces a "mommy brain" (Weise, 2006 p. 9d)? How would you evaluate the credibility of these claims? The short answer is research. If you were going to describe this phenomenon for your friends, you might do a Google search or look for information on Wikipedia. For an academic paper—because your audience is an academic audience—you need more reliable sources, and to find those sources you would conduct a literature search, that is, a search for material written by professionals. Table 4.1 outlines some additional purposes for and benefits of doing a literature search.

Because the sources you find may end up as references in your paper, you want to use search engines—such as the library book catalog and article databases—that catalog scholarly sources. In this chapter we offer suggestions for doing literature searches more efficiently, specifically regarding the resources you can find through your school's library, and different techniques for using search engines.

Table 4.1
Conducting a Literature Search

Purpose of a literature search	How this helps your research
Identify studies related to a topic	• Prevents you from repeating research that has already been done • Familiarizes you with common theories and different perspectives • Shows your reader the extent of your research
Identify key studies related to a topic	• Using key studies in your paper can strengthen your credibility • Missing key studies can weaken your credibility
Identify gaps related to a topic	• Helps you develop a thesis that offers new insight into the topic • Enables you to consider participant populations that have not been studied by psychologists
Identify methods that others have and have not used	• Helps you develop your own methodology • Helps you find gaps in published research that your research can address
Show the value of your research	• Using existing scholarly sources lets your reader know that other psychologists have found the topic to have academic merit
Identify useful directions for future research (and for your own research)	• Scholarly sources often discuss what their research does not do; from these discussions you can develop an innovative thesis for your own research

UNDERSTANDING LIBRARY RESOURCES

The idea that libraries only store and lend books oversimplifies the role that a library can play in your research. With advancements in communication and information technologies, libraries offer access to much more than print publications. Libraries, especially those that are a part of a college or university, subscribe to article databases that catalog the contents of scholarly journals, newspapers, and magazines. Additionally, academic libraries often have research resources, such as subject reference guides and links to Web-based information.

Using Search Engines
A search engine is a tool for finding something. The library catalog has a search engine so that you can find books; in databases such as PsycINFO and LexisNexis, search engines enable you to find articles;

and Internet search engines such as Google, AltaVista, and Lycos catalog Web pages. Because academic papers need support from scholarly
sources, we recommend that you rely more heavily on the library catalog and article databases that catalog academic research.

Different search engines may look different, and there may be differences in the kinds of searches you can perform; however, search
engines often share one important characteristic: they recognize certain
search engine commands, such as *and, or, near,* and *not.* When you use
one of those commands, you are telling the search engine to limit the
results in a specific way, and skillful use of these commands can make
your research more efficient. See Table 4.2 for a list of different search
engine tools and how they may be used in a search.

Academic Journals

Generally, you will find the most current research in psychology published in academic journals. Journals have editing processes designed
for rapid publication, and because an individual journal article is much
shorter than a book researchers are able to write journal articles more
quickly than book-length manuscripts. Therefore, journals are useful
for familiarizing yourself with recent developments.

If a database such as PsycINFO catalogs an academic journal, there
is a good chance that you will be able to access an article in that journal. However, we want you to be aware of the limits of using journal
articles that you can access only through the Internet. Firstly, many
journals have a lag time between the date when an issue is published
and the date when the contents of that issue are available through
article databases. If your library subscribes to that journal, the most
current issue will be in the current periodicals section. You will not be
able to check out the journal, but you will be able to photocopy an
article from it. Second, even though some references may result from
an article database search, you may be able to access only the citation
information and abstract for the article because the article is either too
recent or too old to have been digitized. Nevertheless, if your library
subscribes to the journal, you will be able to find it in the library stacks
and photocopy the article. Instructions for learning if your library subscribes to a journal are in Box 4.1; Figure 4.1 shows you how to read
the information in a library catalog journal citation.

Library Books

Although books may not be as current as journal articles, the length
of a book enables it to explore a theme or area of research in depth.
In your paper you will probably cite more articles than books, but we

Table 4.2
Using Different Search Engine Tools

Search tool	What the search tool does
Quotation marks	If you enclose a phrase within quotation marks, your search results will contain that exact phrase (e.g., "mental health"), whereas the same search terms without quotation marks will give you results that have the word "mental" somewhere and the word "health" somewhere else
Truncation	Truncation enables you to find sources that contain words that begin a certain way. For example, if you are interested in constructivist theories in psychology, then searching for the term construct* will bring up search results that also include the words constructive, constructivism, and constructivist
And	Using "and" enables you to search for sources that contain both one term and another term (e.g., "memory" and "word recognition")
Or	Using "or" enables you to search for sources that contain one term or another term. For example, if you are interested in adolescent psychology, it might be useful to search for "adolescent or teenager"
Not	Using "not" enables you to search for sources that do not contain a word or phrase. For example, if you are interested in memory and want to search for studies that only use human participants, it may be useful to add "not rats" when you search. Doing this will ensure that studies involving rats are not included in the search results (although other nonhuman animals may be included).
–	In addition, using a minus sign in Google will exclude the word following the minus sign
…	This feature (three dots) searches for a range of numbers. So if you wanted to know about treatment for depression from 1930 to 1950, you could search for "treatment depression 1930…1950"
~	Using the tilde (~) tells Google to search for words similar to the one you enter into the search engine
Link	Using this word tells the search engine to look for Web pages that contain a link to a Web site of interest to you. So typing "link:www.ithaca.edu" will result in a listing of Web sites that reference www.ithaca.edu, the Web site of Ithaca College

encourage you to include a library catalog search when you look for scholarly sources. Figure 4.2 describes how to read the information in a library book citation. We will briefly discuss the characteristics and uses of textbooks, edited collections, and books that present an author's own cumulative research.

In psychology, many books are published as textbooks. Textbooks are useful when starting a literature search because they contain a large amount of information and because the information is generally

Box 4.1 Performing a Journal Search in a Library Catalog

Library catalogs list only the titles of journals and newspapers they receive, so you cannot search for individual articles. Therefore, you can use the library catalog to find out if the library subscribes to a particular journal or magazine, either electronically or in print form.

1. Go to the library's catalog search page.
2. Type in the journal title (for example *Political Psychology*). Note that if a journal begins with the word "The" you should not include it in the title.
3. When specifying the search category, make sure that you choose a journal or periodical title, not a book title or general keyword search.
4. Locate the journal using the information in the Location and Holdings sections.

Figure 4.1 shows a sample journal citation with information about the different parts of the citation and how to find the journal.

credible. Although textbooks do not contain primary literature (the publication of original research), as you read them you will find references to primary literature that will help you develop your own research project. In other words, you will be able to read summaries of psychologists' research, and from those summaries you can identify which studies you would like to read.

The textbook *Health Psychology: An Introduction to Behavior and Health*, 6th ed. (Brannon & Feist, 2006) offers information about posttraumatic stress disorder and other health-related issues. In contrast, the book *Posttraumatic Stress Disorder: Malady or Myth* (2003) by Chris Brewin, a clinical psychologist, explores the possible causes of posttraumatic stress disorder and its relation to memory and identity. Although both texts address posttraumatic stress disorder, in the textbook the authors do not go into as much depth about the disorder as Brewin does. Therefore, the book by Brewin gives you a more complete picture of posttraumatic stress disorder than the textbook would.

Finally, there are edited books in which different authors write separate chapters. These books focus on a theme that the different essays explore, and they often present a variety of perspectives about that theme. For example, *Posttraumatic Stress Disorder: Issues and Controversies* (2004) edited by Gerald M. Rosen contains 12 chapters, each with a different author. In this book, two chapters explore risk factors: "Risk Factors and the Adversity–Stress Model" and "Risk Factors and PTSD: A Historian's Perspective." If your research asks

Title
The title is the title of the journal, not a book or article

Title: **Political psychology.**

Publication info: **Cambridge, MA [etc.] Blackwell Publishers [etc.]**

Subject
The subject terms are the words or phrases that describe the themes of the journal. They are hyperlinks, so if you click on a term you will be directed to other journals that are described by the same theme.

ISSN: **0162-895X**

Subject: **Political psychology--Periodicals.**

Electronic Access
This section indicates that you may access journal articles online. Clicking on the hyperlinks will bring you to the article databases that catalog articles in this journal. Note the time constraints for EBSCO: full-text articles are not available if they were published before March 2003 or within the previous 12 months.

Electronic access: **http://www.blackwell-synergy.com.proxy.libraries.rutgers.edu/ope nurl?genre=journal&stitle=pops Access from campus or login via Rutgers account.**

Electronic access: **EBSCO-a: Full text available: Mar 2003-. (Due to publisher restrictions, the most recent 12 months are not available.) http://search.ebscohost.com.proxy.libraries. rutgers.edu/direct.asp?db=aph&jid=%22B55 %22&scope=site Access from campus or login via Rutgers account.**

Electronic access: **EBSCO-b: Full text available: Mar 2003-. (Due to publisher restrictions, the most recent 12 months are not available.) http://search.ebscohost.com.proxy.libraries. rutgers.edu/direct.asp?db=buh&jid=%22B55 %22&scope=site Access from campus or login via Rutgers account.**

ALEXANDER
Location: **PER -- Current -- Shelved by title**
Holdings: **v.27:no.4 (2006:Aug.) – v.27:no.5 (2006:Oct.)**
ALEXANDER
Location: **PER -- Bound -- Shelved by title**
Holdings: **v.22:no.3/4 (2001) – v.24:no.3/4 (2003), v.25:no.1/3 (2004) - v.27:no.1/3 (2006)**
Holdings: **v.1 (1979) - v.22:no.1/2 (2001)**

Library Holdings
The Location indicates where the library puts the journal: the current issues are in a different section than the older issues. For older issues, each year of issues (the volume) is bound into a separate book. Holdings indicates which issues the library has. The information: v.1 (1979) – v.22:no.1/2 (2001) means that the library has all issues starting with volume 1 in 1979 through volume 22, issue 1/2, in 2001.

Figure 4.1 Sample library catalog journal citation. Comments in boxes describe items in the citation.

questions about risk factors, reading both chapters will give you a sense of how different authors explored them.

Other Library Resources

Not all the library resources that will help you in your literature search will be in the form of a book or article. In this section we will briefly discuss reference librarians, subject research guides, and interlibrary loan services.

Personal author: **Jensen, Robert, 1958-.**

Personal Author This indicates the author(s) of a text. It is a hyperlink, so if you click on the author's name you will be directed to the other books he has written or edited	Title: **The heart of whiteness: confronting race, racism, and white privilege/by Robert Jensen.** Publication info: **San Francisco, CA: City Lights, c2005.** Physical description: **xx, 98p.; 19 cm.**
Contents This section is the table of contents, and it lists the book's chapter titles. Often in an edited collection, the authors of each chapter are listed with the chapter titles.	Contents: **Introduction: just a joke -- Race word and race stories -- Facing the truth: past, present, and future -- The emotions of white supremacy: fear, guilt, and anger -- Playing the fool -- Against diversity, for politics -- Conclusion: white people's burden.** Subject: **Jensen, Robert, 1958-.**
Subject The subject terms are the words or phrases that describe the themes of the book. They are hyperlinks, so if you click on a term you will be directed to other books that use the same terms to describe a theme.	Subject: **Jensen, Robert, 1958 -- Relations with Africa.** Subject: **Whites -- Race identity -- United States.** Subject: **Whites -- United States -- Social conditions.** Subject: **Whites -- United States -- Psychology.** Subject: **Whites -- United States -- Biography.** Subject: **Men, White -- United States -- Biography.** Subject: **United States -- Race relations.**
Electronic Access This link takes you to a Library of Congress page where you can see the table of contents, not the entire book.	Electronic access: **Table of contents http://www.loc.gov/catdir/toc/ecip059/2005007522.html.**

Archibald S. Alexander Library (College Avenue)	**Copy**	**Sub-location**	**Status**
call number: **E184.A1J425 2005**	1	STACKS	IN-LIBRARY

Call number This number tells you where to find the book in the library. Ask a librarian for directions if you are having trouble understanding how to locate the book.	**Sub-Location and Status** The phrase "in-library" means that the book should be in the library, and looking under the Sub-location tells you that the book is in the library's stacks. It is important to look at both the Sub-location and Status because a book may be in the library, but if it is on reserve for a class you will not find it in the library's stacks.

Figure 4.2 Sample library catalog book citation. Comments in boxes describe items in the citation.

Although reference librarians may not have a background in psychology, they are familiar with what the library has to offer and they can help you access these resources. At any stage in the research process, you can draw upon a reference librarian's expertise to help you perform a search or find a particular source; and if you are having trouble finding sources that relate to your topic, a reference librarian can suggest different kinds of searches and direct you to a variety of search engines. Before going to your psychology professor to tell him or her that you cannot find a specific source or that you cannot find information about a topic, ask a reference librarian. Librarians are trained professionals who may be more familiar with the library's resources than your professor.

Subject research guides list different resources related to a specific topic. The Rutgers University Library system has developed research guides for topics such as jazz, religion, Latino studies, and alcohol studies; there is also a topic labeled *psychology*. The psychology subject guide includes links to article databases, electronic journals, general resources (scholarship opportunities and a guide to finding tests and measures), print resources available at Rutgers, psychology organizations, and career and professional services. You can also access a page, which a reference librarian developed, that offers suggestions about how to do research in psychology. Many of the links on these pages are available only to Rutgers students, but the library at your college or university may have its own set of subject research guides.

You can visit the Rutgers library's psychology subject guide at the following link:

- http://www.libraries.rutgers.edu/rul/rr_gateway/ research_guides/psych/psych.shtml

You can access the Ithaca College psychology subject guide through the following link:

- http://www.ithacalibrary.com/subjects/display.php

Once you have found books or articles that you would like to use in your research, it is possible that the library will not own those resources, either in print or in electronic form. In this situation you can make an interlibrary loan request. Because a library cannot own every book or journal that has been published, libraries lend books and make articles accessible to other libraries' patrons upon request. The only drawback to interlibrary loans is that it may take several weeks for you to get a book. (Check with your library for the average time it takes to get an item though interlibrary loan.)

To request journal articles you first need to make sure that the library does not have the article (either because it does not subscribe to the journal or does not have the issue you need) and that you cannot access the article through an article database. Because articles often are provided electronically through interlibrary loan, they usually arrive more quickly than books do.

USING ARTICLE DATABASES

Databases such as PsycINFO and PsycARTICLES, the Social Science Citation Index, and Academic Search Premier (EBSCOhost) catalog scholarly articles in psychology and other social sciences. Through PsycINFO you can find academic journal articles, book chapters, monographs, dissertations, and technical reports. Social Science Citation Index provides a list of published works that have cited a particular article. Academic Search Premier is an interdisciplinary database that catalogs journals in the sciences, social sciences, and humanities.

Psychologists probably use PsycINFO and PsycARTICLES more than they use any other database, although psychologists who study areas related to medicine or animal behavior may use databases such as Biological Abstracts. There are similarities in search strategies across the different databases, but each one has its own specific characteristics. We will concentrate on psychology databases in this chapter because they catalog an extremely wide range of areas that interest psychologists. PsycINFO does not provide full-text resources; rather, it generates a description of the research, the names of authors, descriptors for the item, and a number of other, more technical, details. On the other hand, PsycARTICLES includes full-text articles, but it covers a narrow range of journals.

There are various strategies for searching. If you search for a single word anywhere in a document, the results will contain that word somewhere in the listing. Searching for a word anywhere in a document is not an efficient search strategy much of the time. For example, if you wanted to find out what psychologists have discovered about how we learn, you could search for the word *learning*. At this writing, a search for *learning* resulted in 579,062 hits. You couldn't (and wouldn't want to) read through all this material. Furthermore, most of the hits are not relevant to learning. Box 4.2 shows the titles of the first 10 citations that the search generated. As you can see, only 1 of the 10 (the last one) actually relates specifically to the topic of learning.

The first citation is listed because it includes the phrase "21st Century Community *Learning* Centers (CCLC) Program." When you search for a term anywhere in a citation, you end up with irrelevant citations like this. An alternative is to use *keywords* or *descriptors*, which narrow down the search so it is more focused on what interests you. Table 4.2 indicates some ways to focus your search if you get too many hits. Table 4.3 shows other ways to direct your search.

Box 4.2   Titles of the First 10 Hits in a PsycINFO Search for "Learning" Anywhere in a Citation

1. "Data for a democracy: the evolving role of evaluation in policy and program development"
2. "Forty years of research knowledge and use: from head start to early head start and beyond"
3. "Beyond baby steps: promoting the growth and development of U.S. child-care policy"
4. "From visions to systems of universal prekindergarten"
5. "Strategies to ensure that no child starts from behind"
6. "Poverty and child development: new perspectives on a defining issue"
7. "Intervention and policy implications of research on neurobiological functioning in maltreated children"
8. "The sexually mature teen as a whole person: new directions in prevention and intervention for teen pregnancy and parenthood"
9. "Family support: a force for change"
10. "Education, psychology, and the brain"

USING THE INTERNET

Because of the Internet's global reach, you have access to an enormous amount of information. Through this medium, information may travel extensively and quickly; and often you can find very current information about an issue. These benefits make the Internet seem like an attractive place to perform research, and for the reasons listed above the Internet may be useful for the initial stages of research. However, as we note in chapter 3, critical evaluation of Internet content is especially important because most Web sites do not have a peer review process to check the accuracy and validity of a writer's research. (Refer to chapter 3 for guidance on using the Internet.) Furthermore, the Internet sites you are likely to find through a Yahoo, Lycos, or basic Google search will probably not be scholarly sources and, thus, probably would be of limited utility.

Search engines such as Alta Vista and Google are limited in several other ways. First, they catalog only a small percentage of the Web pages available on the Internet. Second, sources that have not been published recently are less likely to be cataloged, or even available, online. Third, the Internet is constantly changing, and popular search engines do not always keep up; thus, your searches may lead you to links that are no longer available and you may miss new information. Lastly, your search may provide you with thousands of results, and it would be an extremely time-consuming task to sort through all of them to find the relevant sources.

Table 4.3

Strategies for a More Efficient Search in PsycINFO Using "Set Other Limits," the Thesaurus, and the Index

Search strategy	What the strategy accomplishes
Limit the publication years you want to search by using *Other Limits*	You can limit the search through PsycINFO to a certain year or range of years. Many users eliminate older references when they use this option
Limit the hits to work published in English by using *Other Limits*	You can eliminate publications that appear in languages other than English
Limit the hits to published work that is relatively easy to access by using *Other Limits*	You can limit your search to citations from journals and books by specifying this choice in the options for *Publication Type*. This removes from your search hard-to-find materials such as dissertations or technical reports. There are several options from which you can choose
Limit the search to empirical research (rather than review articles) by using *Other Limits*	You can select for *Methodology* only empirical studies. There are several other options you could select, such as literature review articles
Limit the search to human or nonhuman subjects by using *Other Limits*	You can specify the population of interest, such as female, male, animal, inpatient, etc.
Limit the search to a specific age range of participants by using *Other Limits*	You can direct the search to include such groups as *Neonates* (birth to 1 month) all the way to *Very Old* (85 years and older)
Use the Thesaurus in PsycINFO	This feature allows you to type in the word of interest and to see what search terms PsycINFO uses for this concept. You may find multiple relevant terms
Use the Index in PsycINFO	The index allows you to search for authors, for publications dealing with certain age groups, specified populations, various methodologies, etc.
Use a wild card to expand your search to related terms	If you put an asterisk (*) after a word, PsycINFO will search for hits that begin with the letters of your word. So if you search for *learn**, PsycINFO will search for all instances that begin with those letters, including *learn*, *learning*, *learner*, etc.

Remember, the main purpose of a literature search is to learn about other *academic* research. This means that you will need to understand how researchers approached their studies, chose their methods, collected their data, and interpreted their results. It is unlikely that popular sources will provide you with the information you need to evaluate each facet of research. As a result, we suggest that you limit your Internet searches to library article databases, such as PsycINFO, Medline, and Academic Search Premier. If you do want to use general search engines, the following Web pages offer suggestions for performing academic research on the Internet:

- http://nutsandbolts.washcoll.edu/evidence.html
- http://www.lib.berkeley.edu/TeachingLib/Guides/Internet/About.html

What about Google Scholar? Google Scholar's search results are often academic sources; however, for many of the results you can access only the source's citation information and abstract, so you will have to use an article database or the library before you will be able to read the entire source.

USING SOURCES TO FIND SOURCES

A final method that you can incorporate into your literature search involves using the scholarly sources that you have already found relevant to your own research topic. When you find sources that you plan to cite in your paper, look at the References section of these publications to identify other sources that may be useful. If the authors have done a thorough job, their references should cite other significant scholars, and you can use those references to add to your list of sources.

5

How to Read and Summarize a Journal Article

Many students . . . have almost literally to be taught to read intelligently.

Whipple (1910)

Reading is a means of thinking with another person's mind; it forces you to stretch your own.

Charles Scribner, Jr.

You have probably been reading for one or more decades by now. Has it occurred to you that you might still need to learn how to read? According to the quotation above, Whipple (1910) was not very optimistic about college students' abilities to read. His assessment of students is not entirely realistic—college students today would not be in college if they were poor readers. Still, reading scientific articles is different from casual reading.

People do not often pick up journal articles for casual reading. One of the major reasons is that scientific writing often involves complex ideas that are unfamiliar to many readers. In spite of the complexity of journal articles, it is important for you to read about research if you are ultimately going to write about your own research.

When you read a journal article, you will be reading slowly. There is a lot of information in an article, and that information is densely packed. You will also need to read most journal articles more than once because it will be very difficult to take in all the details with just one reading.

In order to help your memory for the material in the article, you should take notes. This can be more useful than highlighting the material because, when you compose your own notes, you engage in more complete processing of the information. In this chapter, we hope to give you some pointers that will help you navigate successfully through research articles. You can use *argument mapping* to help keep track of related topics. It is related to idea maps and involves identifying the claims that authors make, the statements that they use to support their claims, the counterarguments that others have raised, and so forth.

This approach provides a trail of ideas that allows you to see if an argument is sound or if it falls prey to logical fallacies (as described in chapter 3).

Most psychologists produce manuscripts that follow the style of the American Psychological Association (2001) in its *Publication Manual of the American Psychological Association*. You might initially see APA style as being rigid and incomprehensible, but there are good reasons psychologists have adopted it. APA style provides a blueprint for structuring a research paper. If a writer adheres to this style, you will know that the paper includes appropriate information. Furthermore, you will know where to look to find that information.

Every section in an APA-style article has a specific purpose. If you are aware of the purpose of each section, you will understand what authors are saying and why they are saying it. For instance, if you want to get a sense of how the ideas in a given paper have developed, you look in the Introduction. If you want to know what types of measurements the author has used and what kind of materials were important for a study, you will go to the Method section. For a description of the data, you look through the Results section. Similarly, if you want to understand where an author's ideas are leading, you go to the Discussion section.

AN OVERVIEW OF THE RESEARCH—THE ABSTRACT

The abstract is a short presentation, with a maximum length of 120 words. This section provides you with a brief, but complete, description of the research—what question it addressed, what methodology it involved, the outcome of the study, and the conclusions that the researchers drew.

After you read the abstract, you generally have a sense of whether it would be helpful to read the entire article. If the abstract seems to relate to the question you want to address, you should read the entire article. Reading only the abstract does not give you enough detail about the research. It is worth noting that a boring or confusing abstract may drive readers away. You should keep this fact in mind when you write an abstract of your own.

IDENTIFYING THE ISSUES—INTRODUCTION SECTION

The Introduction to a paper establishes the importance of the topic. The author identifies the nature of the question to be addressed and how it connects to other research. This connection is important because virtually no interesting research project stands alone; there are always other studies that relate to the topic.

An author introduces the reader to the importance of the research question and to previous research that bears on the same topic. Thus, after the opening statement that introduces you to the nature of the question, the author engages in a review of the literature. This discussion of earlier research will not be exhaustive, but it will give a sense of what psychologists think about the issue. If there is controversy, a good Introduction section will give an objective look at all sides of the argument. After describing the current state of knowledge, the author will develop hypotheses supported by a logical argument that calls on existing research.

Table 5.1 indicates some of the relevant questions you should be able to answer. Again, we stress the importance of taking notes. If

Table 5.1
Important Questions to Answer from the Introduction

Question	Why the question is important
What general topic is the researcher addressing?	This question puts the research into context. Knowing the topic lets you create a schema so you can understand how different concepts in the article relate to one another
What have other researchers already discovered about this topic?	Research proceeds one step at a time. The research in the article you are reading is more understandable if you know what other questions researchers have asked and what they have found
How does this study follow from earlier research?	Knowing about earlier research lets you establish the logical connections among studies so you can tie the current article to the previous research
What is new about this study compared with other research?	Why is this study worth doing? How does it break new ground? Scientists recognize research as valuable if it contributes to new knowledge. You will have a better understanding of the researcher's logic if you can see how it extends beyond other research
What are the researcher's hypotheses?	If you understand what other researchers have accomplished and how they interpreted their results, you can comprehend why the researcher has developed certain hypotheses that follow from previous ideas

you address the questions in Table 5.1, you should have a firm grasp of the author's topic, the current state of knowledge in the area, what disagreements exist, and why the author believes that certain results will occur.

UNDERSTANDING WHAT WAS DONE—METHOD SECTION

The Method section typically consists of three subsections that describe the research subjects or participants, the implements of the research, and what actually went on during the study. Each of these subsections provides a partial picture of the nuts and bolts of the study. The Method section has little to do with theory or psychological concepts; instead, it deals with details that give a complete picture of how the research proceeded. When you read this section, you can develop a feel for who participated and what they experienced.

Subjects and Participants
In this subsection, you will read about the nature of people or animals that took part in the study. As a rule, *participant* refers to people and *subject* to animals. You can read about the details in chapter 11. Authors generally present characteristics of their participants and subjects that might help the reader understand the results. So when you read this subsection, you will learn about the number of female and male participants, their race or ethnicity, their age, and other salient characteristics. For instance, if the research involved a study of behaviors of depressed people, all of the previously mentioned characteristics could be important; in this example, further characteristics of participants that could be important in understanding the study might also include their histories of hospitalization, length of treatment, use of legal or illegal drugs, and so forth. Such characteristics should appear in the Participant subsection.

However, most psychological research involves college students, so the descriptions of these participants is likely to be limited to their sex, race or ethnicity, and age. A greater range of participants and, sometimes, more extended descriptions of participants may appear in applied, nonlaboratory research (Beins, 2004, pp. 85–86). If the research involves nonhuman animals, you will find out what kind of animals, including genus and species, and the source of the animals. These characteristics might influence the results.

Apparatus and Materials
Any study necessarily involves data collection. In this subsection you

will read about any tests or surveys, word lists, pictures, and so forth that are part of the research. In this subsection, you also learn about any electronic or mechanical apparatus that the researchers used. When you take notes, you should make sure you understand how the materials and apparatus helped the investigators address their research question.

You will later be able to relate the apparatus and materials to the results. If participants completed a personality inventory or engaged in some task, you will be able to get a feel for what they did, based on the materials, and how it related to the behaviors that the researcher measured.

Procedure

This subsection details exactly what the researchers did and, as importantly, what the participants did. When you read this material, you get a detailed depiction of the important aspects of the research session. When you later read the results, you can imagine what the participants did and how it affected their behaviors.

Most of the details would be relevant if you were planning on replicating the research. If you are not planning to reproduce the study, you may be satisfied with a cursory reading, extracting enough detail so that you understand what went on.

There are a lot of seemingly minor details in the Method section. You can get the essence of a study by reading through the procedure and noting the major features. You can always return to it for more detail later. Some of the major questions that will help understand the study appear in Table 5.2.

Table 5.2
Important Questions to Answer from the Method Section

Question	Why the question is important
What are the characteristics of the participants and subjects?	The results might be affected by whether participants are female or male, how old they were, etc.
What apparatus and materials were used in the study?	By knowing what kinds of tests, surveys, and other stimuli the participants were exposed to, you can evaluate whether there is a valid connection between measurements and the researcher's conclusions
What did the participants actually do?	If you have detailed knowledge of what the participants experienced, you will understand the results better and be able to evaluate why the results occurred as they did

You may want to take notes on the Method section, answering the questions in the table. Until you read about the results, these details might seem fairly unimportant. As you read the results, these details help you make more sense of the results.

WHAT HAPPENED—RESULTS SECTION

The Results section contains some of the most technical information of any section of the journal article. It will describe the outcome of the study and present the technical aspects of statistical tests. A well-written Results section will be comprehensible independently of the numerical results. That is, good writers present their findings in understandable English, using the numerical information to support their descriptions.

As you take notes on the results, you should review the hypotheses that appeared in the introduction. Then pay attention to whether the results supported the hypotheses, making note of which results did or did not lend support. You may have to evaluate several hypotheses but, at the end, you should have a list of notes that indicate "These results

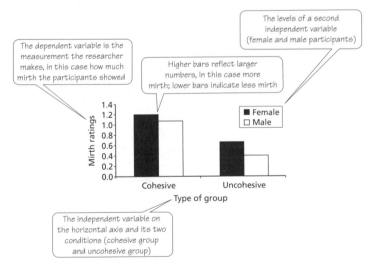

Figure 5.1 Example of a figure in a results section. Participants viewed humorous pictures, and observers recorded the amount of mirth (e.g., smiling, laughing, etc.) the participants showed. The researcher manipulates the independent variable to see if behaviors, as measured on the dependent variable, change. The height of each bar indicates the degree of mirth shown by participants. The results show that there was more laughing and smiling in cohesive groups than in uncohesive groups. In addition, female participants showed more mirth than male participants (Pashka, Agnitti, Bubel, MacNaughton, & Beins, 2005). ©Bernard C. Beins.

supported Hypothesis A, because the means of one group were greater than the means in another group. But these other results failed to confirm Hypothesis B because the means of these groups were equal."

Often authors will summarize their results in tables and figures that present a lot of data in a small amount of space. An example of a relatively simple graph appears in Figure 5.1. It documents participants' mirth responses (e.g., laughing, smiling, chuckling) to humorous pictures. The participants were either in cohesive or in uncohesive groups and included both women and men. The figure illustrates the main points of a graph.

When you read through a Results section, it can be easier to understand if you read and summarize small amounts of the section rather than trying to capture the whole set of results in a few sentences. Taking this reduced approach will also let you work for shorter periods of time at one sitting. It will also keep you from being overwhelmed by the sheer volume of information.

Table 5.3
Important Questions to Answer from the Results Section

Question	Why the question is important
For each hypothesis: What results relate to the hypothesis? Do they support the hypothesis?	You can get a sense of how closely the researchers' expectations matched the actual results. Sometimes hypotheses are completely supported, sometimes only partially supported, sometimes not at all
What statistical tests did the researchers use when they analyzed the data?	If researchers use tests like the t-test or the analysis of variance, you know that they are looking for differences across groups. If they use tests of correlation or association like the Pearson or the Spearman correlation, the chi-square test, or regression analysis, you know that they are looking for associations between variables
In everyday English, what do the statistical tests tell you?	If you can translate the numerical results into everyday English, they will make more sense
Are the results consistent with those of earlier research?	This question is relevant to the Discussion section, but in the Results section authors sometimes compare their data with those of other investigators
What do the figures and tables convey? Do they lend support to the hypotheses?	Tables and figures support the researchers' verbal statements. So a table or a figure will present detail that goes beyond the text

Finally, keep in mind the characteristics of the participants. Does their gender matter to the outcome of the study? Their ages or their cultural backgrounds? Also, do the measurements as described in the Method section relate to the researchers' goals? The details of the Method section might begin to fall into place as you read the results.

WHAT IT MEANS—DISCUSSION SECTION

What do the results really mean? Authors use the Discussion section to explain why their results are important and interesting. If you think back on the Introduction, you will recall that one of the purposes of that section is to tell the reader why the topic is interesting and important. Now, in the Discussion, the researchers explain why their results contribute to our knowledge of thought and behavior. There should be a link between the concepts in the Introduction and the conclusions that appear in the Discussion.

Furthermore, in the first part of the paper, the authors discuss how their research plan related to previous studies. Now, in the Discussion, the investigator explains how the actual results connected to the results of those studies.

Table 5.4
Important Questions to Answer from the Discussion Section

Question	Why the question is important
Do the present research findings agree with previous research and with accepted theory?	Research can point out limitations in previous research or correct flaws in those studies. New studies can also show where theories are strong or weak
If there are any unexpected findings, why did they occur?	Research can lead to surprising outcomes. If something occurs that an investigator did not anticipate, it could lead to new research projects that others have not pursued
Why do the researchers think their findings are important?	When researchers discuss their findings, they tell why their study extends what psychologists already know, creating new knowledge
What are the implications of this research?	Research is important not only for what new knowledge it generates, but also for what new lines of research it can foster

Writers also take the opportunity in this section to explain any unexpected findings. What happened that was surprising? What might the participants have been doing that led to unanticipated results? Such findings can lead to new research.

Finally, in the Discussion section, the researchers note the limitations of their research and how future studies might overcome those weaknesses. The researchers also speculate on new lines of research that could extend from their study.

The important questions that authors address in the Discussion section appear in Table 5.4. These questions relate to the psychological concepts and principles that interest the researchers.

WHERE THE IDEAS ORIGINATED—REFERENCES SECTION

All new research flows from previous research, so scientists document the path of ideas by citing previous work. Any time authors mention a publication or presentation in their article, they cite the work in the References section. The value of this section is that it allows you to track down other research that you might not already know about. It also gives credit to those researchers for their work.

The References section is not the same as a bibliography. In the list of references, authors include only the work that they refer to. So if research is not mentioned in the article, it does not go in the References section.

FIGURING OUT WHAT IT MEANS

After you read a journal article, you should know why the researchers did their study, how they did it, and what it means. Because of the complexity of research articles, you should take careful notes so that you understand how all the different pieces of the research fit together.

You can use the questions listed in Table 5.5 as a worksheet. It can be copied and enlarged so you have enough space for your ideas. At the end, you should write your own summary of the study, just to make sure that you maximize your understanding of the research.

Table 5.5

Worksheet with Important Questions to Answer when Reading a Journal Article

Question	Answer
Introduction	
What general topic is the researcher addressing?	
What have other researchers already discovered about this topic?	
What is new about this study compared with other research?	
What are the researcher's hypotheses?	
Method	
What are the characteristics of the participants or subjects?	
What apparatus and materials were used in the study?	
What did the participants actually do?	
Results	
For each hypothesis: What results relate to the hypothesis? Do they support the hypothesis?	
What statistical tests did the researchers use when they analyzed the data?	
In everyday English, what do the statistical tests tell you?	
Are the results consistent with those of earlier research?	
What do the figures and tables convey? Do they lend support to the hypotheses?	
Discussion	
Do the present research findings agree with previous research and with accepted theory?	
If there are any unexpected findings, why did they occur?	
Why do the researchers think their findings are important?	
What are the implications of this research? What new research does it suggest?	

6

Organizing a Paper

Do not write so that you can be understood, write so that you cannot be misunderstood.

Epictetus

It doesn't matter what you write. But don't think that just because you wrote it that it's good.

Neal Pollack

Although academic writing might appear unfamiliar and intimidating, it is merely a variation of certain discussions you might have in your daily life. For example: you are going out to eat with some friends, but there is disagreement about where to eat. To persuade your friends to go to a particular restaurant, you might describe the quality of the food, the cost of a meal, its proximity to where you are now, any coupons you might have, and so on. Knowing your audience (your friends), what would convince them (are they more concerned about how close the restaurant is or how much a meal would cost?), and where to get the information to convince them, you can choose how to present the support for your position, or thesis, "We should eat at X restaurant." Although you might not think about this situation in terms of "thesis" and "development and support," it follows a process similar to the one you would use to persuade a reader that your position in a research paper is valid.

Most academic papers are exercises in influencing your reader that your thesis is accurate. In order to do this, you must know and use the conventions of the field, the audience for whom you are writing, what you are hoping to achieve through your writing, the parameters of the writing task, and what kind of support you need to achieve credibility as a writer.

ORGANIZATION

Think of organization in academic writing on three levels. The *global level* refers to the overall organization of the paper, or the order in which you present your main points. For much writing in psychology, you will split the body of your paper into sections, although different writing assignments do require different kinds of global organization. The *sectional level* refers to the organization of a section (e.g., "Introduction," "Method," and "Results"). At the *local level* your concerns relate to the organization of paragraphs and sentences.

As you start organizing and drafting your paper, there are several techniques you can use to help you set up the structure on a global, sectional, and local level. When you begin thinking about your paper's overall organization, an idea map can usefully build on the results of a brainstorm and prepare you for making an outline at the sectional level. To make an idea map, use your general topical area (such as "Nightmares") or your focal question ("What are the best ways to stop nightmares from recurring?") as the starting point of your idea map. Write the topic or question in the middle of a sheet of paper and circle it. Near the main idea, write and circle another idea that relates to the main idea. Then, draw a line connecting the two ideas; if you can, along the connecting line write *how* the two ideas are related. Some ideas might clearly fit with others at this stage, and if you are not sure where an idea or piece of evidence fits, include it anyway. As your ideas develop, new relationships will emerge, and the placement of ideas might become clearer. Figure 6.1 offers a sample idea map, which is an elaboration of an outline by Professor John Richard Suler of Rider University.

Some Internet sites offer additional examples of idea maps and suggestions for how to make them:

- http://modena.intergate.ca/personal/gslj/ideamap. html#MAKING
- http://library.humboldt.edu/owls/owl2-Map.htm

As groups of ideas become apparent, you can start thinking about how these groups might be written in paragraph form. At this stage, think about transitioning to an outline. Not only will a good outline get you closer to a draft of your paper by refining the paper's organization, it will also help you explore the relationships between ideas that you used to construct the idea map.

Outlines are versatile because you can employ them to clarify global,

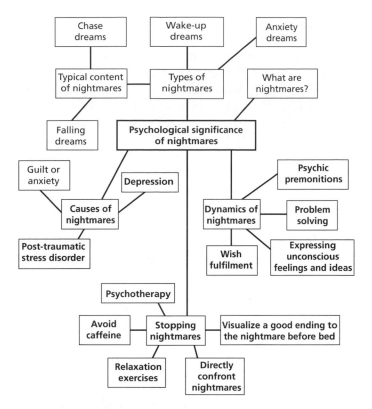

Figure 6.1 Example of an idea map.

sectional, and local levels of your paper. For example, first you can label the top of a page with a section heading and then free-write or brain-storm a list of items you might include in that section. At this stage it can be productive not to censor your ideas. Rather than spending a lot of time deciding exactly where a topic or idea will be in the final draft, when making a broad outline such as this, we suggest that you focus your attention on listing possible ideas.

As you start making more detailed outlines and rough drafts, you can be more strategic about the placement of information. To organize a section, you might make an outline that contains the main idea for each paragraph and which sources or evidence you will use to sup-port the main idea. On a paragraph level, the outline may look more like traditional outlines that use uppercase roman numerals for the topic sentence or main idea, uppercase Arabic letters for supporting ideas, and Arabic numerals for specific evidence, such as the one below (Sommers & Ellsworth, 2001):

I. Racial factors may affect jurors' decisions in a trial
   A. Society has changed and discrepancies in conviction rates between white and black defendants have diminished, but not been eliminated, in the last century
      1. Racial norms have changed in society (Devine, 1989)
      2. Interracial crimes may results in harsher sentence recommendations than same-race crimes (Hymes, Leinart, Rowe, & Rogers, 1993)
   B. Claims by some researchers that racial prejudice has been eliminated in the judicial system do not withstand scrutiny
      1. Death penalty cases may disfavor black defendants because of failure of jurors to comprehend instructions (Lynch & Haney, 2000)
      2. Race may constitute an important factor when a crime does not involve obviously racial issues (Sommers & Ellsworth, 2000).

Remember, this outline is only one model. Paragraphs in your papers might have only one supporting idea with several pieces of specific evidence, or you might have a paragraph with more than two supporting ideas.

USING THE WORK OF OTHERS TO SUPPORT YOUR ARGUMENT

In general, there are two things to keep in mind when using sources: how the sources are physically included in your paper—are they summarized, paraphrased, quoted; and what rhetorical role the source plays in your paper. The former area involves technical skills, such as knowing APA style and how to summarize an entire research paper in one sentence. The latter, however, asks you to take into account the broader rhetorical situation: your audience, conventions of academic writing, and effective techniques for constructing an academic argument.

Sources: Credibility and Tone
As an academic writer you are trying to persuade your reader, first, that you are a credible writer and, second, that your thesis is a valid one. Both are critical. A reader can agree with your thesis that, for example, all-girl schools do not significantly increase girls' scores on achievement tests in mathematics but not be convinced that you are a credible writer. That is, this reader will not necessarily agree with *how*

you reached your conclusion after reading your paper. To strengthen your credibility and develop a strong paper, we offer three suggestions when drawing from sources: use more scholarly sources than popular sources, use your sources fairly and respectfully, and present information from your sources in a way that allows your audience to engage your argument.

Scholars who have spent years studying and researching a specific topic will already have established their own credibility and reliability regarding this topic. Including scholarly sources in your paper allows you to benefit from the credibility of other psychologists. In contrast, if you omit the work of a scholar who contributed significantly to your area of study, readers will probably realize it, and they might be skeptical that you have done high-quality research. Moreover, if you rely too heavily on popular sources—sources whose credibility is not guaranteed—your argument could suffer.

In order to benefit from scholarly sources we encourage you to use those sources fairly and respectfully. By this we mean that you should cite the sources when appropriate, accurately represent the content of the sources, and avoid referring to sources in a way that distorts the author's intended meaning. Of course, you cannot read the author's mind, but you can attempt to understand the author's position.

Finally, be aware of the tone you use when referring to sources. Even if you disagree with some part of a source, treat it and its author with respect. We have mentioned elsewhere that all sources can tell us something about the world in which we live. Furthermore, most scholars do not intend to produce information that is incorrect; rather, they truly hope to make a positive impact in the field and, perhaps, positively impact people's lives. If you disagree with a scholar's argument, you can summarize his or her argument and then show a gap in logic or misinterpretation of data. This kind of refutation will be taken more seriously than a complete dismissal of someone's work without any support. Derogatory terms, such as "dumb" and "stupid," are inappropriate descriptions of the sources you use.

On the other hand, be careful about relying too heavily on only one source or using a source uncritically.

Just as most arguments will have some merit, most arguments will have some limitations as well. No theory can account for all cases and no study can represent all populations. Thus, presenting a source as completely infallible can weaken your argument as much as prematurely rejecting a source. Make sure you note the limitations of the work you cite; if others recognize those limitations and you have not mentioned them, a reader may see your writing as biased, and thus less credible.

Sources: Quoting, Paraphrasing, and Summarizing

When using sources, you can quote, paraphrase, or summarize. Quoting involves using language directly from the source and placing double quotation marks around those words (" "). The disciplinary conventions of psychology generally discourage the extensive use of quotes. Because psychologists (and other scientists) rely on an accumulation of research findings to guide the development of ideas, it is better to summarize the body of work related to your topic rather than using a single quotation. Therefore, if you choose to use direct quotations, consider the following criteria:

- Use quotes for particularly memorable language.
- If paraphrasing would make the idea more complicated or difficult to understand, a quote might be more appropriate.
- Use quotes if the author's wording is important for supporting a point you are trying to make.

This is *your* paper. Including too many quotes can also make it seem as though others have written your argument for you. Even though you might be heavily influenced by several sources, you can paraphrase and summarize rather than quoting from them.

Paraphrasing and summarizing are similar because both entail putting someone else's ideas in your own words. To paraphrase, take a passage from a source and put it in your own words so that the paraphrase is about the same length as the original passage. Paraphrasing can be useful because it shows your readers that you comprehend potentially complex ideas. Additionally, consider paraphrasing if the language used in the original passage is not appropriate for your audience. The language could be too formal or too informal, too technical or not technical enough, or just not well written. Phrases such as "according to" and "_____ argues that" let your reader know that you are describing someone else's ideas.

Because you are working with a limited amount of space and because research papers usually reference many sources, summarizing is an invaluable skill to develop. Summarizing is a process whereby the main points of a passage are condensed into a shorter space than the original. The purpose of summarizing is to give your reader a clear and concise version of the original source. Your argument may benefit because you can refer to a number of sources succinctly, which lets your reader know the extent of your research.

In the social and natural sciences, authors also may refer to a number of sources parenthetically. That is, they will make a general claim about research, such as "personality (Eysenck, 1991; Friedman & Booth-Kewley, 1987), lifestyle (Jacobs, Spilken, & Norman, 1969), and environment (Haggerty, 1980) have varying effects on the development of an infection for different individuals (Kemeny & Laudenslager, 1999)" (Ray, 2004, p. 32).

Summaries can be anywhere from one sentence to one paragraph; there is no pre-set length. Keep in mind what a reader needs to know in order to understand the points you are making. For some sources, you might want to summarize the whole text; however, if you are interested only in the researchers' methodology, you can summarize how they did their research without needing to describe other parts of the text. (However, see chapter 2 for information about plagiarism.) As you decide what to include in a paper—rhetorically and tactically— you also want to keep in mind your readers' expectations, as is shown in Table 6.1.

EDITING AND REVISING

We offer two initial suggestions after you have completed a rough draft of your paper: spend some time away from the draft, and revise strategically. Ideally, you would complete a draft of your paper a week or two before it is due. Then, you could put the draft away and read it later with a different perspective. However, because you do not always have that much time between the first draft and final draft, it is important to revise and edit in a way that will most benefit your paper. For example, save your editing of mechanics (grammar and spelling) until the end because after you make other revisions you will need to work on mechanics again.

As with other aspects of research and writing, as you gain more practice writing and revising, you will find the strategies that work best for you. In this section we specifically explore four areas to consider when revising: *focus, organization, development/support*, and *mechanics.*

Focus
At global and sectional levels you will ask yourself similar questions to guide your content revisions. Globally, you want to think about how

Table 6.1
Knowing Your Readers

Question	Reasons for asking
1. Who are my readers?	Are your readers lay readers with almost no knowledge about psychology, an audience of psychologists from across the field or researchers who specialize in the field you are writing about? Or perhaps your reader is your psychology professor. Writing with your readers' expectations in mind can help you decide what information to include and exclude, the tone that would be most effective, and what kind of language you should use
2. What do my readers already know about my research topic?	Knowing your readers' level of knowledge about your topic will help you decide when you can paraphrase or summarize information and when you need to offer more detailed explanations
3. What is my objective—or, what do I want my readers to think about this topic after reading my paper?	If your primary purpose is persuasive or informative, you might choose to use different tones in your writing. Also, keeping in mind your thesis statement—which states the purpose of your paper to your readers—can help you stay focused during the writing process
4. What will convince my readers that I am a credible writer?	As a writer, your credibility is related to how well you can convince your reader that you have authority to write about a specific topic. Authorial credibility is shaped by your tone, language, command of the material, and ability to meet your readers' expectations and needs (see question 1)
5. What will convince my audience that my argument is credible?	Topical credibility is related to the larger significance of your argument. Therefore, you want to show your reader that what you are doing is important and that your research can have an impact on the outside world. Note that if your readers see you as a credible writer, it will probably be easier to convince them that your argument is credible. Conversely, developing a strong argument can strengthen your authorial credibility

the sections fit together and to evaluate the focus of your paper. By *focus*, we mean the scope of your paper, or the breadth and depth of information presented.

One way to approach global revisions is to look at your thesis statement and assess how well you support it in your paper. A strategy for assessing whether you have included relevant information is to ask, for each paragraph: How does this paragraph contribute to an exploration of my thesis? If you have trouble answering the question, take it as a sign that you might need to revise or omit that paragraph; or if you find several paragraphs that do not seem to support your thesis, you might want to revisit your thesis statement. Even though you may not want to delete sentences or paragraphs you have written, if they don't contribute to the message that you want to convey, they will weaken your paper.

In addition to the global focus, each section will have a focus. For example, in the "Method" section, your objective is to describe how you conducted your research and why you chose that particular method. Thus, you could ask yourself for each paragraph in the "Method" section: How does this paragraph help me explain how and why I chose a particular method?

Development and Support

If you have divided your research paper into sections, you will need to address development and support more critically at the sectional level than at the global level. During your revisions, you can think about the main points within that section and how you provide support for those points. Each claim you make should have some support, and all of your main arguments should have support from a scholarly source (either an outside source or your own research results).

Because each paragraph makes a claim, each paragraph needs evidence or support. At this level, organization and development and support work very closely together. As a unit, a paragraph works somewhat similarly to your whole paper: there is a topic sentence (like a thesis) making a claim about what you will do in the paragraph, and you spend the paragraph offering support for the idea (as the body of your paper supports your thesis). Therefore, in your revisions you can ask the question: How does this sentence help support the topic sentence of this paragraph?

Organization

If you find yourself struggling with the support or organization of a particular paragraph or series of paragraphs, making a reverse outline can be helpful. A reverse outline takes what you have already written in your draft as the content of the outline. Using the outline format, try to plug in each sentence in the paragraph. Because the outline forces you to identify one main idea and shows the connections between sentences in a paragraph, it can highlight sentences that do not relate to the topic sentence or it can help you revise the topic sentence. Although this might seem like a tedious project, the cut and paste functions in computer programs make it relatively easy to turn a paragraph into an outline.

Table 6.2
Revising and Editing Activities

Activity	Benefits
Peer review	Those less familiar with the topic can point out where you need more support or explanation. A new set of eyes will read your paper with a new perspective to help evaluate the logic of your argument and support. However, not all suggestions might be useful; you can decide whether or not to make a peer's suggested changes
Read out loud	Because you cannot skip over words, this can help you see awkward grammatical constructions and typos
Reverse outline	This can help you work on tough paragraphs. Outlines make you put all your ideas into relationship with each other, so you can more clearly see what is not needed and where you might need more support
List paragraph main ideas	Listing the main idea of each paragraph, first, asks you to make sure each paragraph has only one main idea and, second, makes it easier to address how each main idea helps support your thesis
Spell-checking programs	These programs do highlight words and phrases, drawing your attention to them, but they do not recognize many discipline-specific words, and their grammar suggestions do not always clarify a sentence
Go back to the assignment parameters	Remember to revisit the paper's constraints and requirements before turning in the final draft. You do not want to be penalized for missing a simple formatting requirement or using the incorrect citation format

MECHANICS

Editing for mechanics, or for spelling and grammar, should be the last step before you print out a final draft. Reading through your text one last time seems like the obvious way to go about editing. However, if you read silently, especially if you are rushed, you are less likely to catch grammatical errors and typos. Also, you will probably read your paper as if what you have written matches what you intend to say. Because what you actually write is not always what you intend, we suggest that you read your paper out loud, or—even better—have a friend read your paper out loud to you. When someone must pronounce every word, there is a greater chance that you will hear incorrect grammatical constructions and that the reader will notice typos.

These suggestions for revision and editing strategies are somewhat formulaic, but we realize that papers do not always fit into formulas. For example, not all paragraphs have the topic sentence as the first sentence; and longer papers might have a transition paragraph—rather than a transition sentence—that does not necessarily incorporate evidence or support from outside sources. Therefore, we encourage you to use these strategies consciously. Just as spell-checking programs can end up changing words you didn't want to change when you follow all of the program's suggestions, not all revision activities will benefit all papers and all parts of papers. Table 6.2 lists additional editing and revising strategies that may be useful.

7

Elements of Style

Social criticism begins with grammar and the re-establishing of meanings.
Octavio Paz

Easy reading is damned hard writing.

Nathaniel Hawthorne

A panda walks into a café. He orders a sandwich, eats it, then draws a gun and proceeds to shoot through the ceiling.

"Why?" asks the confused waiter, as the panda makes toward the exit. The panda produces a badly punctuated wildlife manual and tosses it over his shoulder.

"Well, I'm a panda," he says at the door. "Look it up."

The waiter turns to the relevant entry in the manual and, sure enough, finds an explanation. "Panda. Large black-and-white bear-like mammal, native to China. Eats, shoots and leaves."

As this joke shows us, just one extra comma changes the entire meaning of a sentence. Consider the difference between *Eats, shoots and leaves* and *Eats shoots and leaves.* Most likely, a misplaced punctuation mark in your paper will not result in the firing of any guns; however, a number of misplaced punctuation marks or stylistic errors may result in a B+ rather than an A. In other words, grammar is not just a series of unfortunate rules that you are supposed to learn. Rather, grammar is what enables us to communicate effectively.

In this chapter we discuss good grammar and elements of style. If grammar symbolizes the tools of construction, then style symbolizes the way you decorate that construction. For more information about style consult Parts II and III of this book and the *APA Publication Manual.*

RECOGNIZING THE IMPORTANCE OF GOOD GRAMMAR AND STYLE

Generally, grammar and style do not seem to be exciting topics. They involve rules that don't make sense (e.g., why is it considered improper to end a sentence with a preposition?) and seemingly obscure terms that confuse more than they clarify. Furthermore, knowing the difference between a subordinating and a correlative conjunction does not necessarily mean that a writer is able to use them correctly (the latter connects two independent clauses and the former joins an independent clause with a dependent one).

Communication, however, does not occur only at the level of grammar. Through your style of writing, your words also convey a specific tone that carries beyond the denotative meaning. Consider that the style you use to describe your research paper to a friend and to your psychology professor would probably be different. Academic tone tends to be more formal than that of daily conversation. For example, you should avoid the following:

- contractions (use *do not* rather than *don't*);
- colloquial expressions, such as *you know* and *got to*;
- vague expressions, such as *practically all*, *most of them*, *a lot*, *some*;
- shortcuts used for instant messaging or text messaging such as *lol* or *omg*;
- hyperbolic language, such as *stupid*, *dumb*, *awesome*, *shocking*;
- ridiculing another person's work.

Another facet of grammar and style relates to APA guidelines. APA has a citation style that differs from what scholars in the English department would use; and APA style has specific rules for the use of acronyms and for formatting a paper.

As you can see, grammar and style are shaped by both the requirements for basic meaningful communication and the specific expectations of your readers. In other words, your writing should be stylistically fluent and technically proficient. Errors in grammar can make your reader expend a lot of effort trying to understand the meaning of a sentence.

CHOOSING EFFECTIVE WORDING

Although writing in the sciences might seem dry and uncreative, there are subtle gestures you can make to increase the power and readability of your writing. For example, in addition to employing good grammar and active verbs, you can vary the kind and length of your sentences. It is not grammatically incorrect to write with sentences that are the same length or with sentences that begin in the same way, but this style of writing can be tedious to read. Furthermore, if you present your information in an unvarying manner, it can be easy for your reader to overlook important information. Therefore, varying sentence length is a tool to guide your reader. Following a long sentence with a brief sentence will draw attention to the information in the brief sentence.

The way you construct a sentence also enables you to emphasize different pieces of information. Hyde (2005) wrote, "In an important experiment, Lightdale and Prentice (1994) demonstrated the importance of gender roles and social context in creating or erasing the purportedly robust gender differences in aggression" (p. 588). The examples below are phrased differently, and, as a result, highlight different information.

1. Surprisingly, the purportedly robust gender differences in aggression can be created or erased in different social contexts, according to an important experiment by Lightdale and Prentice (1994).
2. Social context is an important factor in determining levels of aggression for both men and women (Lightdale and Prentice 1994).
3. The purportedly robust gender differences in aggression need to be analyzed within their social context, as shown by Lightdale and Prentice (1994).
4. Although one may believe that gender differences are innate, Prentice and Lightdale's research demonstrates the importance of gender roles and social context in creating or erasing the purportedly robust gender differences in aggression.
5. Research by Lightdale and Prentice (1994) has shown that levels of aggression, generally thought to be higher in males, are affected by social context as well as biology.

The way you start a sentence can give your reader clues about how to read the sentence and to connect it to other ideas. Words like *surprisingly* and *although* signal a relation between ideas that may be one of contrast (examples 1 and 4). Also, note that example 2 mentions the researchers only in a citation, whereas the original sentence and examples 1 and 5 emphasize the role of the researchers. Lastly, compare the tone of sentences 2 and 3. Sentence 2 offers information in a relatively neutral tone, whereas sentence 3 expresses a more persuasive tone with the phrase *need to be*.

Another aspect of effective wording involves the skillful use of transitions that show a relation among ideas or concepts in your writing.

Transitions bridge ideas, signaling the kind of statement you are making. Table 7.1 offers a series of situations in which you might use transitions as well as a list of transition words or phrases you can use to illustrate a relation. Transitional words and phrases in each row can take on slightly different meanings. Thus, it is important that you use transitions deliberately.

USING INCLUSIVE AND APPROPRIATE LANGUAGE

By *inclusive language* we mean language that does not unnecessarily exclude or single out groups of people. We emphasize inclusive language because of concerns about precision and ethics.

Regarding precision, we mean simply that good research requires accuracy. Accuracy is critical not only to the validity of your results, but also to your credibility as a researcher. If your pool of participants

Table 7.1
Transitions and their Uses

Purpose	Transition words
To add	accordingly, in addition, equally important, further, furthermore, moreover, not only … but also
To show contrast	although, but, in contrast, conversely, despite, meanwhile, on the other hand, notwithstanding, otherwise, rather, whereas, yet
To show similarity	in the same way, likewise, similarly
To show exception	despite, however, in spite of, nevertheless, still, yet
To show that you are elaborating on a point	that is, in fact, to illustrate, in other words
To show a result	because, as a consequence, consequently, hence, for this (these) reason(s), as a result, therefore, thus
To show the passage of time or sequence	after, afterward, at this point, before, concurrently, earlier, finally, following, formerly, immediately, meanwhile, next, previously, prior to, simultaneously, subsequently, then, thereafter, thus, while
To give an example	to demonstrate, for example, for instance, in another case, to illustrate, in particular, in this case, in this situation, specifically, such as
To emphasize	actually, certainly, extremely, emphatically, in fact, indeed, most importantly, unquestionably, without a doubt, without reservation
To summarize or conclude	as I have shown, in brief, to conclude, in conclusion, hence, on the whole

includes men and women, using masculine pronouns (*him*, *his*, or *he*) to refer to an average participant does not accurately reflect your research.

Exclusive language pertains also to the ethical representation of those who have participated in and are affected by your research. For example, words such as *man* (the noun and the verb *to man*), *mankind*, and *man-made* have been used instead of *people*, *humankind*, and *synthetic* or *manufactured*. Although you may think masculine words refer to or include all people, the exclusion of women from this kind of language is based on sexist assumptions that men *could* stand for all people or that *only* men are the ones who manufacture products. Consider that in the United States women have traditionally had lower status than men in just about all areas of life. For example, women have been able to vote for fewer than 100 years and for a long time could not even own property.

Appropriate and accurate writing practices also consist in avoiding language that might be offensive to participants and to readers or that might unnecessarily single out a group of people. For example, the phrases *female doctor* or *Black scientist* single out women and Black people. Unless gender or racial identity is important to your research, using those phrases may imply that *doctor* means *male doctor* and *scientist* means *White scientist*.

If you do need to describe a person's identity characteristics (gender, race, sexuality, ethnicity, religion, etc.) be sure that you single out only those characteristics that are relevant to the topic about which you are writing. If all your participants are male, then it is not exclusive to write *The rise in blood pressure for a participant correlates with his level of stress*. Nor do we suggest that you merely replace masculine language with feminine language. *The rise in blood pressure for a participant correlates with* her *level of stress* is not more inclusive if your participants include men and women.

Below are some suggestions for revising prose that contains gender-based exclusionary language or language that may be inappropriate.

- Inappropriate: The rise in blood pressure for a participant correlates with his level of stress.
- Appropriate:
  - The rise in blood pressure for a participant correlates with his or her level of stress.
  - The rise in blood pressure for all participants correlates with levels of stress.
  - The rise in blood pressure for all participants correlates with their levels of stress.

- A rise in blood pressure correlates with one's level of stress.
- Instead of chairman, layman, and fireman use chair, layperson, and firefighter.
- Use parallel nouns. For example, instead of man and wife use husband and wife.
- Be aware of how you label groups of people. Decisions may not be easy, though, because labels continue to evolve. You might consult published research to find what other authors have used.
- Use identity labels only when they are an integral part of your research.

DECIDING ON THE USE OF TECHNICAL LANGUAGE

As we discuss in chapter 6, the kind of language you choose should be appropriate for those who will be reading your writing. If you reader needs to look up a number of words or concepts in order to understand your ideas, then your writing is probably too obscure. If you devote too much space to defining concepts that are already familiar to your readers, then you may end up sacrificing the development of your argument. Consequently, it is important that you use technical language as you use grammar—as a tool to more clearly convey information to your reader.

The purpose of technical language is twofold: it serves as a kind of shortcut and it reflects your proficiency with discipline-related concepts. Because you use technical language to avoid explaining at length some aspect related to your work, it is a shortcut. Consider the following sentence: "The scale assessed satisfaction with amount of time spent together, communication, sexual activity, agreement on financial matters, and similarity of interests, lifestyle and temperament on a 4-point Likert-type scale" (Gallo, Troxel, Matthews, and Kuller, 2003, p. 455). The sentence refers to "a 4-point Likert-type scale" without offering further explanation of what a Likert-type scale is. *Health Psychology,* where this article appears, is a scholarly publication, so the authors can legitimately assume that their readers already know what a 4-point Likert-type scale is.

Using technical language without knowing exactly what it means can weaken your argument. There is a greater chance that you will apply the term(s) incorrectly, and if it appears to your audience that you do not understand part of your writing topic, a reader may assume that other parts of your thesis are flawed, as well. Technical language does not replace critical thinking or grammatical clarity.

AVOIDING COMMON PROBLEMS

Apostrophe Use

Apostrophes have two primary grammatical functions: to indicate possession without the use of "of" and to indicate a contraction. Table 7.2 lists the different rules for using apostrophes to indicate possession, and how these rules might be applied correctly and incorrectly.

Although APA style discourages the use of contractions, it is better to use a contraction correctly than to incorrectly use a word that should

Table 7.2
Apostrophe Dos and Don'ts When Indicating Possession

Rule	Correct usage	Incorrect usage
Add 's to the end of the word if the word is in singular form, even if the word ends in the letter *s*	the rat's behavior, James's discussion	the rats' behavior, Jame's discussion, James' discussion
Add *'s* to the plural form of a word if the word does not end in the letter *s*	the children's expectations, the mice's brains	the childrens' expectations, the mices' brains
Add an apostrophe to the end of a plural noun that ends in the letter *s*	the subjects' responses, the students' musical training	the subject's responses, the students's musical training
To attribute joint ownership, follow the above apostrophe rules, but add an apostrophe only to the last noun	Thomas and Blackmun's experiment (this indicates that Thomas and Blackmun worked together to develop the experiment)	Thomas's and Blackmun's experiment
If you want to show possession without joint ownership, each noun needs to be given an apostrophe according to the above rules	Thomas's and Blackmun's experiments (this indicates that Thomas and Blackmun conducted different experiments separately; note that experiments is plural)	Thomas and Blackmun's experiments
Do not add an apostrophe to the end of possessive pronouns	yours, hers, its	your's, her's, it's or yours', hers', its'

be a contraction. Table 7.3 lists some contractions that are commonly misused.

Pronoun Use

A pronoun is a word that replaces a noun. It is important to use pronouns carefully. Below are two basic guidelines for pronoun use.

- The pronoun must agree with the noun or nouns to which it refers (the pronoun's *antecedent*). By *agreement*, we mean that a pronoun needs to be singular or plural, depending on whether it replaces something that is singular or plural.
- It must be clear to the reader which noun or nouns the pronoun replaces, or what the pronoun's antecedent is.
- Inclusive language can make pronoun–noun agreement more complicated. Often, to avoid using a masculine pronoun to refer to all people, a writer may use a pronoun that does not agree with the noun it replaces. Table 7.4 offers a sentence with pronoun misuse related to inclusive language.

If you are not sure if a pronoun is singular or plural, use the pronoun in a sentence with the verb *is* or *are*. The pronouns *everybody* and *they* both could refer to more than one person. However, you would write *everybody is happy* rather than *everybody are happy*, indicating that *everybody* is a singular pronoun. On the other hand, you would write *they are happy*, not *they is happy*, which shows you that *they* is a plural pronoun.

In addition to agreement in number, clarity of reference is important when using pronouns. As the writer, the meaning of a sentence might be clear to you; however, for a reader pronouns can make meaning ambiguous. Table 7.5 offers an example of a pronoun-related problem and a solution.

Table 7.3
Frequently Misused Contractions

Contraction	Uncontracted form	Similar word	Meaning of the similar word
you're	you are	your	Belonging to you
it's	it is	its	Belonging to it
they're	they are	their	Belonging to them
they're	they are	there	indicates location/where something is

Table 7.4
Pronouns and Agreement in Number

Sample sentence	Agreement in number	Reference to the antecedent
Everyone should do their homework.	*Everyone* is a singular pronoun, and *their* is a plural pronoun. Therefore, the pronoun and its antecedent do not agree	*Their* can refer only to *everyone.* Therefore, *their* has a clear antecedent
Possible revisions Everyone should do his or her homework. Everyone should do homework. You should do your homework. All students should do their homework.		

Table 7.5
Pronouns and Antecedent References

Sample sentence	Agreement in number	Reference to the antecedent
We think that beliefs shape religious people's decision-making processes; therefore, we examine them in this study.	*Beliefs* and *people* are plural nouns. As *them* is a plural pronoun, there is not an error in agreement	*Them* could refer either to *beliefs* or to *people.* Therefore, *them* has an unclear antecedent
Possible revisions We believe that beliefs shape religious people's decision-making processes; therefore we examine beliefs about an afterlife in this study. In this study we examine how beliefs shape a religious person's decision-making process.		

VERB FORMS

For clarity and brevity use the active voice when possible and use the passive voice only when necessary. Sentences written in an *active voice* have an *active verb*, or a verb whose subject is doing the action. For example, in the sentence *The participants answered 10 questions*, the verb is *answered* and the subject is *participants*; and it is the participants who are doing the action. In the sentence *The 10 questions were answered by the participants*, the subject becomes *10 questions*, and the verb *were answered* is passive. For another example, see Table 7.6.

Table 7.6
Active and Passive Verbs

Sample sentence	Analysis
"The social-cognitive observational learning model suggests that normative beliefs about aggression, hostile biases about the world, and aggressive social scripts are all learned from observing violence" (Huesmann, Moise-Titus, Podolski & Eron, 2003, p. 217).	It is clear that the subject is *model* and the verb is *suggests*
That normative beliefs about aggression, hostile biases about the world, and aggressive social scripts are all learned from observing violence *is suggested* by the social-cognitive observational learning model.	The subject is beliefs and the verb is *is suggested*. This passive voice construction makes the reader work harder to find the verb and is more wordy than the active voice construction
It has been suggested that normative beliefs about aggression, hostile biases about the world, and aggressive social scripts are all learned from observing violence.	The verb is *has been suggested*, but because the subject is *it* we do not know who is doing the suggesting. Passive voice constructions allow you to omit the agent of the verb, so your sentence may be less precise and more confusing

We also encourage you to limit your use of forms of the verb *to be* (e.g., *is, are, am, was, were*). Compare the following two sentences:

1. There is a lot we can learn from this research.
2. We can learn a lot from this research.

Both sentences are grammatically correct, yet, *there is* in the first sentence adds words needlessly. Besides ease of reading, an advantage of avoiding forms of *to be* is that your prose is crisper and more dynamic.

SPELLING

As a language, English has borrowed from many other languages, so rules of spelling are sometimes inconsistent from one word to another. The rules in Table 7.7 will give you a good sense of how to deal with many words that you are likely to use, but when you are in doubt, you can consult a good, college-level dictionary for further information.

Table 7.7
Rules for Forming Plurals

Rule	Examples
Nouns ending in *is* often form plurals by changing the *i* to an *e*	Correct: *hypothesis* becomes *hypotheses* Incorrect: hypothesises Examples following this rule: hypothesis, thesis, crisis, diagnosis
Nouns ending in *us* often form a plural by changing the *us* to *i*	Correct: *stimulus* becomes *stimuli* Examples following this rule: focus, fungus, nucleus, syllabus
Nouns ending in *on* may form plurals by changing *on* to *a*. This holds true for nouns that come from Latin or Greek, but not for nouns that come from English, such as *coupon*, which form plurals simply by adding *s*	Correct: *phenomenon* becomes *phenomena* Examples following this rule: *phenomenon, criterion* Note: Traditionally, the plurals of foreign words such as *schema* and *stigma* were formed by adding *ta*, as in *schemata* and *stigmata*. It is common now to see such plurals as *schemas* and *stigmas*
Some nouns have the same form in singular and plural	Examples following this rule: *species, sheep, fish*
Some nouns have a plural form but take a singular verb	Examples following this rule: *news, linguistics, athletics* Note: *Statistics* as a discipline is singular; as an *application, statistics* is plural. Examples: *Statistics is a quantitative discipline,* but *In this research, the relevant statistics are the mean, median, and mode.*
Compound nouns may form plurals by making the initial noun plural	Correct: mother-in-law becomes mothers-in-law Incorrect: mothers-in-laws Examples following this rule: attorney general, mother-in-law
Words that end in *ex* used to form plurals by changing the *ex* to *ices,* but the current form is simply to add *es*	Correct: *index* becomes *indexes* (rather than the old-fashioned *indices*)
Words from Latin and Greek retain their original forms in the plural	Correct: *datum* becomes *data* Note: Never use *data* or *media* as singular nouns; instead use *datum* or *medium* Examples following this rule: *datum* becomes *data, medium* becomes *media, alumnus* becomes *alumni, alumna* becomes *alumnae* Note: In classical Latin, *alumni* and *alumnae* were pronounced identically, with a long *i* at the end. So in speech, they were not differentiated. Most speakers now would pronounce them differently. With the current attempt to avoid language that some might consider sexist, writers often use genderless terms such as *graduates* or *alums*

Continued overleaf.

Table 7.7
Continued.

Rule	Examples
Words that end in *o* often form plurals by adding *es* after the *o*, although words associated with music often do not	Correct: *motto* becomes *mottoes*; *cello* becomes *cellos* Examples following the *es* rule: hero (heroes), memo, potato Examples following the *s* rule: cello (cellos), radio, stereo, quarto Note: There are many exceptions (e.g., *typos*, *albinos*, *tacos*) to rules about forming the plural, so unless you are absolutely certain about the form of the plural, look it up in the dictionary
Collective nouns are sometimes used as singular nouns and sometimes as plural nouns	When the group referred to acts as a unit, the noun is singular Example: *The faculty is on strike.* When the people constituting the group are acting as individuals, the noun is plural Example: *The faculty are going home after their meeting.* Note: Words and phrases such as *a lot* and *a number* are often plural in meaning, so it is appropriate to write that *A number of people are on the street* even though the subject of the sentence is *number*, which usually takes a singular verb such as *is* rather than the plural *are*
In extremely rare situations, it is appropriate to use an apostrophe to form a plural	Sometimes people may use an apostrophe to form the plural of a letter of the alphabet or a number if including the apostrophe would prevent ambiguity. Regardless of which style you use, write the letter or the number in italics and add the letter *s* not in italics. Example: *A*'s *are hard grades to earn in classes.* By not using the apostrophe, a reader could think you were using the word *as*
Words that end in *s* or *s*-like sounds form plurals by adding *es*	Correct: *hex* becomes *hexes* Incorrect: hex's Examples following this rule: *sex* (used as a noun), *scratch*, *kiss*
Nouns and verbs ending in *y* form plurals by using *ies*	Correct: try becomes tries, penny becomes pennies Incorrect: penny's Examples following this rule: penny, baby, cry Note: Do not change the *y* to *ies* for family names like *Kelly*, which would be *Kellys* in the plural, or for nouns with a vowel before the Y (e.g., *day* becomes *days*)

SPECIFIC WORD USE

In APA style, there are some rules regarding specific word use. Although these rules may not pertain only to APA style, they are considered important enough (and are violated enough) that the publication manual singles them out for special attention. These rules appear in Table 7.8.

If you have further questions about spelling (or definitions), the following links will take you to useful online dictionaries:

- http://www.m-w.com/
- http://www.websters-online-dictionary.org/
- http://dictionary.reference.com/

Table 7.8
Specific Guidelines for Specific Word Use in APA Style

Word	Guideline
that and *which*	*That* is appropriate for restrictive clauses that are necessary for the meaning of a sentence. Example: *The word that was in the wrong place changed the meaning of the sentence.* *Which* is appropriate for nonrestrictive clauses that merely provide more information. Example: *The participant identified the word, which was partially obscured.*
who and *that*	*Who* refers to people, whereas *that* generally refers to nonhuman animals, objects, or ideas Example: *The girl who dropped the ball frightened the dog that ran away.*
while and *although*	*While* is a temporal conjunction, so use it only when referring to time. Example: *He ate an apple while he waited* versus *Although he made a mistake, he was able to recover.* (Not *While he made a mistake ...*)
since and *because*	*Since* is a temporal conjunction, so use it only when referring to time. Example: *He has not eaten since breakfast* versus *She was angry because he insulted her.* (Not *... since he insulted her*)
using the subjunctive mood	Actions that did not occur or that are improbable take subjunctive verbs, which look like plural, past tense verbs. Examples: *If I were 12 years old again, I would do things differently* and *If she were prepared for the test, she would have passed it.*

Continued overleaf.

Table 7.8
Continued.

Word	Guideline
between and *among*	*Between* is appropriate when discussing two things, whereas *among* is appropriate for three or more things. Example: *The poet had to decide between love and hate as a theme of her work* and *The poet had to decide among love, hate, and death as a theme of her work.*
sex and *gender*	In APA style, *sex* refers to biology, but *gender* refers to cultural considerations Example: *Estrogen is present in the bodies of people of both sexes* and *Promotion to executive positions in corporations does not occur equally in both genders.* Note: In some disciplines, scholars do not accept this usage.
female/ male and *woman/ man* or *girl/ boy*	In APA style, *female* and *male* are usually adjectives, whereas *woman, man, boy,* and *girl* are nouns Example: *People expect stereotypically female behaviors from girls and women.* Exception: If the age range of people being discussed is considerable, the general words female and male may be used as nouns
Black and *White*	When referring to people of African descent as *Black* capitalize the word; similarly, when referring to people of European descent as *White*, capitalize the word. All words designating racial or ethnic groups are capitalized
Black or *African-American*, *Native American* or *Indian*, *Asian* or *Oriental*	Social norms change, but current conventions are such that *Black* or *African-American*, *Native American* or *Indian* are considered acceptable. People of Asian descent should be called *Asian* (or a more specific, appropriate term, such as *Laotian*); the term *Oriental* is considered pejorative and should not be used to label people or groups. *Oriental* is acceptable as an adjective describing objects, such as an *Oriental carpet*. APA style specifies that, ideally, researchers should describe people as those people wish to be described
Sexual preference and *sexual orientation*	In APA style, *sexual orientation* is preferred over *sexual preference* unless you are explicitly talking about a person's choice. *Gay* is appropriate as a generic term to describe people, although some might consider it sexist because it is a general term used to describe men. If there is any ambiguity in meaning, use the term gay men. The appropriate term for gay women is *lesbian*. The term *homosexual* is not considered appropriate because it has been used in a generally negative sense in the past
disability and *handicap*	Avoid referring to people as being synonymous with challenges they face, such as referring to them as *schizophrenics* or *anorexics*. Instead, refer to them using wording such as *people with schizophrenia*. Use *handicap* to refer to physical limitations, such as being handicapped by lighting that is too dim, curbs that are too high, and so forth

8

Communicating Statistics

If you want to inspire confidence, give plenty of statistics. It does not matter that they should be accurate, or even intelligible, as long as there [are] enough of them.

Lewis Carroll

When you can measure what you are speaking about and express it in numbers, you know something about it.

Lord Kelvin

If you can't fall asleep, you might try counting sheep. As everybody knows, numbers can put your mind into a stupor that is every bit as deep as sleep. When you are reading and you see a set of numbers, does your mind go numb? If so, you know exactly what you want to avoid in your writing. Your own numbers should support your arguments, but most of the time people are going to be more interested in the words you write.

Statistics have a reputation that, to most people, is more negative than positive. People try to avoid them because statistics involve numbers, because statistics can be hard to understand, and because statistics can be deceptive. We too often forget that, when we use them properly, statistics can be highly informative. In the end, they are merely tools that people can use well or poorly.

The problem is that too many of us are so intimidated by them that we fail to evaluate them critically. We need to remember that people use statistics just as they use words—to communicate a message. A good speaker can persuade an audience with well-chosen words. Politicians are very adept at creating messages to convince people that the politician is looking out for their welfare. It is not the fault of the words when the politicians end up lining their own pockets at taxpayers' expense. The problem lies with the failure of people to evaluate critically what the politicians are saying.

The same dynamic occurs with statistics. If people are willing to accept statistics at face value, there is no limit to the chicanery that others can perpetrate with numbers.

Fortunately, when social researchers use statistics to bolster their arguments, they are generally not trying to deceive. Rather, they are using statistics as a tool to help them understand behavior and to let them generate logical and believable conclusions. After drawing their inferences, researchers then use statistics to convince others of the validity of those conclusions.

In your own work, effective communication requires that you know your audience. If you are writing for a statistically sophisticated readership, you can probably assume that people reading your material will possess the technical information necessary to understand the statistics you have used. So a complete and thorough presentation of those statistics would be entirely appropriate. On the other hand, if your audience is less sophisticated about research and statistical techniques, presenting technical jargon will probably only confuse and distract them from the message that you are trying to convey.

When you write, it may be very helpful for you to imagine what a reader will think when reading your words. This strategy is useful when you decide how you want to convey your message.

WHY DO WE USE STATISTICS?

Psychology is an empirical discipline, so we gather information to answer our questions. Most of the time, this information goes by the name *data* and most of the time it involves numbers. If we study a large group of people (or rats, pigeons, etc.), we generate a lot of information and we have to make sense of it. The most common way of reducing the number of data so we are not swamped with too much information is to find the average score. There are several distinct averages, each computed differently. The common averages are the mean, the median, and the mode. The most frequently used is the *mean*, which is the technical term for the score you obtain by adding all your numbers and dividing by the number of scores you added. In everyday language, most people use the word *average* to reflect the mean. Sometimes we also want to find out whether the scores are bunched together or spread apart, so we find the *standard deviation*. Together, these two statistics give us a sense of the typical score (the average) and how far from the typical score we can expect other scores to be (the standard deviation).

A second use of statistics is to allow us to evaluate the similarities and differences of groups. So if we have a group of, say, 100 measurements from one group and 100 measurements from another group, we can compute two numbers for each group, the mean (the average score) and the standard deviation (an indicator of the spread of the scores), to find out if the two groups are similar or different. There are other ways to assess the relations among the numbers, but they all have the same goal of allowing us to put measurements in context or to create a perspective that helps us think about what they mean.

A third use of statistics is to draw inferences about whether we should believe that our numbers are reliable. That is, if we gather our data from one group of people, can we expect the same result if we took the same measurements from a different group of people? The purpose of these inferential statistics is to establish a level of confidence that what holds true for the groups we measured will be true for different groups as well.

If you keep these three general uses in mind when you read about statistics, you will have an easier time understanding what a writer is trying to convey. Similarly, if you make clear to your reader why you are using a particular statistic, you will be helping your reader to understand the points you are making.

WHAT POINT ARE YOU TRYING TO MAKE?

Using numbers to make a point is not much different from using words to make that point. In both cases, you introduce an assertion that you subsequently support with logical argument. The difference between statistics and words is that statistics involve a shorthand way of making your case.

To use one of the simplest types of statistics, the average, you are able to tell the reader what is typical. An average simply depicts what you can generally expect. To cite an average, however, hides a significant amount of background information. Specifically, when you give an average, you are relying on the reader to understand that you had a group of measurements and that you used some kind of arithmetic or numerical action to come up with a single number to represent the entire group. In addition, if you are communicating with a lay audience, you might want to point out that nobody may actually have scored precisely at the mean, even if a lot of scores might be close to it. Furthermore, there are different types of averages, so your reader should know that there are various ways to come up with the average. So when you say that "The average is X", you are only giving the final step in a sequence.

To make your point effectively, it is important not to let the reader lose sight of that point or why each statement you make relates to it. Burying readers in a bunch of numbers and symbols whose relevance they do not understand is a good way to divert their attention from your message, reducing its impact.

So how can you make sure your readers know where you are taking them? You must give them sufficient detail to allow them to assemble a complete picture. This means writing a verbal statement of your point, presenting relevant statistics, and creating a verbal statement of what the numbers mean. Presenting only the numbers poses a risk that readers will not connect them to your main point; presenting only words poses the risk that readers will not be able to evaluate the cogency of your argument.

For each statistic that you provide, you need to include four elements for the benefit of the reader.

- a statement of the point you are addressing;
- a verbal summary of your statistic;
- the numerical presentation of statistical information;
- how the numbers relate to your point.

Your language should be as simple as possible, while allowing you to make your point. Some writers, particularly beginning writers, believe that using complex terms and difficult vocabulary will lead to more credible prose. The reverse may be more likely. If readers do not understand the point you are trying to make, your writing will have no effect on them at all.

UNDERSTANDING YOUR NUMBERS

Numbers, by themselves, are not particularly interesting or informative. As psychologists use numbers, those numbers take on meaning only when they link to an idea. We use our statistics as tools to help us understand thought and behavior. As such, the numbers should take second place to your ideas when you write.

So you should strive to make your prose complete and comprehensible even without the numerical information. The statistics reinforce your writing in much the same way that quotations support writing in the humanities. In both cases, the writer creates an argument and then buttresses it with numbers (in the sciences) or with quotations (in the humanities). Table 8.1 provides two examples of how the technical information complements the verbal presentation but is not necessary for understanding the ideas. Naturally, the more information you include, the greater the understanding that your reader will gain. But you should be able communicate the main points of your research without reliance on any statistical presentation whatsoever.

Table 8.2 illustrates the most frequently asked questions that psychologists pose in their research and the statistical tests that are appropriate for those questions. If you ask whether the averages of different groups are comparable and if your statistical test tells you that the answer to the question is "no," you have a significant effect. Basically, *significant* means *reliable*; a significant difference means that the difference is reliable—you can count on it happening again. So *t*-tests and

Table 8.1
Examples of Text With and Without Statistical Information. Each version should communicate the same basic information; the numbers should not be necessary for the reader to understand your message

Statistical information included	Statistical information excluded
Participants rated how offensive they found a set of jokes. The average rating was highest for jokes victimizing women ($M = 3.6$), with jokes victimizing men ($M = 2.1$) and neutral jokes ($M = 2.3$) showing lower levels of perceived offensiveness. This effect was significant, $F(2,160) = 91.782$, $p < .001$[1]	Participants rated how offensive they found a set of jokes. The average rating was highest for jokes victimizing women, with jokes victimizing men and neutral jokes showing lower levels of perceived offensiveness
Participants in the different groups expected jokes that varied in humor level. People who believed that they would read very funny jokes found the jokes the funniest ($M = 4.8$), followed by participants in the neutral, no-information condition ($M = 4.0$), and then by participants who expected very unfunny jokes, who found the jokes least funny ($M = 3.2$). When we led participants to expect either horrible jokes or hysterical jokes, the ratings did not differ significantly from the neutral group ($M = 3.5$ and 3.9, respectively), $F(4,85) = 8.59$, $p < 001$[2]	Participants in the different groups expected jokes that varied in humor level. People who believed that they would read very funny jokes found the jokes the funniest, followed by participants in the neutral, no-information condition, and then by participants who expected very unfunny jokes, who found the jokes less funny. When we led participants to expect either horrible jokes or hysterical jokes, the ratings did not differ significantly from the neutral group

[1]Beins, B. C., Agnitti, J., Baldwin, V., Yarmosky, S., Bubel, A., MacNaughton, K., & Pashka, N. (2005, October). How Expectations Affect Perceptions of Offensive Humor. Poster presented at the annual convention of the New England Psychological Association, New Haven, CT.

[2] Wimer, D. J., & Beins, B. C. (2000, August). Is this joke funny? Only if we say it is. Presented at the annual convention of the American Psychological Association, Washington, DC.

Table 8.2
Common Research Questions and the Statistical Tests Associated with them.
Each type of test has variations that are appropriate for different circumstances.
You can refer to statistics and research methods books for details on appropriate
use of these tests

Question	Statistical test
Do two groups have the same averages?	*t*-test, *z*-test
Do three or more groups have the same averages?	Analysis of variance (*F*-test)
When two scores are paired, are the two scores independent? Or does knowing one score give you a clue about the other score, reflecting that the scores are dependent and related to one another?	Correlation (ρ, *r*, ϕ)
For paired scores, if you know the score of one member of the pair, can you predict the second score at above-chance levels?	Regression analysis
If you have multiple categories into which different observations can fall, does the number of observations in each group match your expectations?	Chi-square (χ^2)

F-tests let you know if the difference between groups is likely to appear again if you do your research a second time.

Similarly, if scores are paired so that knowing something about one member of the pair helps you predict the second, there is a significant relation between the two variables. Again, significant means reliable. So if you were to conduct your study a second time, you could reasonably expect to see a similar pattern in the data.

The term *significant* is a technical term, one that psychologists would probably change if we could. It means something very different in statistics and in everyday life. In a casual conversation, if somebody tells you a significant fact, it is probably an important fact. But if your results are significant, they may or may not be important; they are simply reliable, that is, likely to recur if you replicated your original study.

As an example, if standardized aptitude test (SAT) scores increase nationwide by only a few points from one year to the next, that difference is going to be statistically significant because huge sample sizes make it easy to spot small, but reliable, differences. The difference is significant in a statistical sense, but it is not particularly significant in a real-world sense. This is why psychologists have recently started reporting a statistic called an effect size. The effect size can tell you if an experimental manipulation produces a large, medium, or small effect. The larger the effect size, the more meaningful it is in a real-world sense.

HELPING READERS UNDERSTAND YOUR STATISTICS

A number of authors (e.g., Best, 2001, 2004; Huff, 1954; Tufte, 1983) have perused the research literature and the popular media and have found examples of poor statistical communication. Fortunately, we do not need to be victims of poor statistics. Huff (1954) suggested that experts at statistical deception know how to mislead people with numbers, so it would be a good idea for the rest of us to know about these tricks. Best (2001) stressed that the cure for the so-called "bad statistic" is a recognition that we must evaluate numbers.

One of the most effective strategies to avoid giving your reader the wrong message with your numbers is to keep your presentation as simple as possible. As the information becomes more complicated, you need to include more statistics, but your goal should be to minimize the likelihood that your information will distract the reader from the point you want to make. Tufte (1983) has coined the term *chartjunk* to describe elements that appear in graphs that distract the reader from understanding the content in the graph. He suggested that, if you create a figure, you should maximize the amount of relevant information and minimize anything that would distract the reader. For example, differentiating the bars in a bar chart or a histogram is more effective when you use darkness of shading rather than thin lines that produce a distracting, moiré effect like the one in Figure 8.1.

A useful principle that Tufte identified is the maximization of the data-to-ink ratio. That is, graphs become more useful when the amount of data grows and the amount of ink decreases. Another way of saying this is that you will communicate more effectively if you present the critical statistical information and as little else as possible in a graph.

Sometimes you can miscommunicate with words, too. Best (2001) identified what he described as "The Worst Social Statistic Ever." He pointed out that a graduate student made the claim, based on research by the Children's Defense Fund (1994) that "Every year since 1950, the number of American children gunned down has doubled" (pp. 1–2). This statistic is patently impossible because if a single child had died by gunfire in 1950, the number of children in the United States felled by gunshot in the year 2000 would exceed 2 trillion. The message here is that you need to be very careful in selecting your wording. The original claim by the Children's Defense Fund about gunshot

(a)

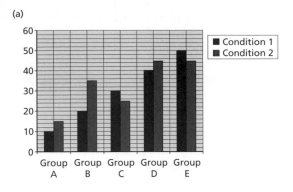

(b)

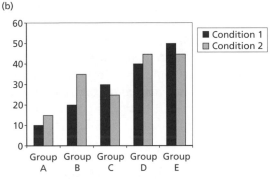

Figure 8.1 An illustration of (a) a graph with uninformative gridlines that clutter the figure and bars with a moiré effect that Tufte (1983) asserts will distract the reader and (b) a graph with a less cluttered, more easily comprehensible format.

deaths was that "The number of American children killed each year by guns has doubled since 1950" (Children's Defense Fund, 1994, p. x). This claim is very different from the misstatement by the graduate student. You need to be very careful in your wording so that your claim matches the data.

Another common problem is presenting data out of context. For instance, Best (2004) pointed out that during a news broadcast in 2001, CBS anchor Dan Rather commented on the "epidemic" of school shootings after a student in California had killed two students and wounded several others. Obviously, deaths of children are tragic; multiple, violent deaths are worse. But the truth is that the rate of school-based violence had decreased by around 50% in the past decade. Rather's comments were based on the California shooting and a few other well-publicized tragedies rather than on the mass of data that showed the schools were safer than a decade previously and pretty safe compared with nonschool locations. This incident exemplifies the concept of missing data and relates to the concept of hasty generalization discussed in chapter 3.

In another instance, Daniel Okrent, who worked for the *New York Times*, noted that health workers and activists had criticized the administration of President Ronald Reagan for scant funding for AIDS research. An official in the Reagan administration, Gary Bauer, asserted that AIDS funding had increased during Reagan's tenure as president. In assessing Bauer's claim, Okrent explained that AIDS had not existed as a public health issue prior to the Reagan administration, so there would have been no need for funding. Obviously, comparing contemporary funding with a time when no money was needed does not help resolve arguments. Bauer's statistics were misleading, whether or not his failure to present the whole picture was intentional (Gross & Miller, 2006).

Obviously, a few examples here cannot exhaust the ways that somebody can present a distorted message with statistics. But these examples can alert you to the need to be cautious in presenting your statistics and in assessing the statistics that others present to you.

DIFFERENTIATING RESULTS AND INTERPRETATIONS

When you analyze your data, the results provide a description of what has happened. You conclude that the groups you compared are significantly different or they are not. Or the relation between two variables is significant or nonsignificant. Or the number of observations in different categories matches your expectations or it does not.

If statistical results tell you what happened, it is now up to you to figure out why things occurred as they did. This is the realm of interpretation. In an APA-formatted paper, the description of what happened belongs in the Results section. The interpretation and speculation goes in the Discussion section.

Your statistics support your description of what happened. At some point, though, you need to figure out why the data emerged as they did. In your discussion, you are using your knowledge of the area, your creativity, and your insights and intuitions to speculate regarding what it all means. For just about any data set you generate, there will be more than one feasible interpretation. Your job is to generate the most plausible interpretation based on your statistics and on what previous researchers have discovered. For questions that are complex, there will always be explanations that differ from yours. Further research will resolve the issue of whether your interpretation or some other interpretation is most reasonable.

Part II

Preparing APA Format Papers

9

Writing a Thesis or a Term Paper

Science is facts; just as houses are made of stones, so is science made of facts; but a pile of stones is not a house and a collection of facts is not necessarily science.

Henri Poincaré

That is what learning is. You suddenly understand something you've understood all your life, but in a new way.

Doris Lessing

Because most colleges and universities have writing requirements and general education requirements, it is nearly impossible for a student to graduate without writing a term paper. Although writing a term paper can produce a certain level of anxiety, we hope that this book, and specifically this chapter, will provide some guidelines for writing them effectively (and efficiently!). In psychology, a term paper is the paper you write specifically for a class. Rather than being a paper based on original research, a form of primary literature, a term paper is based on your own review of existing primary and secondary literature. In other words, in a term paper it is your job to identify a topic, search for scholarly sources that address your topic, and use those sources to support your claims.

The process for writing a term paper will be similar to the process you use for writing other research papers; however, the research process will differ slightly. Table 9.1 outlines the steps involved in writing a term paper. Depending on the amount of guidance your professor gives, you may skip some of the steps. Additionally, the steps are listed in a chronological order—for example, it is important to do research before choosing your thesis—however, activities done for each step may overlap with the activities involved in another step, and you may move back and forth between different steps (that is, after developing and supporting your paper's main ideas, you may realize that the ideas need additional support or additional focused research).

Table 9.1
Writing a Term Paper

Step	Activities
Understand the assignment	Read the assignment closely. Ask the professor if you have any questions (even if it is a few days before the due date)
Invention	Brainstorm ideas for the topic, freewrite about possible ideas, use techniques such as broad outlines and idea maps to try out different ideas
Pre-research	Skim scholarly and popular sources for ideas; it is useful to use your pre-research to inform your brainstorming and freewriting
Preliminary research	Once you have a general topic, read a wide variety of sources about your topic, start narrowing your focus, ask of the topic: why would an academic audience be interested
Thesis development	Narrow your research questions so that you can address them within the paper's parameters, ask why an academic audience would be interested in your thesis
Focused research	Once you have outlined your thesis, look for scholarly sources that relate to the thesis, look at the sources' reference lists to find additional relevant resources, take clear notes to avoid unintentional plagiarism
Organization	Use outlines to organize your paper (outlines can be useful at different levels, from the scale of the entire paper to a single paragraph), start drafting the paper
Development and support	Use sources and your notes to make sure that all of your claims have scholarly support, put this evidence into your outlines, do additional research if some points need more support
Drafting	Use your outlines, brainstorms, freewriting, and idea maps to draft the paper
Revision	Read the draft of your paper with the following questions in mind: do all the paragraphs in my paper relate to my thesis, does my paper address the audience appropriately, do I provide evidence for each claim, do I have transitions between the main sections of the paper and the paragraphs
Check your sources	Make sure that you have all the information you need for your reference list, make sure that each idea from a source is cited in the paper
Proofreading	Read your paper to check for typos, grammatical errors, and sentences that might be confusing for your reader (we suggest reading the paper out loud or having a friend read it out loud to you)

DEVELOPING YOUR IDEA

Rather than coming up with a thesis statement and then looking for articles that support that thesis, use the articles to give you ideas for your thesis. You do not want to unintentionally repeat what somebody has already published; nor do you want to develop a thesis that is flawed because you failed to read important studies about the topic. Familiarity with published research is also important because you can locate studies whose ideas you can build on. We offer some general descriptions of different approaches below.

Filling in a Gap

In a study about unintentional race bias, the authors discussed a gap in the body of research:

> Much research has been focused on elucidating the mechanisms of race-bias control in an effort to understand why control sometimes fails (Devine & Monteith, 1999). A key feature of existing models of prejudice control is that the regulation of behavior follows the conscious realization of having unintentionally made a race-biased response (Monteith, 1993; Monteith, Ashburn-Nardo, Viols, & Czopp, 2002). However these models do not account for how race-bias activation may be detected and controlled as a response unfolds "in the moment." (Amodio et al., 2004, p. 88)

Through their research the authors realized that models of prejudice control can explain only some facets of race bias, but they cannot necessarily explain how a person's prejudices may surface, despite that person's attempts to be nonprejudiced. In other words, studies about race bias frequently explore a person's conscious reaction to his or her own racism. As a result, biological changes in a person's body receive no attention because the individual may not recognize those changes. Therefore, the authors propose that a neural model might offer information about prejudice that prior models cannot. They performed research about race bias, identified a gap in the field, and then developed a study that could start to fill that gap.

Building Upon a Particular Study or Studies

In a study about the risk of violence among patients in a forensic psychiatric hospital, de Vogel and de Ruiter (2005) described why they chose a particular sample population for their study:

> The HRC-20 was primarily developed on the basis of research in male samples and most research into the psychometric properties of the HCR-20 has been done in male samples. Therefore, the question of whether the HCR-20 is also suitable for use with females seems important. (de Vogel & de Ruiter, 2005, p. 227)

Because male patients had been the primary sample population, the authors decided to explore the validity of this model in assessing risk factors for violence among female patients. They developed a study to supplement a previous study of male patients in a Dutch forensic psychiatric hospital. They write,

> In this article, we will present findings on the inter-rater reliability and predictive validity of the HCR-20 in a sample of 42 female patients who have been admitted to the Dr. Henri van der Hoeven Kliniek, a Dutch forensic psychiatric hospital. The findings are compared with those for a matched sample of 42 male forensic psychiatric patients from the same hospital. The aim of the present study was to examine whether there are differences between female and male forensic psychiatric patients regarding mean HCR-20 scores, inter-rater reliability and predictive validity for violent outcome. (de Vogel & de Ruiter, 2005, p. 228)

Note that the authors do not imply that their study invalidates the study of male patients; rather, in their study they assess the usefulness of a model to explain the behavior of another population. As you read different articles about your topic, ask yourself how research could be modified to test the validity of a theory about human behavior. The answers to this question can provide fruitful places for you to start developing your thesis.

Exploring Competing Theories

Often when psychologists ask a question there is no single answer. As a result, some studies survey and evaluate different ways to address an issue or problem. For example, in a study about people's motivations for giving to strangers, the authors explore the debates between an empathy-altruistic (i.e., caring) basis and an egoistic (i.e., self-oriented) basis, which are the two main theories to describe why one individual gives to another. The two sides of the debate informed the authors' study in the following way:

One common resolution to these contradictory findings is to acknowledge that there are two basic reactions to another person's need: personal distress and empathetic concern. And, as seen by the plethora of research on both sides of the issue, both personal distress (self-oriented reactions to another's need) and empathetic concern (other-oriented reactions to another's need) can motivate an individual to give aid to someone who is in need (Batson, 1991). Although many laboratory experiments have yielded evidence in favor of both egoistic and altruistic motives of giving, fewer non-laboratory studies have been examined to investigate motivations for giving. The present study examines motivations for giving within the context of a real-world, non-laboratory event. (Piferi, Jobe, & Jones, 2006, p. 174)

In addition to building upon previous studies by shifting from a laboratory to a nonlaboratory setting, the authors used the debate between egoism and altruism to shape their research. They identified a contradiction—that seemingly altruistic behavior has an egoistic basis—and evaluated how the two sides of the debate could help them understand the patterns of giving in their sample population.

Reviewing Published Work

Review articles constitute a legitimate area of publication for psychologists, and they can be useful to your research because they are scholarly sources that review other scholarly sources. In one review article about the efficacy of narrative therapy (i.e., telling stories) for treating psychosis, the authors outlined their research project:

Although we suggest that narrative changes should be considered in the context of psychosis, it is unclear how such changes are best systematically assessed and/or studied. In this paper, we begin to address the above question by reviewing recent findings in which narratives have been utilized as potential measures of outcome in the treatment of psychosis. (France & Uhlin, 2006, p. 56)

They continue:

In this paper, we do not seek to construct a definitive taxonomy of important narrative elements. Instead, our primary goal is to review the efforts of various authors to utilize narrative elements as a means to assess outcomes in psychosis. (France & Uhlin, 2006, p. 57)

In their conclusion, after reviewing a wide range of studies about treating psychoses, the authors affirmed their commitment to narrative therapy. Because they cited over 70 sources in their "References" section, they demonstrate the extent of their research and, thus, increase the credibility of their argument. Their "References" section also provides you with a list of sources that may help you develop your own ideas about this topic.

Because you are not doing empirical research in a term paper, you will not be able to follow all of the above models. However, the models do offer varied ways to place your voice into academic discourse. That is, you can use the frameworks to start thinking about how you want to develop your own ideas. In Table 9.2 we describe how the different categories can be applied to a term paper by offering different questions that each enables you to ask.

Table 9.2
Different Research Models

Type of model	Possible questions
Filling in a gap	• What kinds of research questions have been asked about a topic? • What kinds of research questions have not been asked about a topic? • What study or studies are important for the way they fill in a gap that had existed?
Building on a study or studies	• How does a study attempt to build on existing literature? • Does the study successfully add another dimension to the existing literature? • If it is successful, why? If it is not successful, why not? • Why might the authors of the study have chosen to add to the literature in the way they did?
Exploring competing theories	• What are the existing perspectives about a topic? • What are the assumptions that shape the different perspectives? • Is there one perspective that dominates the field? Why? • In your mind, which perspective is most useful? Why?
Reviewing published work	• Why are the authors writing this review article? Would you arrive at the same conclusions that the authors did? • What are the benefits of reviewing a specific body of literature? • How are the different articles in the body of literature "speaking" to each other? Which are attempting to fill in a gap? Which are building on prior studies? Which are exploring competing theories?

ORGANIZING YOUR PAPER AROUND THE CENTRAL QUESTIONS

The central questions of your paper are the ones that you are attempting to answer. Every part of your paper should contribute to answering those questions or to giving your readers the background information they need to understand your paper topic.

In this section we will briefly present some strategies that may be useful for keeping your paper focused on the questions you are addressing. (See chapter 6 for more information about organizing a paper.)

Use Index Cards

This strategy allows you to see your ideas and can help you develop themes that may eventually become the main ideas of your paper. In practice, write one idea per index card and include citation information for that idea. When you have a set of index cards with different ideas you can start categorizing them at different levels. For example, if your topic relates to morality-driven behaviors, you could group your index cards by fields of psychology that have contributed to this topic, such as social psychology, cognitive psychology, evolutionary psychology, and neuroscience (García & Ostrosky-Solís, 2006). Subsequently, you can identify subgroups within each field and organize index cards on a more specific level.

Develop Outlines

You can make outlines at different levels of detail, from the most general main ideas of your paper to the individual sentences of a paragraph. When you start your paper, make an outline with your thesis and the main ideas that help you support the thesis. The next step is to focus on one of the main ideas and outline the points that support that main idea. Later in your writing process you could outline a particular paragraph that has been difficult to write.

For each paragraph you should be able to answer the following questions:

- What is the main idea of this paragraph?
- How does this main idea help me answer the questions I am addressing?
- How does this paragraph help strengthen the credibility of my argument?
- Is there more evidence I should provide to support the main idea of this paragraph?
- Is there evidence in the paragraph that does not relate to the main idea?

If you have difficulty answering these questions for a particular paragraph, that paragraph may need revision. You may want to rewrite the topic sentence to change the focus or use different evidence to support the topic sentence; however, you might decide to change your thesis to accommodate the important idea in that paragraph.

FINDING DIFFERENT PERSPECTIVES ABOUT YOUR IDEA

As we note throughout this book, all academic studies and publications are partial. Scholars must choose what to include and exclude in their research and writing. They make decisions about their samples, the sources they cite, and the methods they use, all of which add limitations to the conclusions that they can make. Furthermore, the results of a single study can lead to different conclusions. Because academic arguments are often complex, finding different perspectives about your idea may strengthen your paper in several ways: regarding your credibility as a writer, the credibility of your argument, and the validity of your conclusions. See Table 9.3 for a brief explanation of how you can improve your argument through this kind of research.

Through your research you will not only find a variety of perspectives about your topic, you will also find perspectives that might challenge your thesis. As we note in Table 9.3, if study X shows the limitations of study Y, study Y is not necessarily invalid. Similarly, if you find a study that challenges your own argument, your argument is not necessarily invalid. However, it is important to acknowledge these counterarguments and to show your reader how they have helped you strengthen your own argument. In other words, you want to consider at which places in your paper your reader could ask, "But what about _____?"

For example, if you claim that teachers must consider a child's classroom performance in conjunction with SAT scores to determine if the child has a learning disability, your reader could legitimately ask, "But what about the neurobiological factors related to learning disabilities?"

Rather than dismissing the question, consider its strengths. Perhaps the neurobiological studies in this area are not conclusive and because of that you do not want to rely on what may be inaccurate evidence. Or perhaps the scope of your paper is limited to the social factors that affect learning disabilities, not the biological factors; if this is the case, you may acknowledge that neurobiological research would enhance your argument, but that the exclusion of that research does

Table 9.3
The Benefits of Including Different Perspectives

Kind of benefit	How it benefits your writing
Increase your credibility	Including a variety of perspectives in your paper gives you a more complete understanding of your topic and increases the chances that you will be referencing important scholarship about your topic. You are also showing your reader that you have done a thorough job in your research, which may make your argument more credible
Strengthen your argument	If you have a more complete understanding of your topic, it may be harder for your reader to find gaps or holes in your argument
Identify others' biases	Part of a critical academic paper involves identifying the biases and assumptions of other scholars. If you read a variety of perspectives about your topic, you can use one perspective to help you find the limitations of another perspective
Strengthen your conclusion	Being able to identify others' biases and assumptions will help you reach a more valid conclusion because you can avoid repeating those biases. Being familiar with different scholars' conclusions also prevents you from making the same argument that others have made. Additionally, your readers may be more likely to believe your conclusion to be credible because you have already shown them the breadth and depth of your research

not necessarily invalidate your argument. Regardless, we urge you to consider counterarguments carefully; they may help you understand your topic from a different perspective.

You may address counterarguments by refuting them or conceding to them. That is, you could respond to some counterarguments by showing that you do not consider them to be valid arguments. For example, researchers have performed many different studies trying to identify the cause of a person's sexuality, and some of those studies may not be credible because they are not replicable or because other studies have shown their inaccuracy. You can *refute* counterarguments of this type. However, some research that challenges your thesis may be valid. To these perspectives you should *concede*. You can acknowledge their credibility and validity, and then you can describe how your own argument is still strong, nevertheless. For example, if you are exploring the impact of race on criminal stereotypes, your reader may ask, "But what about gender? Doesn't gender also impact criminal stereotypes?"

Rather than refuting this perspective, it could be useful to acknowledge that, yes, gender may impact criminal stereotypes, but it is outside the scope of your project. Additionally, although research about gender may usefully add to knowledge about criminal stereotyping, your own conclusions still can be valid.

DEVELOPING THE LOGIC OF YOUR ARGUMENT

Most academic research papers involve making an argument. In academic writing, an argument is not a belligerent or contentious statement; rather, it is the point that you want your readers to consider credible and valid. In a term paper your argument is the claim, or the conclusion, that you support with evidence from previous research. In addition to using credible evidence to support your argument, you must also use sound logic.

One example of a well-known logical argument (with a slight modification) is:

1. All people are mortal.
2. Socrates is a person.
3. Therefore, Socrates is mortal.

If you were using the statements about Socrates as the basis of an academic paper, the third statement would be your thesis, the claim that you want to support in your paper. Perhaps you would formulate it this way: "In this paper I am going to argue that Socrates is mortal." The first and second statements would be your evidence or support. You would use the premises "All people are mortal" and "Socrates is a person" to help you show your reader that your thesis is valid and accurate. Consequently, you must make sure that your premises are clear, accurate, and truly logical. Consider the following syllogism, which appears to have a logical structure but which leads to an invalid conclusion:

1. Birds can fly.
2. A moth can fly.
3. Therefore, a moth is a bird.

Even though it is not false to state that birds can fly, there are birds that cannot fly, and some animals that fly are not birds. This syllogism shows that relying on an idea that is imprecise may affect the rest of your argument. For this reason, you should familiarize yourself with the ideas and perspectives that already exist. By knowing the different arguments—as well as the strengths and limitations of those arguments—you will be less likely to base your own argument on a premise that has already been disqualified by other psychologists.

Building a logical argument also involves making your conclusions valid. It is possible to start with credible, precise premises and still develop an inaccurate conclusion. Most academic arguments are more complicated than the three-statement arguments above, so you must consider a wider variety of premises and premises that are more complex. In Table 9.4 we offer several suggestions for making valid claims based on evidence from your sources.

One purpose of this chapter is to show how writing a term paper may be different from performing original research. Despite these differences, both kinds of writing share similar strategies. For this reason, we encourage you to review other chapters when you are working on a term paper. For example, you still need to narrow your focus to a specific question or set of questions (chapter 2), do research and assess sources (chapters 3 and 4), use effective wording and follow the rules of grammar (chapter 7), and understand and summarize statistics (chapter 8).

Up to this point in the book we have addressed different aspects of communication that are relevant to a number of different disciplines. Whether you are taking an English, psychology, or physics class, in your writing you will need to consider topics such as grammar, the difference between popular and scholarly sources, how to effectively summarize and analyze the information in graphs and statistics, and how to organize your ideas. In the following chapters we will shift the focus and present material that relates more specifically to communicating the way that psychologists do. In these chapters, for example, you can learn how to organize the different sections of a psychology paper, the APA guidelines for formatting and citing sources, and how to create a poster according to APA style.

Table 9.4
Strengthening the Logic of Your Argument

What to consider	Why to consider it
Avoid generalizations	Using the words *always*, *all*, *none*, *never*, *forever*, may lead you to a claim that is impossible to support. Additionally, making a claim about a group of people based on their identity means that you are applying that claim to all members of that group. For example, the sentence, *Females have more highly developed verbal skills than males*, is making a claim about *all* women and *all* men, which you cannot support
Be specific	One way to avoid generalizations is to be specific. When you are discussing a population, clarify its boundaries. Furthermore, we encourage you to use specific examples from sources to support your claims. You do not want to rely on an inaccurate generalization to support your argument
All studies are limited	Remember, all studies have limitations. Therefore, you want to be critical of studies, regardless of whether they support or challenge your claims. Do not rely on the results of only one study to support or refute an argument. Additionally, your own paper will have limitations; being aware of those limitations can strengthen your credibility as a writer
Do not rely on the accuracy of only one study	You may find a study whose conclusions provide strong support for a claim you make. *However, the results of one study are not necessarily a convincing demonstration of a claim*. If one study concluded that a specific population of girls tended to have stronger verbal skills than a specific population of boys, it does not prove that females have more highly developed verbal skills than males
A study may be limited but not invalid	You may find a study (study A) whose conclusions contradict the conclusions of another study (study B). Although study A demonstrates the limitations of study B, study B is not necessarily completely illogical or inaccurate. You may use study B in your paper while recognizing its limitations
Become familiar with logical fallacies	Logical fallacies result from mistakes in reasoning, and being aware of different fallacies may prevent you from making them. See chapter 3 for more information about logical fallacies
Do not use opinions to support a claim	It will weaken your argument to use an opinion as evidence to support a claim. An opinion is a claim that does not have evidential support, and without evidential support you cannot verify the opinion's accuracy or inaccuracy. Therefore, if you use an opinion as support (a premise) for a claim (a conclusion), you may be relying on an inaccurate premise, which will invalidate your conclusion
Acknowledge counterarguments	In a term paper, a counterargument is an argument that in some way challenges the argument you are making. Rather than ignoring the studies that present a different perspective, you should analyze those studies and respond to them, showing your reader that your own argument has validity, despite these other perspectives

10

The Introduction Section

One good paragraph at the very start, indeed, accomplishes all sorts of magic.

Katherine Frost Bruner

Writing your Introduction is simple. All you have to do is answer the following questions: What are you doing? Why are you doing it? What do you expect to happen? Why is it interesting? When you answer these questions, you have finished your introduction. This chapter will help you organize the Introduction section of your APA-style research paper so you have addressed the four questions above. After finishing this section, your reader will be able to understand how your ideas developed and what sources contributed to your ideas. In subsequent chapters, you will see how you can develop the other sections of your research paper.

The introductory section provides a blueprint for the ideas you are developing in your paper. Your job in this section is to (a) identify your topic (i.e., what are you doing?), (b) to discuss what psychologists already know and don't know about that topic and to explain how your research will advance our knowledge even further (i.e., why are you doing it?), and (c) to provide the logic of your hypotheses (i.e., what do you expect to happen?) You should (d) try to accomplish these goals while engaging the reader with clear and cogent writing (i.e., why is it interesting?). One of the most difficult aspects of writing the Introduction is to offer enough detail for readers to develop a good grasp of the material without distracting them with irrelevant information.

INTRODUCING THE TOPIC

Authors typically structure the Introduction section so that broad, more general, ideas appear first, with details specific to the author's research coming later. Writers can capture the reader's interest by starting the Introduction in any number of ways. You will be more successful in engaging your reader if you begin with a compelling and original opening statement; you will be less successful if you make an uninspired statement. For instance, suppose you want to study people's sense of humor. You might begin your introduction with one of the ways given below.

- Just about everybody claims to have an above average sense of humor. This is an impossibility because, although some people possess a clear sense of humor, one can spot a great many humor-impaired people.
- Researchers have conducted many studies concerning people's sense of humor. The present study will investigate that trait in individuals.
- Humor is an important part of people's social lives. Consequently, psychologists have studied this trait extensively.

How effective would they be? The first example would probably be the most enticing. It states the general topic of the paper (sense of humor), and the idea of somebody being humor impaired might pique a reader's interest. The second example establishes the general topic, but it is not very interesting. The third example might not draw the reader to the topic. After reading it, the reader would know the article is about humor, but not what aspect of the broad topic of humor; furthermore, the writing is not particularly engaging.

DIFFERENT APPROACHES TO STARTING THE INTRODUCTION

You will encounter some standard approaches to the Introduction section as you read journal articles. Other authors have made additional suggestions (e.g., Kendall, Sills, & Chou, 2001) about ways to begin your writing. In the end, you should select a way that fits the message you want to convey.

Citing an Actual Event
Some authors describe actual events that relate to the focus of their research. One study that reflected this approach involved people's inability to recognize their own incompetence.

In 1995, McArthur Wheeler walked into two Pittsburgh banks and robbed them in broad daylight, with no visible attempt at disguise. He was arrested later that night, less than an hour after videotapes of him taken from surveillance cameras were broadcast on the 11 o'clock news. When police later showed him the surveillance tapes, Mr. Wheeler stared in incredulity. "But I wore the juice," he mumbled. Apparently, Mr. Wheeler was under the impression that rubbing one's face with lemon juice rendered it invisible to videotape camera. (Kruger & Dunning, 1999, p. 121)

Creating a Fictional Scenario

Another approach is to create a fictional scenario (i.e., a brief story) introducing the general point of the study. An example from a journal article exploring how people try to understand the behaviors of others illustrates this approach.

Sylvia is a typical college student. She does, however, have persistent doubts about her ability to understand the reasons for people's behaviors. Five minutes into the first lecture of her social psychology class, a male student stands up and loudly demands to know why the class is not meeting in a different room. The professor gives a reasonable answer, but the student rejects it and stomps out of the lecture hall. Aghast, Sylvia (like the rest of the class) infers that the student is emotionally unbalanced. Several minutes later, the professor welcomes him back and introduces him as her T.A. She then explains to all that the T.A. had no choice about what kind of part to play in this class demonstration. Most of the class still perceives their T.A. to be slightly unstable, thereby showing the correspondence bias (an overattribution of behavior to dispositional causes). Does Sylvia? Or, do her chronically accessible causal uncertainty (CU) beliefs influence how she processes the available information? We sought answers to such questions in the current research. (Weary, Vaughn, Steward, & Edwards, 2006, p. 87)

Identifying the Scope of Previous Research

In most journal articles, authors simply establish the main topic in a straightforward way, giving the reader a sense of the paper's focus as it relates to the related research topics. For example, one study of college student suicide began by referring to the general nature of previous research.

The literature on suicide, suicidality, and suicide risk factors is extensive. The research includes clinical reports, intervention strategies, identification of individual risk factors, demographic patterns of suicide and estimates of base rates in different ages and cultures. A subset of this literature has examined suicide in college students. College student suicide research is longstanding and an increasing number of articles address the topic each year. (Stephenson, Belesis, & Balliet, 2005, p. 5)

Presenting a Statistic

Another approach is to cite an interesting statistic that will engage the reader. This tactic can be successful, but you should take care not to start with statistics that will bore the reader. One research report on health and disease opened with a statistic that might capture the interest of somebody who is interested in health psychology.

- Health outcomes are increasingly recognized as socially patterned. In 2001–2002, the leading three causes of death in the United States were heart disease, cancer, and stroke (Jackson, Kubzansky, & Wright, 2006, 21).

Another study focused on statistics associated with AIDS:

- South Africa is the center of the AIDS epidemic today, with approximately 28% of the population infected (Baron, Bazerman, & Shonk, 2006, p. 123).

Citing a Quotation

Sometimes, a quotation around which an article focuses can raise a reader's interest, as illustrated in an article on Freudian repression. Because the quotation below came from Sigmund Freud, it could attract a reader's interest.

Freud once wrote, *"the essence of repression lies simply in turning something away, and keeping it at a distance, from the conscious."* [italics in original] (Boag, 2006, p. 74)

Describing Common Occurrences

Another tactic to generate interest in your ideas is to describe a common experience to which the reader can relate. A description of gender-based discrimination in hiring as the focus of an opening paragraph serves as a good example.

For traditionally male jobs, . . . women are less likely to be hired than men. They are also paid less, given less authority, and promoted less often . . . . Conversely, male applicants are discriminated against for jobs that are considered feminine. (Uhlmann & Cohen, 2005, p. 474)

In composing your Introduction, you should ask yourself whether you would enjoy reading it. If you wouldn't enjoy your own writing, it is pretty certain that nobody else will. As a rule, readers are not going to be captivated by writing that begins with names of authors they don't know, and they won't care about the date an article was published (e.g., "In 1999, Dunning and Kruger found that . . ."). Instead of starting with this type of mundane fact, you should try to entice your reader with your opening statement. The adage that you only get to make a first impression once certainly holds for your Introduction.

HOW TO BEGIN

The opening paragraphs of a journal article are likely to include references to books, journal articles, and conference presentations. In the first part of the Introduction, there will be little detail about actual research projects. Instead, the references will be related to the overall question being addressed in the paper you are reading.

For example, in a research article about true and false confessions in the legal system (Russano, Meissner, Narchet, & Kassin, 2005), the authors began their Introduction with a very broad set of ideas:

- goal of police interrogation;
- power of a confession on jury decisions;
- value of confession in avoiding trials;
- prevalence of false confessions;
- psychological processes at work in police interrogations.

The authors addressed all of these elements in three paragraphs, citing 11 references. Two points are important here as they relate to your Introduction section. First, in a few paragraphs, you are not going to be able to include the details of the research you mention. You have to limit your presentation to the most important, global issues in that research. Second, you have to make it clear how the ideas interrelate and where they are going. You don't want to give your reader the impression that you are talking about unrelated facts and ideas, merely listing one study after another.

REVIEWING THE LITERATURE

No matter how novel your research idea, it is very likely that some-body has already addressed a similar question. You may remember from chapter 4 that you can conduct systematic literature searches to identify research related to yours. Depending on your topic, you might locate many more articles that you could possibly read.

You should not try to read everything. Your literature review does not need to be exhaustive, but it should be illustrative. That is, you should read enough background material so that you can discuss the research and theory, giving a reasonably complete account of our knowledge of the topic.

Your treatment of the topic should address any controversies in the area. What are the sources of disagreement among scholars and researchers? You can use selective examples that represent what psy-chologists have found. You might have your opinion regarding the subject you are studying, but stating your opinion is not the purpose of the Introduction. Rather, in this section you are supposed to present ideas that are based on data and theory, including conflicting views of different researchers.

In short, you should avoid simply listing a number of studies, describing each one as if it were unrelated to the others. The task is to make it easy for the reader to understand how all of the studies interrelate.

REASONS FOR REVIEWING THE LITERATURE

What might happen if you do not locate relevant references? One pos-sibility is that you could plan and carry out a study that somebody has already done, maybe better than you did. There are few rewards for simple replication of an existing study (Beins, 2004, pp. 66–69).

A second reason for perusing the existing literature related to your topic is that a reader will want to know where your idea fits in with other research. Science proceeds one small step at a time; we accumu-late knowledge from one project to the next. Your research is one of those small steps. Failure to cite previous research might also lead the reader to question your expertise in the area.

A third reason for becoming familiar with the research in your area is that you might spot limitations in early work that you could remedy. Every research projects answers some questions but leaves other ques-tions unanswered.

Finally, an advantage associated with a thorough literature search is that you may be able to adapt others' methodologies, their materials and apparatus, and their statistical analysis for your research. Creating a sound methodology on your own is difficult because there are many details you have to consider. It is completely legitimate to use techniques that others have developed. You just need to make sure to credit them for their ideas. (See chapter 2 for a discussion of avoiding plagiarism of others' ideas.) Generally, you do not present great detail about methodology in the introduction, but if methodological details are important in how you set up your study, you might want to introduce them here.

CLARIFYING TERMS IN THE RESEARCH

Like any discipline, psychology has developed its own language. There are terms with specific meanings to a psychologist that might have a different meaning to a layperson. For instance, *schizophrenia* is a diagnostic label relating to people with inappropriate affect and behavior, but to the general public, schizophrenia means a split personality (which a psychologist would call *dissociative identity disorder*).

Similarly, in different areas of psychology, terms may not reflect the same concepts. For instance, different psychologists who see the abbreviation SSRI could interpret it differently. Within the realm of treatment for psychological disorders, those initials stand for *selective serotonin reuptake inhibitors*, whereas in studies of emotional intelligence, the initials refer to the *Schutte Self-Report Inventory* (Schutte et al., 1998).

In your Introduction, you can let your reader know how you are using important terms. Sometimes you might be discussing a relatively obscure concept that is generally known within a limited domain of psychology, such as Schutte's Inventory. Your reader might need help understanding the concept. If you are not making use of any unusual terms or definitions, you probably don't need to clarify your terminology, but you can let your reader know about any such instances here.

In the same vein, you can use your introduction to discuss the operational definitions that previous researchers have used if you believe you can generate different and better operational definitions or if there is disagreement among professionals about how to measure a construct. As an example, in studies of emotional intelligence, it appears to make a difference how the researchers measure (i.e., operationally define) this concept (Zeidner, Shani-Zinovich, Matthews, & Roberts, 2005).

INTRODUCING YOUR RESEARCH: GENERATING A HYPOTHESIS

In many cases, your hypothesis will be based on what a theory predicts or what other researchers have discovered. Your hypothesis will carry more weight if you present a logical argument based on existing knowledge.

As an example of how to generate a hypothesis, consider how a research team studying terror management theory (TMT) introduced their ideas (Goldenberg, Pyszczynski, McCoy, Greenberg, & Solomon, 1999). They noted that TMT deals with people's feelings of mortality, that is, knowledge that we will die some day, and how we cope with those feelings. The investigators explained that one theorist had posited that neurotic people are highly conscious of their mortality (Rank, 1936). In addition, neuroticism appears to be related to discomfort with sex (Eysenck, 1971). Further, thoughts of sex seem to be associated with thoughts of death (Becker, 1973). Finally, if the spiritual or romantic aspects of sex are emphasized, the connection to death is removed. Based on these ideas, the research team generated a hypothesis regarding the tendency to link sex and death among people with high levels of neuroticism.

In this research, the logic of their hypothesis was clear and orderly. Previous psychologists had provided the building blocks for the hypotheses; these researchers connected the ideas.

Idea 1 People with high levels of neuroticism associate the physical act of sex and death.

Idea 2 People with high levels of neuroticism do not connect romantic or spiritual ideas of sex with death.

Hypothesis: If people with high levels of neuroticism are induced to think about the physical aspect of sex, they will mentally transform neutral stimuli into death-related responses. On the other hand, if they are primed to think about the romantic aspect of sex, they will be less likely to transform neutral stimuli into death-related responses.

This is an interesting hypothesis, but how would you go about testing it? The researchers created a clever research task in which participants completed words when given word fragments (e.g., COFF_ _). These words could be completed to create either death-related words or more neutral words. Thus, COFF_ _ could be rendered either as *coffin* or *coffee*. The researchers' hypothesis was supported. Neurotic individuals tended to form death-related words twice as often when given a prime about the physical aspect of sex than about the spiritual aspect of sex.

The researchers' study included more variables than we have discussed, but the example illustrates how they developed this particular hypothesis. They had reviewed the research and theoretical literature on this topic and used a logical connection between ideas as a basis to predict the outcome of their study.

In your research project, your hypotheses should be based on what previous research has documented. Your hypothesis will be more credible if it follows logically from these established ideas, like Goldenberg et al.'s (1999) did. Using intuition or hunches is not particularly helpful because people may consider the same ideas but generate very different intuitions.

Finally, you should spell out the implications of your study. In their study of TMT, Goldenberg et al. essentially said, "This is what we expect to find (i.e., their hypothesis) and this is what it will mean regarding support for terror management theory (the implication)." In your writing, you should also give the reader a preview of what it will mean if your data support your hypothesis.

At the end of your Introduction, the topic of your study should be obvious, the current state of knowledge about this topic should be apparent, your expectations should be unambiguous, and the potential impact of the study should be defined. Obviously, there is no simple formula for accomplishing all of this, but a well-constructed introduction will contain all of these elements to some degree. Thus, the reader will know where your ideas came from and where you are going to take them.

11

The Method Section

Research is formalized curiosity. It is poking and prying with a purpose.
                                                Zora Neal Hurston

It doesn't matter how beautiful your theory is, it doesn't matter how smart
you are—if it doesn't agree with experiment, it's wrong.
                                                Richard Feynman

Psycholinguists like to use the following example: Time flies like an arrow, but fruit flies like a banana. At first, the beginning and the ending don't seem to go together, but if you puzzle through it, you can get its meaning. When you write a paper, your introduction and your conclusions should go together, but your reader should not have to work hard to figure out the connection. Your Method section shows how the ideas in the beginning are linked to the ideas at the end.

This chapter will highlight the points that you should include in the description of your methodology. These points link the more general or abstract concepts in your introduction to the specific means you used to investigate the concepts critical to your research.

The Method section provides your reader with a detailed picture of exactly what you did. It is oriented more toward technical details and much less toward the subject matter of your study, and it serves two basic functions. First, it allows readers to evaluate how well your methodology answers your research question and leads to your conclusions. Second, the description of your methodology provides other researchers with the information they need to be able to replicate your study.

As such, you should offer the reader sufficient detail to permit comprehension and reproduction of your research. It seems that providing such a description should be fairly easy, but in reality, you have to make quite a number of choices about what to include and what to omit. If you give too little detail, your reader will not have sufficient knowledge to assess your study or to replicate it. If you give too much detail, you will lose your reader in boring and meaningless facts.

When you write your Method section, keep your readership in mind. You have planned and conducted your study, so you know just about everything important about it. However, what you are writing may be the first exposure that the readers have to your topic, so concepts that are completely clear to you are largely unknown to others. Similarly, the methodology for your study may be obvious to you because you may have tested many participants. It will not be so clear to a naive reader.

A good strategy is to regard your audience as consisting of people who are intelligent but uninformed. Your writing should call upon their intelligence as you teach them about your research.

PARTICIPANTS AND SUBJECTS

Human Participants

Much psychological research entails studying college students (Plous, 1996; Thomas & Blackman, 1992). These students have some generally predictable characteristics: they tend to be young, often first-year students; White; middle class or higher, socioeconomically speaking; female; intelligent and well educated; cooperative; and responsible. Even though most research involves people, some psychologists study nonhuman animals.

As a rule, researchers refer to people who volunteer for psychological studies as *participants*. According to APA style, it is appropriate to refer to people you study as *subjects* if you are observing them without interacting with them. When psychologists study nonhumans, the appropriate term is also *subjects*.

The difference in designation relates to the fact that a research situation is also a social situation. Participants interact with experimenters, and participants have expectations about how they should act. In addition, experimenters can communicate subtle expectations to participants. Consequently, it makes sense to refer to the people who volunteer for research as participants because they help create the dynamics of the experimental situation. When people are going about their business without knowing that a researcher is studying them, the people are truly a subject of study. The researcher's expectations and perspectives might affect the type of observations made, but the researcher's act of observing will not affect the behavior of the person being observed.

Likewise, researchers generally believe that research animals do not interact with the experimenter in the same sense as humans do. The reality is that an experimenter's expectations can affect a rat's behavior (Rosenthal & Fode, 1963; Burhnam, cited in Rosnow & Rosenthal, 1993). Nonetheless, APA style specifies using the term *subject* to refer to nonhumans in research.

Whether you intend to study people, rats, pigeons, mealworms, or some other species, it is important to inform the reader of the characteristics of those organisms. There are particular characteristics of your participants that you should communicate with your reader. Table 11.1 presents some of the general participant characteristics that you need to provide. This listing is not exhaustive, and you can tailor the information you include to meet the specific needs of your own study.

If your research question involves comparing people in different age groups, you want to emphasize the ages of people in the groups you compare. If your research entails a discussion of cultural differences, you need to tell which cultures you are studying, including enough detail about your participants so the reader is confident that your comparisons are meaningful.

Other information that you should report is the strategies by which you recruited your participants and the number of participants who completed or who failed to complete the study. These elements can be important in understanding your results because a random sample of people from a population may act differently from a convenience sample. For example, in studies of bulimia, samples that consist of people referred to the researchers by doctors show more severe symptoms than do samples of people suffering from bulimia in the general community (Fairburn, Welch, Norman, O'Connor, & Doll, 1996). In addition, people who are persistent enough to complete the study may be very different from those who drop out. Thus, the conclusions you draw based on your research may have a lot to do with your sample.

The particular characteristics you should include will depend on the research question you are asking. Box 11.1 gives some examples of participant descriptions that require varying levels of detail. For instance, Wimer and Beins (in press) studied the effect of misleading information on participants' ratings of jokes. The intent was not to investigate cultural or social factors, so a fairly broad characteristic of participants sufficed.

On the other hand, Vorauer and Sakamoto (2006) studied formation of friendships across ethnic groups. In order for a reader to understand the nature of their research topic, the investigators provided information about ethnicity, but they did not give information about the ages

Table 11.1
Demographics of Research Participants

Characteristic	What to report
Age	Older Children, Adolescents, and Adults • Average age of sample, in years • Range and/or standard deviation of age Young children • Age in months • Range and/or standard deviation
Sex	Number of female and male participants (man and woman, boy and girl are nouns; male and female are typically used as adjectives, although if the range of ages is considerable, APA style permits the use of male and female as nouns.)
Ethnicity	*General designations* • White • Black (or African-American) • Indian (or Native American) • Hispanic (or Latino/Latina) • Asian *Examples of subgroups if different cultures are a focus of the research* Hispanic: • Mexican-American • Mexican • Puerto Rican • Colombian Asian • Chinese • Japanese • Thai • Vietnamese • Indian
Recruitment method	*Nonprobability samples* • Convenience samples (e.g., solicitation in psychology classes) • Notices posted in public spaces, newspapers, etc. • Purposive (judgmental) sampling • Chain-referral sampling *Probability samples* • Simple random sampling (for which you specify your population) • Stratified random sampling
Inducement to participate	• Extra credit in class • Possibility of winning a prize in a raffle for all participants • Money (including amount) • No inducement

Box 11.1   Participant Descriptions from Journal Articles Involving People

General Characteristics for Research that Does Not Study Social or Cultural Variables
We tested 90 undergraduate students in this study. The participants included 61 women and 29 men whose ages ranged from 17 to 23 years ($M = 18.9$, $s = 1.2$) They volunteered in order to receive extra credit in psychology classes (Wimer & Beins, in press).

More Specific Characteristics for Research that Studies Social or Cultural Variables
One hundred and twelve introductory psychology students (56 same-sex pairs) participated in the study in exchange for partial course credit. There were 22 White–White pairs, 19 White–Chinese pairs, and 15 Chinese–Chinese pairs. The ratio of male to female pairs was approximately the same across the three pair types . . . . Students were assigned to pairs on the basis of scheduling convenience . . . . (Vorauer & Sakamoto, 2006, p. 327).

Highly Specific Characteristics Required for Understanding the Research
In the U.S. group, six researchers were each given 20 surveys to distribute, making 120 respondents possible, of which 116 were returned. Two French research assistants sought 50 respondents each, and 99 were completed . . . . Overall, there were 120 female respondents (61%) and 76 male respondents (39%), and 150 (76.5%) were employed full-time. On average, they worked 39.53 hr per week (SD = 11.16) and had held their jobs for over 8.5 years ($M = 106$ months, SD = 113.71). [The researchers also broke down the listing of participants by type of job: managerial, service, sales, etc.] (Grandey, Fisk, & Steiner, 2005, p. 897).

of participants. Although it is common for researchers to identify the ages, Vorauer and Sakamoto simply referred to "introductory psychology students." The implication here is that they were traditional college-aged students, about 18–22 years old.

Sometimes research requires more detailed descriptions of participants. Grandey, Fisk, and Steiner (2005) investigated cultural differences in employees in the workplace. So they presented detail that far exceeds that of laboratory research, including types of jobs in which people were engaged, how long they had been employed, how many hours they worked per week, and nationality.

You should include participant characteristics that relate to your research hypotheses. If you are studying visual memory, you should include characteristics such as age, sex, education level, whether your participants have a background in visual arts, any visual impairments, and so on; in most studies of this type, it is probably not critical to indicate cultural backgrounds of your participants. On the other hand, if you are studying cross-cultural issues, ethnicity would be a critical variable to report. The information that appears in journal articles that you read can provide guidance.

Confidentiality of Participants

In your description of research participants you are supposed to provide detailed information. But, in virtually any project you complete, you need to keep participant identities anonymous and confidential. Data are anonymous when nobody can link a particular piece of data to a single individual; data are confidential when nobody outside the research project has access to information that could link participants and their data. When you present participant information in the Method section, you are legally and ethically bound not to divulge details that will reveal the identities of your participants.

Most psychological research is benign, but some studies do pose risks. You must observe extra caution if your research involves sensitive issues. Revealing behaviors of participants to people who are not part of the research project would be unethical.

Nonhuman Subjects

When projects involve nonhuman animals, there is a subsection of the Method labeled *Subjects* (as opposed to *Participants*). You need to specify the type of organism (genus and species), the age, where you obtained them, and their physiological condition.

Behavior that holds true for one species may not generalize to another, although sometimes you can predict behaviors from one type of animal to another. For instance, in some cases, nonhuman animals such as cockroaches make decisions like humans (Warren, 1965). But you cannot count on such generalizability. The fact that behaviors across species may or may not be similar in a given environment necessitates that you offer information on the species you used.

Some examples of how researchers have described the animals they have used in their studies appear in Box 11.2. As you can see, the authors have presented considerable detail about the animals.

Attrition

Sometimes the humans or animals you are studying do not finish your study, particularly in projects involving repeated testing sessions. People may not return; animals may become ill or die. You should report the attrition rate in the Method section and speculate in the Discussion section how it might have affected your data.

Box 11.2   Examples of Descriptions of Subjects in Research
Involving Nonhuman Animals

Rats
Male Wistar rats from Pasteur Institute (Iran), weighing 180–230 g at the time of surgery, were used. The animals were housed four per cage, in a room under a 12 hr light–12 hr dark cycle (lights on 07:00 h) and controlled temperature (23 ± 1 °C). Animals had access to food and water *ad libitum* and were allowed to adapt to the laboratory conditions for at least 1 week before surgery. Rats were handled about 3 min each day prior to behavioral testing. All experiments were performed between 9:00 and 13:00 hr and each rat was tested only once. Eight animals were used in each group of experiments (Jafari-Sabet, 2006, p. 121).

Monkeys
We studied 32 mated, but nonbreeding, adult cottontop tamarins from a captive colony at the University of Wisconsin-Madison Psychology Department. We housed all colony animals socially throughout their lives, either in family groups or in mated pairs. The tamarins ranged in age from 1 to 6 years old and had all been paired for at least 6 months prior to the beginning of the study. Tamarin pairs live in cages measuring 160 × 93 × 263 cm, furnished with natural tree branches, ropes, acrylic or polycarbonate sheeted nestboxes and various toys for environmental enrichment. We fed the colony three times daily from food platforms at least 1 m above the floor. Water was available *ad libitum*. For further details on colony husbandry refer to Ginther et al. (2001). Testing occurred either between 10:00 and 11:30 hr, before the main feed, or between 15:00 and 16:00 hr, before a high-protein snack (Moscovice & Snowdon, 2006, p. 935).

Pigeons
The subjects were 16 female Carneau pigeons about 1 year old, originally purchased from Palmetto Pigeon Plant. They had previously participated in another autoshaping experiment that had used different stimuli. The assignment of pigeons to groups in the present experiment was random with respect to their previous treatments. They were housed in pairs and maintained at 80% of their free-feeding weights (Rescorla, 2006, p. 139).

The problem with attrition, sometimes called *subject mortality*, is that the subjects or participants who leave your study may be quite different from those who remain. In some cases, researchers can assess the degree of similarity between those who stay and those who leave. When those who drop out are generally similar to those who remain, the outcome of the study may not differ much from what would have occurred without attrition (e.g., LaGreca, Silverman, Vernberg, & Prinstein, 1996). Unfortunately, in many cases, researchers cannot evaluate how attrition has affected their studies. Thus, if you lose participants over the course of your research, you need to specify the attrition in detail.

MATERIALS AND APPARATUS

When you conduct a study, you may need stimulus materials or other implements. If you are studying learning, your participants must have something to learn. If you survey your participants, you need a questionnaire of some kind. If you are observing people for the presence of a behavior, you will need a behavior checklist. If you are performing a surgery on a rat, you will need surgical instruments.

In preparing your manuscript, you need to tell the reader about materials (e.g., questionnaires, stimulus words) and apparatus (e.g., devices to record data, surgical implements) that you used. You do not need to detail ordinary instruments you might use, such as stopwatches and computers, beyond mentioning that you used them. For specialized or unusual equipment, you should produce a clear and complete description of what you used.

Most psychological research involves little apparatus that merits detailed description, but materials appear in virtually all human-oriented studies. The difference in designation between materials and apparatus is that materials are often printed on paper or displayed on a computer screen. Apparatus refers to instruments used by the researcher. Another way to differentiate them is that, if you drop an apparatus, it breaks; if you drop materials, they simply scatter on the floor.

In general, if psychologists are likely to be familiar with your materials and apparatus, you might only mention them. But if you created your own materials, you should give a very detailed depiction of them. If you are using relatively unknown materials or apparatus created by others, you should provide a description of them and indicate to the reader where to obtain them. If you used personality inventories or questionnaires, it is a good idea to indicate levels of reliability reported by previous researchers. Some examples of descriptions of apparatus and materials from published journal articles are given in Box 11.3.

Readers often do not get as interested in this aspect of the methodology as they do in the hypotheses and theories, but knowing about the materials and apparatus can be critical in a reader's decision about whether the research is worthwhile.

Box 11.3   Examples of Details of Apparatus and Materials in Published Research Articles

---

Most psychological journal articles do not involve apparatus, but they do involve materials. Researchers are likely to use different types of apparatus in studies involving children and nonhuman animals, and in those involving perceptual processes. Much human-oriented research involves only materials.

Apparatus

Research with Humans
The apparatus consisted of a wooden display box (106 cm high × 101 cm wide × 35 cm deep) that was mounted 76 cm above the room floor. The floor and back wall of the apparatus were covered with pastel paper, and the side walls were painted white. Each infant sat on a parent's lap and faced an opening (41 × 95 cm) in the front of the apparatus; the opening was hidden by a curtain that was raised at the start of the trial. An experimenter introduced his or her right hand (in a yellow rubber glove) into the apparatus through a curtained window (36 × 43 cm) in the back wall (Wang & Baillargeon, 2005, p. 545).

Research with Nonhumans
The monkeys were tested by using the Language Research Center's Computerized Test System (described in Rumbaugh, Richardson, Washburn, Savage-Rumbaugh, & Hopkins, 1989; Washburn & Rumbaugh, 1992) that consisted of a PC, a digital joystick, a color monitor, and a pellet dispenser. Monkeys could manipulate the joystick through the mesh of their home cages, producing isomorphic movements of a computer-graphic cursor on the screen. Contacting appropriate computer-generated stimuli with the cursor resulted in the delivery of a 94-mg fruit-flavored chow pellet (Bioserve, Frenchtown, NJ) by using a Gerbrands 5120 dispenser interfaced to the computer with a relay box and output board (PIO-12 and ERA-01; Keithley Instruments, Cleveland, OH) (Beran, Smith, Redford, & Washburn, 2006, p. 112).

Materials

Description of Stimulus Materials
Twenty line drawings of nonsense objects were randomly selected from a database of nonobjects (see Fig. 1 for examples). Ten consonant-vowel-consonant (CVC) Dutch nonwords (e.g., bap) were selected as monosyllabic novel words. Ten bisyllabic novel words were constructed by adding a second syllable to each of these monosyllables (e.g., baptoe). These items are listed in Table 1. The nonsense-object pictures were randomly assigned to the novel words (Shatzman & McQueen, 2006, p. 373).

Description of Questionnaires
Marsh's (1990) Self-Description Questionnaire (SDQII) is designed to measure self-concept in adolescents. Three scales, each containing 10 items, were used in this study: the general school scale (academic self-concept), the general self scale (global self-esteem), and the emotional stability scale. The coefficient alpha estimate of reliability of scores on each of the SDQII scales has a median of .87 . . . .

To measure test anxiety, Sarason's (1972) 37-item Test Anxiety Scale (TAS),with test-retest reliability at least .80 (Spielberger,1976) was adapted. It incorporated Sarason's later (1984) work that differentiated the TAS into four components—test-irrelevant thinking, worry, tension, and bodily reactions (Matters & Burnett, 2003, pp. 243–244).

PROCEDURE

A thorough and detailed description of the actual behaviors of participants and of researchers is critical for complete understanding of research. The trick is to include the important material and to omit the details that are irrelevant to the outcome of the study.

You should specify the sequence of steps associated with the data collection, including what the researcher does and what the participants do. This information is likely to merge the actual procedures with the materials and apparatus because it is hard to say what the participants were doing without indicating what they were doing it with.

There are some fairly standard elements in the procedure. They include:

- variables that are manipulated and measured, including independent and dependent variables;
- any conditions or groups that you intend to compare;
- how participants are assigned to or placed in groups;
- the role of the researcher in the session;
- the directions that participants received;
- the activities in which the participants engaged.

In essence, you should present only detail that relates to the data you collect. So if your participants are learning something, you describe the nature of the stimuli that they are learning. The nonsense words that Shatzman and McQueen (2006) created for their research, as described in Box 11.3, might produce very different learning than actual words.

As a rule, you do not need to report verbatim the directions to the participants. A summary will suffice unless there is something unusual about the instructions. If your instructions are part of a manipulation, you might want to report exactly how you instructed the participants. You should ask yourself if somebody could conduct your research in all its important aspects from the information you provide. If the answer is no, you should provide more detail.

Finally, sometimes writers include a statement with the procedure that participants provided informed consent. When you write your own procedure section, you can determine whether to include how you obtained informed consent. Strictly speaking, it is not part of the data collection process, so you can logically argue that it does not belong in this subsection. However, for purposes of establishing that the researcher followed ethical guidelines, writers sometimes discuss how they obtained informed consent during the study.

DESIGN

The final, common subsection regarding methodology offers a statement of the design of your study. The reader will benefit from a clear statement of your independent variables (IVs), the groups that constitute the IVs, and your dependent variables. You also specify

Table 11.2
Common Elements in the Design subsection

Element of design subsection	Possible examples
Design	• Experiment with (manipulated) variables • Quasi-experiment (measured or categorical variables) • Mixed design (experimental and quasi-experimental variables) • Correlational design • Observational study • Archival study
Variables	• Independent variables • Dependent variables • Matched variables • Extraneous or confounding variables
Assignment of participants	• Random assignment • Systematic assignment • Assignment by pre-existing characteristics (e.g., sex, age)

here whether you tested your participants more than once (repeated measures) or only once (independent measures). If your design is not yet apparent to the reader before this subsection, you have one final chance to indicate how many variables are of interest in this research and how you set up your study.

Table 11.2 identifies common elements that appear in the design subsection. The guidelines presented in this chapter are not fixed rules. If it makes more sense for your presentation to identify your variables in the Procedure subsection, you may not need to include a design subsection. The important point is that the reader be able to find information critical to understanding your research.

12

The Results

Without data, all you are is just another person with an opinion.

Unknown

Statistics may be defined as "a body of methods for making wise decisions in the face of uncertainty."

W.A. Wallis

Everybody likes a good story. An interesting plot will leave you satisfied at the end, particularly if there are surprises along the way. In the story of your research, your hypothesis is the plot, and your results provide the surprises.

In this chapter, you will learn how to present your results so the reader can see whether your data support the ideas you presented in your Introduction section. Your Results section also prepares your reader for your conclusions, which appear in the Discussion section and which is the subject of the next chapter.

You can't just make things up, though. Each element in your story should be interesting, but each provide a glimpse at the truth. In your Results section, your interesting story comes through your words; the sense and truth of your words comes through your statistics.

Your ideas are the most critical aspect of the paper you are writing; the statistics are merely a tool that provides support for your ideas. If you keep this relation between ideas and statistics in mind, you will find it easier to communicate with your reader.

Creating an outline or an idea map (as described in chapter 6) can be very sound because it forces you to think of your main ideas. If you have generated a reasonably complete outline or idea map, you will have a good sense of your main points and how you will support them.

Both of these approaches takes a top-down approach (Salovey, 2000). This means that you are beginning with an overall sense of where your ideas are going. If you simply line up your statistics one after another, it will have the meaning (and interest) of listings in a phone book.

If you have not noticed, there has been no mention of statistics or numbers so far. The reason is that your first responsibility in the Results section is to convey the ideas of what happened in your study. The numbers can wait. If you understand the purpose of the statistics from your data analysis, you can tell the reader in words what the numbers have revealed. The words give the idea; the numbers, which come later, support your idea and provide an element of precision to your presentation.

YOUR HYPOTHESES

In your Introduction, you will have presented your hypotheses. Normally you talk about your hypothesis in the Results section in the same order as you offered them in the introduction.

A good example of a research report that describes support for a hypothesis involved testosterone level and aggression (Klinesmith, Kasser, & McAndrew, 2006). The investigators noted that previous researchers had discovered that insults or challenges to status can be associated with increases in testosterone levels in males. So Klinesmith et al. hypothesized that the presence of a gun (compared with a child's toy) would increase testosterone levels in men. The researchers created a task in which participants handled for 15 minutes either a child's toy or a pellet gun that resembled an automatic handgun. The investigators measured testosterone level before and after the 15-minute period. The data confirmed their hypothesis. As they reported,

> Our first hypothesis was confirmed: Subjects who interacted with the handgun showed a greater increase in testosterone from Time 1 to Time 2 than did those who interacted with the children's game. Thus, interacting with the gun increased testosterone levels. (Klinesmith et al., 2006, p. 571)

This verbal presentation of the results is clear and straightforward. After reading it, you know what happened. The researchers mentioned that they tested a hypothesis, how they tested it, the pattern of results, and the fact that the data confirmed their hypothesis. You don't need statistics to understand their point.

In a research report, though, a reader expects the technical, statistical information that supports their conclusion. Here is how those researchers included the statistical information:

Our first hypothesis was confirmed: Subjects who interacted with the handgun showed a greater increase in testosterone from Time 1 to Time 2 (mean change = 62.05 pg/ml, SD = 48.86) than did those who interacted with the children's game (mean change = 0.68 pg/ml, SD = 28.57), $t(28)$ = –4.20, p_{rep} = .99, d = 1.53. Thus, interacting with the gun increased testosterone levels. (Klinesmith et al., 2006, pp. 571–572)

As you can see, the technical information supports the verbal statement, but you don't need the statistics to understand the authors' point. When you create your own Results section, you should try to make your point using words. Then insert the technical part. This advice is a little simplistic, but as a strategy, starting with ideas instead of numbers is a good idea.

In addition, you should begin your presentation of the data with descriptive statistics. The authors who studied testosterone level presented the means and standard deviations, then the inferential statistic, a t-test.

There are numerous ways to present your data. Examples of how authors present descriptive statistics appear in Table 12.1.

DECIDING WHAT TO PRESENT

The main point of the Results section is to let the reader know what happened. Start this section with the most interesting, important, and surprising results. You should present as much detail as required in order to inform the reader adequately.

Generally, theoretical and empirical reports are meant for a readership that is versed in psychological research techniques. You can expect the reader to know the difference between experimental and nonexperimental methods, the uses of various statistical tests, the norms for hypothesis and significance testing, and so forth. When you present your data and statistics, you don't need to belabor the obvious. For example, all competent psychologists know that t-tests tell us whether two groups differ significantly. So don't bother explaining that fact to the reader.

Unless a statistical approach is fairly obscure, you should expect the reader to know what you are talking about. Similarly, if you use standard data analysis software such as SPSS® or Minitab®, you don't need to mention it specifically.

Table 12.1
Examples of presentations of descriptive statistics.

Type of presentation	Example
Means in the text with standard deviations presented in parentheses	The proportion of leg kicks occurring after post-tasting was similar whether the object had tasted sweet or bitter. The mean for the sweet condition was 0.584 (sd = 0.165), and for the bitter condition it was 0.604 (sd = 0.223). (From Rader & Vaughn, 2000, p. 537)
Means and standard deviations presented in parentheses	An independent t-test was conducted to explore absolute differences between men and women in reported levels of suicidality. There was a significant difference between genders, $t(630) = 2.47$, $p < .05$, with women reporting more frequent suicidal ideation than men ($M = 1.23$, $SD = .738$, $M = 1.10$, $SD = .522$). (From Stephenson, Pena-Shaff, & Quirk, 2006, p. 111)
Means referred to in the text but placed in a table (or figure)	As Table 1 indicates, the results show nearly equal means in the traditional-emphasis class and in both moderate-emphasis classes but notably better scores in the high-emphasis class. (From Beins, 1993, p. 162)

REPORTING SIGNIFICANT AND NONSIGNIFICANT RESULTS

Authors tend to devote space in their manuscripts to statistically significant effects and to downplay nonsignificant effects. Significant results suggest that something interesting took place, so it is not surprising for the researcher to detail it. If your data analysis reveals an unexpected, significant result, it is probably worth mentioning, but you should remember that significant effects are sometimes accidental and don't really signify anything. If you see an effect that you cannot explain, mention it, but do not develop a convoluted account of the result that is pure guesswork.

Just as researchers attend to significant effects, they minimize attention devoted to nonsignificant results. Such results let us know that something did not happen, but not why it didn't happen. Most of the time, when results are not significant, it does not pay to discuss them at great length. The problem with nonsignificance is that you don't

THE RESULTS | 135

know if the results turned out they way they did because there is no real effect or because your methodology obscured a real effect.

Incidentally, when your statistical analysis fails to result in a significant effect, the norm is to report it is as *nonsignificant*. Psychologists will recognize this wording in its statistical context. You should not refer to that effect as *insignificant*. If you hypothesized that there would be a significant effect and it turned out not to be, it would be *nonsignificant* statistically but it would not be *insignificant*. After all, the results differed from what you thought would happen—and that would be significant in the normal English meaning of that word.

In recent years, psychologists have recommended that researchers rely on more than merely tests of significance. Recommendations for the statistics that should appear in journal articles include effect sizes confidence intervals (Wilkinson and the Task Force on Statistical Inference, 1999) and the probability that an effect will replicate (Killeen, 2005). These new approaches are gradually appearing in the professional literature as psychologists become more familiar with them. The journal *Psychological Science*, published by the Association for Psychological Science (APS), recommends including effect sizes and confidence intervals, along with the probability that an effect will replicate (p_{rep}) rather than the traditional p-value. The journals of the APA do not yet have a single standard for presenting results.

As you write your results section, it is probably safe to err on the side of more complete information rather than less. Thus, presenting p-values will satisfy traditionalists; presenting effect sizes and confidence intervals will satisfy those who embrace the emerging conventions, and presenting p_{rep} will go one step further, toward new trends (you can learn how to obtain values of p_{rep} at http://www.asu.edu/clas/psych/research/sqab/).

MARGINALLY SIGNIFICANT EFFECTS

Psychologists typically adopt the Type I error rate of 5%; that is, the likelihood of mistakenly concluding that there is a real effect is 5%. For decades, authors claimed significance and rejected the null hypothesis when $p \leq .05$ and did not reject the null when $p > .05$. The analogy researchers often used involved pregnancy: you either are or you aren't. You can't be highly pregnant or slightly pregnant or nearly pregnant.

Some psychologists are more comfortable with the idea that you should not ignore a possibly interesting effect, even if $p > .05$. For example, why should a p-value of .050 be so much more interesting than a *p*-value of .051? Further, there is no logical or scientific rationale for choosing the typical significance levels of .05 and .01; it is merely tradition. In studies with low power (i.e., small sample sizes combined with small effect sizes), it may be more reasonable to adopt significance levels of .20 or .30 (Winer, Brown, & Michels, 1991).

Authors have called potentially interesting effects that do not attain conventional levels of significance *marginally significant* when $.05 < p < .10$. Some writers (e.g., Salovey, 2000) have suggested avoiding such qualifying statements, preferring a simple statement that, for example, $p = .06$. A reader would know that such a value is not significant and can evaluate it appropriately. If you are writing about your results and an effect is not quite at the level of significance but may be important, let the reader know about it and declare that you are discussing the result with caution.

APA STYLE AND PRESENTATION OF YOUR RESULTS

APA-style presentation of results is not difficult to implement, but there are a lot of details that you have to consider. The presentation style for numbers, results of statistical tests, and creation of tables and figures is quite technical. Table 12.2 gives the format for statistical presentation of commonly used tests.

Some common abbreviations that are standard for referring to various measurements appear in Table 12.3. In addition, standard symbols in presenting the results of statistical tests are in Table 12.4. A general rule is that if the measurement is written using Roman letters (e.g., *t*, *F*, *M*), it appears in *italics*; if the measurement is written using Greek letters (e.g., α, β, μ), it is not italicized. You may occasionally see text underlined in a typed or word-processed manuscript; underlining is the old-fashioned manner of indicating that the text should be in italics. Old typewriters were incapable of generating italics, boldface, or any other nonstandard form of print. The need to represent italics by underlining has disappeared because you can actually insert italics with a word processor.

Remember that the focus of the Results section is to present ideas. You are trying to convey to the reader a complete sense of what happened. If you compared two groups to see which one had the higher mean score, your first job is to tell the reader that the average score in one group is different from the average score in the other group. If you are correlating variables, you need to tell the reader that as the scores on one variable go up (or down), the scores on the second variable go up (or down). Most research that you will encounter deals with those

Table 12.2

Format for Presenting Commonly Used Inferential Statistics

Statistic	Example	
Generic	Statistic(degrees of freedom) = value of statistic, p = significance level, effect size	
t-test	$t(45) = -4.35, p = .029,$ $\eta^2 = .14$	For providing the exact probability value, as recommended in APA style
	$t(45) = -4.35, p < .05,$ $\eta^2 = .14$	For simply establishing that the obtained value is less than (or greater than) the cutoff for significance
	$t(45) = -4.35, p_{rep} = .91,$ $\eta^2 = .14$	For providing the probability that the effect will replicate, as recommended by the APS
	$t(45) = -4.35, p = .029,$ $p_{rep} = .910, \eta^2 = .14$	For providing the traditional p-level and the probability that the effect will replicate
F-test (ANOVA)	$F(2,33) = 5.25, p = .01,$ MSE $= 2.95, \eta^2 = .24$	For providing the exact probability value, as recommended in APA style; MSE refers to mean square error
	$F(2,33) = 5.25, p < .05,$ MSE $= 2.95, \eta^2 = .24$	For simply establishing that the obtained value is less than (or greater than) the cutoff for significance
	$F(2,33) = 5.25,$ $p_{rep} = .95,$ MSE $= 2.95,$ $\eta^2 = .24$	For providing the probability that the effect will replicate, as recommended by the APS
Correlation	$r(107) = .13, p = .18$	For providing the exact probability value, as recommended in APA style
	$r(107) = .13, p > .05$	For simply establishing that the obtained value is greater than (or less than) the cutoff for significance
	$r(107) = .13, p > .05$ $p_{rep} = .787, p = .18$	For providing the probability that the result will replicate, as recommended by the APS
Chi-square	$\chi^2(1, N = 46) = 1.39,$ $p = .24$	For providing the exact probability value, as recommended in APA style
	$X^2(1, N = 46) = 1.39,$ $p = .24$	Alternate form using X, a Roman letter, instead of χ, a Greek letter

Note: When reporting a chi-square value, indicate the degrees of freedom followed by the sample size in the parentheses

Note: APA style says that, normally, you should report test values and probability levels to two decimal places, but when a p-value is less than .001 (e.g., p = .0005), you may see it reported as p < .001. In some journals, authors occasionally report p values to three or four decimal places.

Also, insert a space between each element in the statistical presentation. The spaces make it easier to read.

Table 12.3
Some Commonly Used Symbols and Abbreviations Used in Measurement

Symbol*	What it represents	Symbol*	What it represents
f	Frequency	N	Total sample size
f_e	Expected frequency	n	Size of subsample
H_0	Null hypothesis	SD	Standard deviation
H_a or H_1	Alternate or research hypothesis	z	Standardized score
M	Mean	α	Probability of Type I error
Mdn	Median	β	Probability of Type II error

*Symbols appearing in Roman letters (e.g., a, b, c) are italicized; symbols appearing in Greek letters (e.g., α, β, γ) are not italicized. If the symbol or abbreviation has a subscript or superscript, it is not italicized.

Table 12.4
Some Common Symbols Used in Presenting the Results of Statistical Tests

Symbol*	What it represents	Symbol*	What it represents
ANOVA	Analysis of variance	r_{pb}	Point-biserial correlation
ANCOVA	Analysis of covariance	r_s	Spearman's correlation
d	Cohen's measure of effect size	R	Multiple correlation
d'	Measure of sensitivity (psychophysics)	R^2	Square of multiple correlation
df	Degrees of freedom	SEM	Standard error of measurement; standard error of the mean
MANOVA	Multiple analysis of variance	SS	Sum of squares
MS	Mean square	t	t-test value
MSE	Mean square error	η^2	Eta-squared (measure of effect size)
p	Probability; probability of success in binomial trial	ϕ	Phi (measure of association)
p_{rep}	Probability that an effect will replicate	χ^2	Chi-square value
r	Pearson product-moment correlation	ω^2	Omega squared (measure of effect size)
r^2	Coefficient of determination	$\wedge$	Caret (reflects an estimated value when used above a Greek letter)

*Symbols appearing in Roman letters (e.g., a, b, c) are italicized; symbols appearing in Greek letters (e.g., α, β, γ) are not italicized. If the symbol or abbreviation has a subscript or superscript, it is not italicized.

two issues: do averages differ and are variables correlated? It should not be difficult to tell that to the reader.

So what is the difficulty in presenting results? One concern is expressing the technical details in appropriate format. All you have to do is to insert them into your prose in a meaningful place and follow the prescribed format. A second concern is taking your understanding of what the numbers have told you and converting that information into coherent and comprehensible English. This requires more thought.

CREATING TABLES

Tables are an effective way to present a lot of information in a small space. When you have many data, it might be difficult to include them all in the text without overwhelming or boring the reader. The most difficult part of creating tables is generating a format that makes the purpose of your data transparent, that is, clear and accessible.

The first task here is to decide whether you need a table for your results. If you are comparing two or three groups, you would not use a table because the table would take up too much space relative to the information you are presenting. Also, as the APA *Publication Manual* (2001) points out, tables are expensive because a person must take extra time to format it so that it fits into a journal article appropriately. Thus, you should use tables only when you have a lot of information. This situation typically arises when you are dealing with multiple variables that, if presented in prose format, would constitute a string of numbers that are hard for the reader to process.

Suppose you collected data about the way that women and men respond to offensive jokes that victimized either women, men, or neither gender in particular. After you analyzed your results, you would communicate which groups differed in their ratings of the jokes. As such, you could (but you should not) indicate the mean ratings on a scale of 1 (*not funny*) to 7 (*very funny*) using the following dense, text-dependent passage:

> There was a significant interaction between sex of joke victim and sex of rater. Women rated male-victimizing jokes as funniest (M = 3.6, SD = 1.2) followed by no-victim jokes (M = 3.4, SD = 1.0), then by female-victimizing jokes (M = 2.7, SD = 1.2). Men rated male-victimizing jokes (M = 3.2, SD = 0.68) and no-victim jokes (M = 3.2, SD = 0.9) comparably, and female-victimizing jokes funniest (M = 3.9, SD = 1.2), $F(2, 160) = 26.66$, $p < .001$, $p_{rep} > .986$. [data from Beins et al., 2005).

This presentation is factually accurate, but who would want to wade through the string of numbers? Besides, it is difficult to make comparisons across groups based on this presentation. If these were your data, you could create either a table or a figure to depict them. Figure 12.1 provides the structure for a table that would represent the data more coherently.

If you refer to the APA *Publication Manual*, you will read that means and standard deviations normally appear in different parts of the table so it is easier to compare the means separately from the standard deviations. In many published articles, though, the means appear next to the standard deviations, with the latter in parentheses, as illustrated in Figure 12.1. If you wanted to discuss differences between means separately from differences in standard deviations, you could present them in different places in the table, as shown in Figure 12.2.

Figures 12.1 and 12.2 both demonstrate how you can depict numbers showing differences among means. Psychologists use other types of data, however, so you may need tables with somewhat different formats. For instance, if you want to present correlational data, the layout of your table will not be quite the same as when you present averages. If you measured several different variables and computed the correlations among them, a table like Figure 12.3 would illustrate the relations among the variables clearly.

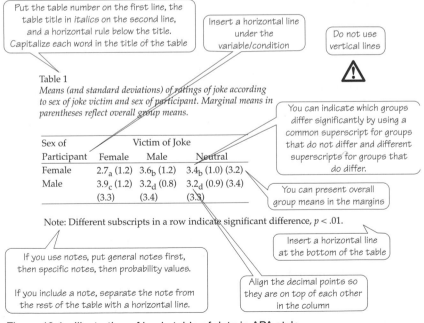

Figure 12.1 Illustration of basic table of data in APA style.

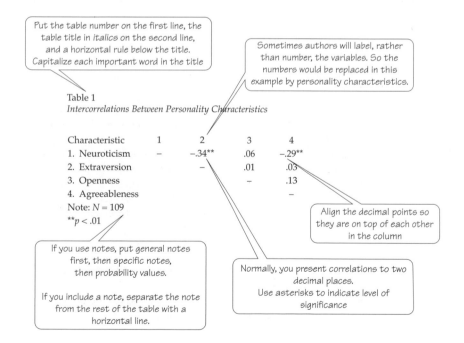

> Put the table number on the first line, the table title in *italics* on the second line, and a horizontal rule (i.e., an underline) below the title. Capitalize each word in the title of the table

Table 1
Means and Standard Deviations of Ratings of Joke According to Sex of Joke Victim and Sex of Participant.

Sex of	Mean rating Victim of Joke			Standard deviation Victim of Joke		
Participant	Female	Male	Neutral	Female	Male	Neutral
Female	2.7	3.6	3.4	1.2	1.2	1.0
Male	3.9	3.2	3.2	1.2	0.8	0.9

> Underline headings that indicate conditions that go together, in this case, means go with means and standard deviations go with standard deviations

> Place a horizontal rule below the labels for conditions and variables

> Align the decimal points so they are on top of each other in the column

Figure 12.2 Example of a table in which different measurements (means and standard deviations) appear separately.

> Put the table number on the first line, the table title in *italics* on the second line, and a horizontal rule below the title. Capitalize each important word in the title

> Sometimes authors will label, rather than number, the variables. So the numbers would be replaced in this example by personality characteristics.

Table 1
Intercorrelations Between Personality Characteristics

Characteristic	1	2	3	4
1. Neuroticism	–	–.34**	.06	–.29**
2. Extraversion		–	.01	.03
3. Openness			–	.13
4. Agreeableness				–

Note: $N = 109$
**$p < .01$

> If you use notes, put general notes first, then specific notes, then probability values.
>
> If you include a note, separate the note from the rest of the table with a horizontal line.

> Normally, you present correlations to two decimal places.
> Use asterisks to indicate level of significance

> Align the decimal points so they are on top of each other in the column

Figure 12.3 Example of a table of correlations in APA style.

Table 12.5
Steps to Use to Create a Table with Word® and WordPerfect® .

Step 1	Type the table number on the first line, then type the table title in italics on the second line
Step 2	Make a 5 × 5 table
Step 3	Leave the upper left cell empty. In the first column, indicate the first variable name (Sex of participant) and, below the variable name, the conditions for that variable (female and male). This is often the variable with fewer conditions
Step 4	On the top line, type the variable name (Joke victim)

	Using Word©	Using WordPerfect©
Step 5	• Highlight the top row of cells	• Highlight the top row of cells
	• Right-click on the mouse and select *Merge cells*	• Right-click on the mouse and select *Join cells*
	• Center the variable name	• Center the variable name

Step 6	On the line below type the second variable name. This is often the variable with more conditions
Step 7	On the next line, indicate the conditions of the second variable (female, male, neutral)

Now that you have established the structure of the table, enter the data

	Using Word©	Using WordPerfect©
Step 8	To erase all lines in the table: • Select *Borders and Shading* • Choose *None*	To erase all the lines in the table: • Move the cursor into the table and right-click the mouse • Select *Borders/Fill* • Select the tab labeled *Table* • Choose no lines where it says *Default cell lines* • Click on *OK*
Step 9	To insert a line under the title of the table: • Highlight cells in the top row of the table	To insert a line at the top of the table: • Highlight cells in the top row of the table

Table 12.5
Continued.

	• Right-click the mouse and choose *Borders and Shading*	• Right-click the mouse and choose *Borders/Fill*
	• Click on the icon on the right that shows a line at the top of the cell	• Select *Top*
	• Click on *OK*	• Click on *OK*
Step 10	To insert a line under the row listing the variables (Sex of participant: female, male, neutral):	To insert a line under the row listing the variables (Sex of participant: female, male, neutral):
	• Highlight the row listing the variables	• Highlight the row listing the variables
	• Right-click on the mouse and choose *Borders and Shading*	• Right-click on the mouse and choose *Borders/Fill*
	• Click on the icon on the right that shows a line at the bottom of the cell	• Select *Bottom*
	• Click on *OK*	• Click on *OK*
Step 11	To insert a line at the bottom of the data:	To insert a line under the data:
	• Highlight cells in the bottom row of the table	• Highlight the bottom row of data
	• Right-click on the mouse and choose *Borders and Shading*	• Right-click on the mouse and choose *Borders/Fill*
	• Click on the icon on the right that shows a line at the bottom of the cell	• Select *Bottom*
	• Click on *OK*	• Click on *OK*
Step 12	To enter any notes below the bottom line:	To enter any notes below the bottom line:
	• Position the cursor below the table and type the notes.	• Position the cursor below the table and type the notes

Note: You can also create a table with only one column, but with rows as shown here. You would then use the space bar to create the spacing you desire.

As you can see in Figures 12.1 and 12.3, you can put notes at the bottom of a table if it helps the reader understand the contents of the table. You insert a horizontal line and put any notes below the line. You may insert more than one note. General notes with a wide scope come first, followed by more specific notes (e.g., referring to individual groups), then probability notes related to significance levels.

When you create your table, you can simply type it, using the space bar to creating the spacing you want. Or you can use your word processor to create the table. Table 12.5 shows how you can use your word processing program, either Word© or WordPerfect© to format the table. Table 12.6 shows the final result.

CREATING FIGURES

Tables summarize large numbers of data efficiently and precisely. Sometimes, though, visual presentations using figures can be helpful. In a graph, it is not always possible to discern the exact values of the data, so using figures may entail sacrificing some precision. Figure 12.4 shows the standard elements of a graph.

Figure 12.5 illustrates the results of a study in which participants' moods were manipulated prior to their rating a set of jokes (data from Cronin, Fazio, & Beins, 1998). It would be possible to present the results in text as follows:

> Participants showed greater mirth in the elevated mood condition; that is, they exhibited more laughing, smiling, and outward signs of humor. In contrast, the participants showed nearly equal levels

Table 12.6

The Result: Means (and Standard Deviations) of Ratings of Jokes According to Sex of Joke Victim and Sex of Participant. Marginal means in parentheses reflect overall group means

Sex of participant	Joke victim			
	Female	Male	Neutral	
Female	2.7_a (1.2)	3.6_b (1.2)	3.4_b (1.0)	3.2
Male	3.9_c (1.2)	3.2_d (0.8)	3.2_d (0.9)	3.4
	3.3	3.4	3.3	

Note: Different subscripts in a row indicate significant differences, $ps < .01$.

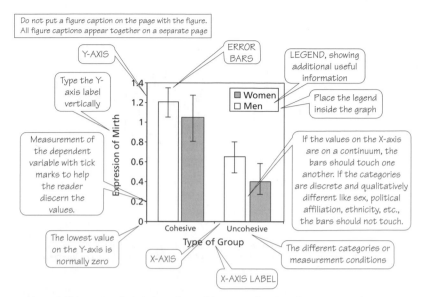

Figure 1. The amount of mirth shown by participants as a function of group type and sex of participant.

Figure 12.4 Graph with labels of common elements of the graph. Specific terms are in uppercase letters. Note that the figure caption appears below the figure. In preparing a manuscript, you would place the caption on a separate page, not on the page where you drew the figure.

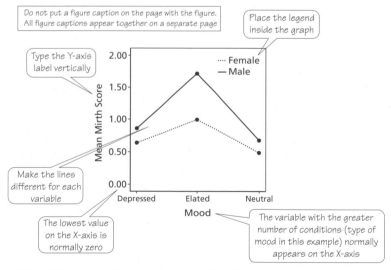

Figure 1. The mean mirth score (e.g., degree of laughing and smiling) as a function of induced mood and sex of the participant.

Figure 12.5 Line graph in APA style. Line graphs are appropriate when the variable on the X-axis is quantitative. The figure caption should include any explanatory information needed to understand the graph. Figures do not generally use notes the way tables do.

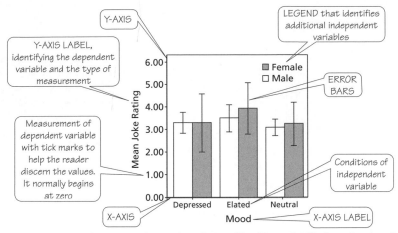

Figure 1. The mean mirth score (e.g., degree of laughing and smiling) as a function of induced mood and sex of the participant. Error bars reflect 95% confidence intervals around the mean.

Figure 12.6 Bar chart showing error bars in APA style and example of a figure caption with an explanation of the error bars. A bar chart is appropriate when the variable on the X-axis is based on discrete categories.

of mirth in the depressed and in the neutral conditions. For women in the depressed mood condition, $M = 0.64$ ($SD = 0.86$); for men in the depressed mood condition, $M = 0.86$ ($SD = 1.08$). For women in the elevated and neutral conditions, $M = 0.66$ ($SD = 0.65$) and $M = 0.67$ ($SD = 0.68$), respectively. For men in the elevated and neutral conditions, $M = 1.70$ ($SD = 1.64$) and $M = 1.22$ ($SD = 1.35$), respectively.

Unfortunately, this presentation does not lend itself to the development of a good overall sense of what the data revealed. If you refer to Figures 12.5 (a line graph) and 12.6 (a bar graph), you will see patterns delineated more clearly. The effect of induced mood on laughing and smiling was significant: elevated mood resulted in greater expression of mirth.

One of the important considerations in creating graphs is that you can alter their appearance greatly by changing the scale of the X- and Y-axes. The data don't change, but their appearance does. The data in Figure 12.7 are based on the same data as Figure 12.6, but the scale on the Y-axis has changed. In Figure 12.7, the Y-axis begins with a

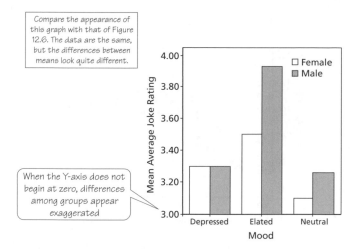

Compare the appearance of this graph with that of Figure 12.6. The data are the same, but the differences between means look quite different.

When the Y-axis does not begin at zero, differences among groups appear exaggerated

Figure 12.7 Bar graph showing the same data as Figure 12.6 but with a different scale on the Y-axis, which exaggerates the differences between groups, and example of a figure caption.

value of 3.00 whereas Figure 12.6 begins at zero. This change in the structure of the graph leads to a drastic change in appearance.

If your Y-axis begins at a number greater than zero, small differences can be magnified. Further, if you extend the Y-axis so that it is quite long compared with the X-axis, the differences between groups will look big; if you compress the Y-axis so that it is quite short compared with the X-axis, the differences between groups will look small.

The appearance of the graph should match the accurate message you want to convey. You need to make sure that you are not deceiving your reader by portraying the data so that they lead to an inaccurate conclusion.

The figures described so far have related to comparison of separate groups, which lends itself to bar and line graphs. If your research involves correlational data, however, your data will probably lend themselves to scatter diagrams. The principles involved in creating a scatter diagram are similar to those for bar charts and line graphs. An example of a scatter diagram appears in Figure 12.8.

One final type of figure to be discussed here is the frequency histogram. It looks like a bar graph, but its main function is to illustrate how many observations fall into different categories. In the histogram shown in Figure 12.9, you can see how many students thought they had unhealthy lifestyles (low ratings) versus healthy lifestyles (high ratings) based on the results of student responses to a question about

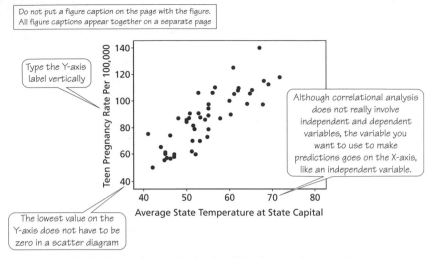

Figure 1. Scatter diagram showing the relation between the average temperature in each of the state capitals in the United States and the teen pregnancy rate per 1,000 teenagers.

Figure 12.8 Scatter diagram in APA style showing the relation between temperature and teen birth rates in the states in the US and example of a figure caption. A scatter diagram is appropriate for showing the pattern of individual cases measured on two different variables.

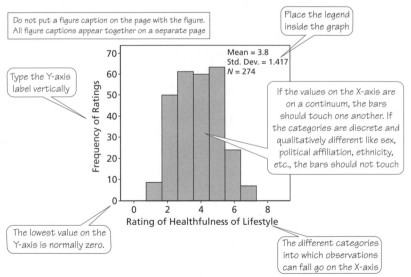

Figure 1. The frequencies of students who rated the healthfulness of their lifestyle in each category on a scale of 1 (*poor*) to 7 (*good*).

Figure 12.9 Illustration of a frequency histogram in which the categories fall on a continuum. In this case, the categories are ratings that progress from 1 to 7. In such a histogram, the bars should touch one another.

their lifestyles. When the X-axis involves a quantitative variable, the bars should touch. When the X-axis involves a qualitative, categorical variable, the bars do not touch, as shown in Figure 12.10.

THE CONNECTION BETWEEN THE TEXT AND THE TABLES AND FIGURES

The advantage of creating tables and figures in your manuscript is that you can present a large number of data in a small amount of space.

You should use them judiciously, though, because journal space is precious. Many more authors submit manuscripts to journal editors than can possibly be printed in the journal. For example, the journal *Teaching of Psychology* rejected 77% of all manuscripts submitted to the editor in 2005. Among APA's primary journals, the average rejection rate was 69% (Summary report, 2006). So the editors returned over two-thirds of manuscripts to the authors with the unfortunate message that the manuscript would not appear in that journal.

As you consider including tables and figures, ask yourself if they are worth including. That is, could you get your point across as easily and effectively by using words rather than pictures? If the answer is yes, you probably do not need tables or figures. On the other hand, if your

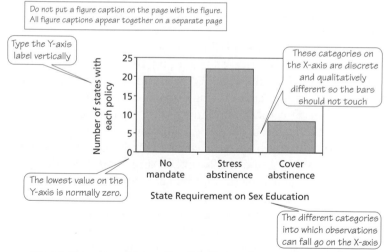

Figure 1. The number of states with policies that are silent regarding content of sex education programs, that mandate stress abstinence, or that simply mandate some coverage of abstinence in sex education programs.

Figure 12.10 Illustration of a frequency histogram with discrete (nonquantitative) categories on the X-axis. When the categories are discrete, the bars should not touch.

reader's work will be easier because of a table or a figure, you should include it.

When you include visual elements in your manuscript, refer to them in your text. Don't just create them and expect the reader to pay attention to them. You must connect the figure or table to the text so the reader knows the relation between the two. Furthermore, if the text gets the point across, you don't need a table or figure. If you can express a result more efficiently in a table or figure, don't include that information in the text. In the end, the text and the tables and figures should complement, not duplicate, one another.

THE DIFFERENCE BETWEEN RESULTS AND DISCUSSION SECTIONS

In most APA-style papers, you create separate sections for describing your data and saying whether those data support your hypotheses (Results) and for talking about what your results mean (Discussion). As such, in your Results section, you should give your data without interpreting what they mean. This does not mean that you give only a cursory presentation of your data; rather, it means that you consider only the data and the statistical results. You offer descriptive statistics such as means and standard deviations, accompanied by inferential statistics such as the ANOVA. At this point, you don't link your results to theory or other related research.

Your Results section should be fairly noncontroversial because you are giving your reader numerical facts and, for the most part, the facts are straightforward. Sometimes, results spark controversy, such as when researchers criticize the statistical approach used by earlier authors. But this type of disagreement is relatively rare because psychologists have generally agreed on most statistical approaches. In essence, there should be no controversy because every statement you make in your results section should describe and be linked directly to your data.

As an example, if you look at Figure 12.7, you will see that participants showed more mirth responses in an elevated-mood condition than in either depressed- or neutral-mood conditions. This is a straightforward result that nobody could deny—the data reflect that pattern of behavior. So it would be appropriate to include this in the results. On the other hand, you would refrain from interpreting the data and saying what is going on in the participants' heads. Your conclusion may have validity, but it is an interpretation. It is not a fact in the same sense as noting that means for the different mood groups differ. Inferences and conclusions belong in the Discussion section, which contains speculation, interpretation, theory, and connection to other research.

SOME FINAL POINTS ABOUT PRESENTING RESULTS

As you have undoubtedly noticed, there are some fairly specific guidelines for presenting the results of research. If you refer to the *Publication Manual of the American Psychological Association* (2001), you will see that it devotes 25 pages to presentation of numbers and statistics. Sometimes the rules seem picky and maybe even nonsensical. But psychologists follow these rules in writing.

Some final points about presenting numerical information appear in Table 12.7. This is an encapsulation of the entire set of APA guidelines about presentation of statistics and data. For presentation involving rare occurrences, you can consult the APA *Publication Manual.* You can also peruse published journal articles to see how researchers have presented this type of information.

Table 12.7
Specific Rules and Guidelines Commonly Used for Presenting Numbers and Statistics in APA Style

Rule	Examples
Write out numbers less than ten. Use a numeral for numbers equal to 10 or more. Exception: If you are giving a series of numbers that includes values greater than 10, use all numerals	• Participants learned six lists. • There were 15 participants. • Participants learned either 6, 8, or 10 lists.
Do not start sentences with numerals. Preferably, start the sentence non-numerically. If you need to start a sentence with a number, write out the number	• Volunteers included 40 students recruited from psychology classes. • Forty students from psychology classes participated.
Use numbers to represent time and dates, number of participants, scores on a scale	• 1 hr 22 min • February 27, 1980 • 8 participants (but eight people) • The Likert-type scale ranged from 1 (low) to 7 (high)
Use numerals for precise measurements. Abbreviate the units of measurement, but do not use periods after the abbreviation except to avoid confusion	• 10 min (for 10 minutes) • 25 cm (for 25 centimeters) • 10 in. (for 10 inches)

Continued overleaf.

Table 12.7
Continued.

Rule	Examples
Put spaces between elements in mathematical copy. For an inferential statistic, do not put a space between the statistic and the number of degrees of freedom	• $t(35) = 1.02$, $p > .05$ *not* $t(35)=1.02$, $p>.05$
If a measurement could be greater than one but is actually less than one, use a zero before the decimal point	• 0.35 (if the value could have been greater than one, such as in measuring length) • .35 (if the value could not be greater than one, such as a probability value or a correlation coefficient)
Carry inferential statistics to two decimal places	• $t(35) = 1.02$, $p > .05$
Use two more decimal places than were used in the raw data	• If the raw data are whole numbers (e.g., 1, 3, 4), report summary statistics like means to two decimal places: $M = 3.67$
Use an uppercase N for total sample size and lowercase n to represent subsamples. You can use a subscript to identify particular subsamples	• $N = 100$ (for a total of 100 participants) • $n = 25$ (for a subsample) • $n_{girls} = 25$ (for the number of girls in a group)
Use the symbol for percent (%) when it is used with a numeral; use the word percentage if there is no number. Exception: Always use the symbol in tables to save space	• 10% • A different percentage of respondents
When symbols are in Roman letters (e.g., N, p), italicize them. When symbols are Greek, do not italicize them.	• $N = 25$ (*N* is italicized) • $\mu = 25$ (mu is not italicized)

13

The Discussion Section

Nothing is so simple that it cannot be misunderstood.

Freeman Teague, Jr.

That is what learning is. You suddenly understand something you've understood all your life, but in a new way.

Doris Lessing

Imagine that you knew something about behavior that nobody else in the world knew. You could do one of two things with the knowledge. You could keep it to yourself or you could shout it from the rooftops.

What do psychologists do in this situation? After doing research, only fairly bizarre psychologists shout their findings from actual rooftops. Instead, they write papers for journals, which is actually a psychologist's way of shouting from the rooftops. After you carry out a study, it is nice to let others know what you have found and what it means. That is what the Discussion section is for.

In this chapter, you will see how you can tie together all the information in the previous sections of your research paper. The Discussion section revisits the basic concepts of interest to you and how you addressed your research questions; this section also shows how your results supported your ideas. Finally, the Discussion allows you to speculate on what you think your data are telling you.

In general, in the Method and Results sections of your paper, you limit your presentation to your research project. In the Discussion section, however, you are beginning a conversation with the reader about your ideas. What does your study have to say about the topics of interest to you, and where do your ideas lead? Your job here is to stimulate your reader to think about larger issues. You have to develop clear explanations that make sense to the reader and that show why your work is interesting and important.

SUMMARIZING YOUR RESULTS

You should refresh your reader at the beginning of the discussion about what you discovered. You will be doing your reader a favor if you present each of your research findings separately, perhaps reserving a paragraph or two for each finding or closely related group of findings. Begin with your most interesting and important results.

The reiteration of the results should not include statistics. Rather, give a verbal description that encapsulates the critical findings. If the reader is interested in the statistics, they are available in the Results section; there is no need to repeat them here.

When you describe your results, connect them to your hypotheses, which you should have developed in the Introduction. That is, did your results provide support for your hypotheses? A simple statement often suffices. For instance, Kaiser, Vick, and Major (2006) studied whether people pay attention to different environmental cues when they expect to experience prejudice. In the Discussion section of their research article, they began their discussion by noting that

> we hypothesized that individuals who chronically anticipate being a target of prejudice, or who find themselves in a situation in which these concerns are salient, are vigilant for cues that their social identity is under threat. Our research findings were consistent with this hypothesis. We found that individuals with chronic or situationally induced concerns about prejudice preconsciously screen their environment for signs of identity devaluation. (Kaiser et al., 2006. p. 337)

If you have developed multiple hypotheses, deal with each one individually. There is nothing wrong with reporting that the results did not match your expectations. As we all know, human behavior is complex and not easy to predict. So your data might confirm a hypothesis entirely, partially, or not at all. Research is a process of finding out the limits to our theories and our predictions.

CONNECTING DIFFERENT ASPECTS OF YOUR RESULTS

If you have included multiple dependent variables (DVs) in your study or if your research report involves more than one study, you should tell how the separate components relate to one another. For example, if you had more than one DV, say how the different DVs combine to give a more complete picture of your participants' behaviors and responses. That is, what do two (or more) DVs tell you that one alone would not?

Sometimes your different measurements complement one another. When this happens, you can make a stronger argument about your conclusions than if you had a single DV. On the other hand, sometimes different DVs lead to different patterns of behavior because those measurements tap into different psychological processes. In your discussion of your results, you should bring together these individual results so you can develop a complete picture of participants' behaviors.

For example, we conducted several projects in which participants read and responded to a series of jokes after their moods were temporarily raised or depressed. One DV was the participant's rating of how funny the joke was; the second DV was the degree of mirth (e.g., laughing, smiling) that the participant showed.

In initial experiments, our only dependent measure had been joke ratings (Cronin, Fazio, & Beins, 1998). The participant's mood (elevated vs. depressed) had no effect on the ratings of the jokes. People in depressed moods rated the jokes just as the people in the elevated group did. But when we added mirth responses as a second DV, we found that mood did have an effect on responses to jokes. People in the elevated mood group showed greater degrees of mirth than the people in the depressed group did; that is, they laughed and smiled more (Martin & McGaffick, 2001).

It appears that mood does not affect the rated funniness of jokes, but mood does affect the overt reactions to the jokes. If we had used only one DV (joke ratings), we would not have seen that mood has a reliable effect on the way people respond to jokes.

Sometimes if you use multiple DVs, they don't cooperate, providing contradictory results. Although, as a researcher, you don't really want to encounter this situation, it is important to recognize when it occurs. You can't simply ignore it. If you can figure out a reason for such inconsistency, you should report it. On the other hand, sometimes you can't figure out why the results occurred the way they did. In that case, simply say so.

DEALING WITH NONSIGNIFICANT RESULTS

Sometimes your data analysis leads to results that are statistically nonsignificant. (Remember that psychologists refer to results that don't achieve statistical significance as *nonsignificant*, not as *insignificant*.)

Such results are problematic because you don't know whether the results are nonsignificant because there is no relation between the variables that you are investigating or because there was a problem with the design of your study.

You might have hypothesized that you would see nonsignificant results because that is what other researchers had discovered or because a theory predicts no relation among variables. If your nonsignificant results were as you expected, that can provide support for your ideas. On the other hand, if you expected significance but didn't see it, it isn't clear what you can say about it in your discussion. You might not be able to say much more than that you are puzzled by the results and have no explanation.

Sometimes, your results are significant, but they are totally puzzling. As you will recall from your knowledge of statistics, researchers usually set a Type I error rate of 5% in their research. So if you conduct enough analyses, some results (i.e., about 5%) will be statistically significant, even though the difference between groups or the correlation between variables does not mean anything and would not replicate if you repeated the study. If you wind up with significant effects that are completely unexpected and totally puzzling, simply state that there is no convincing explanation for the results except that it might be a Type I error. In such a situation, it does not make sense to try and conjure up complex and convoluted explanations. It is reasonable, though, to suggest another study that would determine if the results were reliable.

COMPARING YOUR RESULTS WITH THOSE OF OTHERS

After you draw the connection between your results and your hypotheses, you can take the opportunity to link your research to previous studies. If you haven't found research that relates to yours, you have probably not searched extensively enough. Furthermore, your ideas will have greater credibility if you can connect them to the work of other psychologists.

As an example of how researchers have made such connections, consider the work of Reder et al. (2006) They studied drug-induced amnesia, using the drug midazolam, which blocks memory formation in people; in their discussion, they explicitly linked their data to several previous studies:

Our data are consistent with the results of Huppert and Piercy (1976, 1978), who found that patients with anterograde amnesia can still recognize pictures as long as judgments do not require list discrimination . . . . Our results are also consistent with the priming study of Musen et al. (1999), which showed that it is easier to create an association to a word than to an unfamiliar stimulus. Our hypothesis that familiarity affects the probability of encoding as well as the probability of a false alarm can also explain a finding of Koutstaal et al. (Reder et al., 2006, p. 565)

Just as your results might or might not conform to your hypotheses, they might or might not be similar to those of previous researchers. There are different reasons for this happening. The other research might have had methodological limitations or yours might have. Different types of participants in the studies or different species of subjects might have led to different outcomes. Unfortunately, when differences occur across studies, it can be very difficult to figure out why.

Still, it is important to try and determine why your replication did not achieve the same results. Wang (2006) investigated people's first memories from their childhoods and generally obtained results very similar to expectations and to previous research. However, there was one element of the findings that differed from earlier work; Wang's research involved a slightly different memory task, which may have accounted for the difference.

The ages of earliest memories were substantially later in the current study than in previous studies using free-recall tasks . . . or asking participants to answer questions about targeted events such as the birth of a sibling. . . . The differences between the current study and previous studies . . . are particularly interesting . . . This issue merits further investigation, and examination of both the accessibility and the content of early memories elicited in different experimental paradigms will be necessary to unravel the mystery of infantile amnesia. (Wang, 2006, p. 713)

One temptation is to suggest that a small sample size might have been responsible. In most cases, sample size is not a very sound argument. Issues of sample size can be relevant if the data are quite variable or if an effect is real but weak, but the number of participants is not likely to have led to different patterns of results.

STATE THE IMPORTANCE AND IMPLICATIONS OF YOUR RESULTS

After you conduct your study, you will know something that, literally, nobody else in the world knows. You have created knowledge that did not exist before you completed your project. This can be an exciting thought because, as Francis Bacon wrote, *Nam et ipsa, scientia potestas est*, which means "In and of itself, knowledge is power."

You will probably see the importance of your results more clearly than anybody else will, so you are in the best position to illustrate to the reader how your study has advanced psychological knowledge. The Discussion section is the most appropriate place to write about the importance of your ideas. For example, if a theory makes a prediction, your data could lend support to the power of that theory. Or if your data are inconsistent with the theory, you can help establish the limitations of the theory or, perhaps, to extend it in new directions.

One important task for your discussion is to convince your reader that your question is psychologically meaningful. That is, tell why psychologists would think that your research has contributed to our knowledge base. You can't accomplish this merely by saying that your question is important. You need to connect your research with current psychological thought. That is, how does your research relate to what other psychologists have been studying?

The Discussion section also lets you expand your presentation beyond the confines of your particular research project. Every study leaves questions unanswered, and no single study answers all of the interesting questions in an area. So in your discussion, you can tell the reader how your research has paved the way for new ideas by answering some questions and giving suggestion for others. The research by Wang (2006) on infantile memory cited above provides a good illustration of this. Psychologists are impressed not only by clever and insightful research projects, but also by the implications that those projects have for future research.

So, for instance, if you conducted your study in a laboratory, you could take the opportunity to speculate on how your findings might relate to everyday life. Likewise, you could relate your results to a different population of participants. This kind of conjecture shows that you are conversant with the important issues in the area.

ACKNOWLEDGING THE LIMITATIONS OF YOUR STUDY

No study is perfect. That fact is a reality of life. In your discussion, you should acknowledge the limitations of your study. These limitations can involve different facets of your project.

For example, your methodology might set the limits to generalizability of your data. When planning your study, you have to make decisions about what kinds of measurements to make or what conditions to study. If you make different measurements or create different types of groups, your results might turn out differently. In dealing with this kind of limitation, you should not assume that you made poor choices for your measurements and conditions. Rather, you should simply recognize that there is more work to be done to answer your question fully. Furthermore, when it comes to questions of measurements and conditions, it isn't necessary to belabor the limitations. If you are carrying out your research with measurements that are identical to those of previous researchers, other investigators are probably not likely to question your study because of those measurements.

Another limitation to your study may involve your sample. If your participants were students, your results might generalize well to other students, but maybe not to nonstudents or to people of different ages. Or if your participants included mostly females, your results might not generalize well to males. As always, you should use good judgment and your knowledge of the phenomena you are studying to draw your conclusions. Some phenomena may exhibit themselves similarly for women and for men, so if your study included mostly women, your conclusions might generalize nicely to men. Still, you should make sure that you acknowledge such limitations if they are potentially relevant.

Another potential limitation involves identifying causal relations. If your study was correlational or quasi-experimental, you should avoid suggesting that you can identify the cause of your participants' responses. This caution is particularly important when your study involves a quasi-experimental design that involves intact groups and when participants are not randomly assigned to conditions. A quasi-experimental design looks like an experimental design, which permits causal conclusions, but in reality, quasi-experiments are correlational designs disguised as experiments.

14

References: Citations in the Text and the Reference List

Don't worry about people stealing an idea. If it's original, you will have to ram it down their throats.

Howard Aiken

All of us . . . need to take advice and to receive help from other people.

Alexis Carrell

If no other psychologist had a research idea like yours, you would be the most unusual person in the world. Good research virtually never arises spontaneously and without any earlier work on the topic. So if you come up with an idea, it only makes sense to see who else has had a similar idea. This is where references are important.

In this chapter, you will see how to present the citations for previous work to which you have referred. The References section may very well be the least glamorous part of a research report and the most mechanical, but it is still very important. Each person builds on the ideas of others. When you cite previous work, you are documenting the flow of ideas from one thinker to another. The references you use tell your reader what path you took to arrive at your research question and your conclusions. This chapter deals with the way you refer to citations in your writing and how you list them in the References section.

Choosing the references to use can sometimes be difficult. You may have a great number of potential sources to cite, but you may not want to mention them all because there will be too much redundancy. So you should identify the points you want to make and decide which of your references will help you develop your ideas. Sometimes writers have a tendency to want to mention every single source they encounter. If you do this, you run the risk of overwhelming your reader.

The References section in an APA-style paper has a particular purpose: It lists the work you have referred to in your writing. So if you mention a book, a book chapter, a journal article, or any other source, you should include that source in your References section. If you do not mention a source in your paper, do not include it among the references. In other disciplines, a paper might have a Bibliography that contains work not cited in the paper, but psychologists only include in the References the sources they actually mention in the paper.

There are too many details regarding reference citation to list exhaustively here. However, examples of the major types of citations appear at the end of this chapter. If you need to cite a source that is not included here, you should refer to the *Publication Manual of the American Psychological Association* (American Psychological Association, 2001).

Finally, you should keep in mind that the references begin on a separate page. Other sections of the paper simply start on the line after the final sentence of the preceding section. For example, the heading for the Results section begins right after the final sentence of the Method section, without any extra lines between sections. The References section is different in that it starts on its own page. Like the rest of your paper, it is double spaced. So type the section heading (i.e., the word References, not in bold type) followed on the next line by the first reference. Do not include a blank line after each reference.

CITING REFERENCES IN THE TEXT

There are several ways of citing references as your create your text, but all of them involve mentioning the author or authors and the year in which the source was published or presented. You use last names only unless there are different authors with the same last name, which could confuse a reader; in that case, use the initials of the different authors in addition to the last name. In addition, it is almost never useful to cite an author's affiliation (e.g., Ithaca College) because it generally does not matter where a writer works. So the referencing style is simple: last names and year of the work.

If you want to present an overall sense of the ideas of several writers, you can present your idea, then refer to those writers as a group. When you do this, you alphabetize the references in the parentheses and separate different authors' work with a semicolon. You can see an example of this below.

When you alphabetize names, you alphabetize by the last name of the first author. You never rearrange names of the authors of an individual reference. The order of names in your References section needs to match the order of names in the published article.

As a rule, each time you cite somebody's work, you include the names and the year of publication or presentation of the ideas. However, if you have just mentioned a source, you may not need to cite the year again. The general rule is that, within a given paragraph, you need to include the year only once. In subsequent paragraphs it is often a good idea to repeat the year so the reader is certain which source you are citing. If you are providing a long discussion of a single reference, you may not need to include the year in each paragraph because there is little chance that the reader will be confused as to which work you are citing.

Citing One or Two Authors

Scientific publications very often include more than one author. When there are one or two authors, the format is entirely straightforward. Every time you mention work with one or two authors, you cite name and date.

As an example, consider Scheibe's (2004) discussion of media literacy in which she cited two previous works as follows:

> Even with a growing emphasis on technology skills and critical thinking, there are still only seven states that mandate media literacy as a separate strand in their state standards (Baker, 2004), and even those states have had difficulty grappling with how to assess media literacy as part of standardized state testing.
>
> Kubcy and Baker (2000) have noted, however, that nearly all states do refer to aspects of media literacy education as part of the mandated state standards, although they do not typically use the phrase *media literacy.* (Scheibe, 2004, p. 62)

One of the citations inserts the author within parentheses. The second citation mentions the authors in the text and puts the year of their work within parentheses.

CITING SOURCES WITH THREE, FOUR, OR FIVE AUTHORS

If a publication or presentation involved three, four, or five authors, you identify all the authors when you first mention the work. Then, in subsequent references to them, you list only the first author and follow it with this phrase: et al. (There should be a period after the phrase.) For instance, Stephenson, Pena-Shaff, and Quirk (2006) identified predictors of suicidal ideation among college students, citing the work of previous researchers:

Suicide rates for college students are about 7.5 per 100,000 per year but older students and males are at greater risk (Silverman, Meyer, Sloan Raffel, & Pratt, 1997) . . . In general, while the suicide rates of college student populations are lower than those of their non-college peers, many of the predictors of suicide are the same (Silverman et al., 1997, p. 109)

As you can see in this quotation, the first citation includes all the authors. The second citation mentions only the first author.

CITING SOURCES WITH SIX OR MORE AUTHORS

Occasionally, a large group of people collaborate to create a publication or presentation. If there are six or more such people, the referencing format is a little different than when there are five or fewer. This referencing style, as exemplified by Beins (2006), involves putting all of the authors' names within parentheses:

Academic psychologists are teachers as well as scholars. However, only recently have people noted the feasibility and the importance of linking the two (e.g., Halpern et al., 1998; . . .). (Beins, 2006, p. 11)

In this citation, Halpern is the only name that appears in the citation. The reason for this is that there are 18 authors in the Halpern et al. (1998) article; it would take up space, for no good reason, to include all of the authors. The first time you mention a reference, cite all authors if there are five or fewer. In APA style, if there are more than five authors, you list only the first author, followed by et al., which means *and others*.

When a source involves more than six authors, you type it in the References section a little differently than you would a source with six or fewer. That is, you include the names of only the first six authors, then you indicate that there are additional authors merely by typing "et al."

CITING PERSONAL COMMUNICATIONS

Sometimes you have had communication with a scholar who has provided useful information that has not appeared in print. When this happens, you should refer to the communication in the text, but you do not list it in the References section.

Beins (2006) cited such personal communication, which includes the name of the person, an indication that it was a personal communication, and the date on which the communication occurred:

> Teachers of psychology who submit materials to OTRP need to remember that the focus of materials published in OTRP is utilitarian. Theoretical justification for the project and the background literature are less important for resources in OTRP (Janet Carlson, personal communication, August 10, 2004).

Including this type of information gives appropriate credit to the person whose idea you mention, and it establishes the time, which could be important if the person changes his or her thoughts about the topic at some point.

CITING MULTIPLE SOURCES WITHIN PARENTHESES

If you cite more than one work within parentheses, there are certain rules for ordering them.

- Alphabetize the references by the last name of the first author.
- If you cite the same author more than once, put the author's work in chronological order, with the oldest first.
- If you cite an author who has more than one reference in a given year, add letters to the date (e.g., Davis, 2004a, 2004b, 2004c).
- Separate references to a single author or group of authors with a comma (e.g., Davis, 2002, 2004, 2006).
- Separate different authors or groups of authors with a semicolon (Davis, 2002, 2004, 2006; Smith, 1995).

ORDER OF CITATIONS IN THE REFERENCE LIST

- The most basic rule is to alphabetize the reference list by the last name of the first author.
- If you cite two references for which the first author is the same for each, put them in chronological order.

- If you cite two references with the same first author, but different junior authors, alphabetize by the last name of the second (or third, etc.) author.
- If two references have the same authors, but one of the references has an additional author cited at the end, put the citation with fewer authors first in the reference list.
- Alphabetize names with *Mc*, *Mac*, and *M'* using the exact letters in the name. So *Mac* would come before *Mc*, which would come before *M'*. Similarly, a last name like *Saint James* would come before *St. James*.
- If two different authors have the same last name, alphabetize by their initials (e.g., Smith, R. A. would precede Smith, S. L.)
- If a group has authored a work, use the first important word of the group name as the author's name. (Words like *The* or *An* are not considered important words, so you would ignore them in alphabetizing the work.)

USING YOUR WORD PROCESSING PROGRAM TO CREATE THE CITATION

In APA style references, the first line of the citation falls on the left margin. Each succeeding line is indented five spaces. This format is called a *hanging indent*. You could type in your reference, hitting the *Enter* key at the end of each line. But if you change your margins or insert or remove a word, the spacing of the citation may be inappropriate. It is easier to use your word processor to format the reference.

Using Word® to create a hanging indent	Using WordPerfect® to create a hanging indent
Type the reference in proper format without worrying about the hanging indent	Type the reference in proper format without worrying about the hanging indent
Select *Format* on the menu at the top, then *Paragraph*, then *Indents and Spacing*	Place the cursor at the very beginning of the citation
In the area labeled *Indentation* select the dropdown box *Special*. Highlight and select *Hanging*	Hit <CTRL> 7 or click on *Format* on the menu at the top, then select *Paragraph*, then select *Hanging Indent*
Click on *OK*	

EXAMPLES OF HOW DIFFERENT TYPES OF REFERENCES SHOULD BE LAID OUT

• Alphabetize the references, using last names and initials of authors.
• Use a hanging indent so that the first line is on the left margin and subsequent lines are indented.

When a single author is referenced multiple times, put the oldest citation first.

When a single first author is referenced multiple times, put the citations with fewest co-authors first

When there are more than six authors, cite only the first six, then indicate there are others by using et al.

When there are six or fewer authors, cite them all

References

Beins, B.C. (1993). Writing assignments in statistics classes encourage students to learn interpretation. *Teaching of Psychology, 20*, 161-164.

Beins, B.C. (2006). The scolarship of teaching and pedagogy. In W. Buskist and S.F. Davis (Eds.), *Handbook of the teaching of psychology* (pp. 11-15). Malden, MA: Blackwell.

Beins, B.C. Agnitti, J., Baldwin, V., Lapham, H., Yarmosky, S., Bubel, A., & MacNaughton, K., & Pashka, N. (2005, October). How expectations affect perceptions of offensive humor. Poster presented at the annual convention of the New England Psychological Association, New Haven, CT.

Halpern, D.F., Smothergill, D. W., Allen, M., Baker, S., Baum, C., Best, D. et al. (1998). Scholarship in psychology: A paradigm for the twenty-first century. *American Psychologist, 53*, 1292-1297.

Mathie, V.A., Buskist, W., Carlson, J.F., David, S.F., Johnson, D. E., & Smith, R.A. (2004). Expanding the boundaries of scholarship in psychology through teaching, research, service, and administration. *Teaching of Psychology, 31*, 233-241.

Rader, N., & Vaughn, L.A. (2000). Infant reaching to a hidden affordance: Evidence for intentionality. *Infant Behavior & Development, 23*, 531-541.

Scheibe, C.L. (2004). A deeper sense of literacy: Curriculum-driven approaches to media literacy in the K-12 classroom. *The American Behavioral Scientist, 48*, 60-68.

Stephenson, H., Pena-Shaff, J., Quirk, P. (2006). Predictors of college student suicidal ideation: Gender differences. *College Student Journal, 40*, 109-117.

Articles in Periodicals

Reference to a journal article.

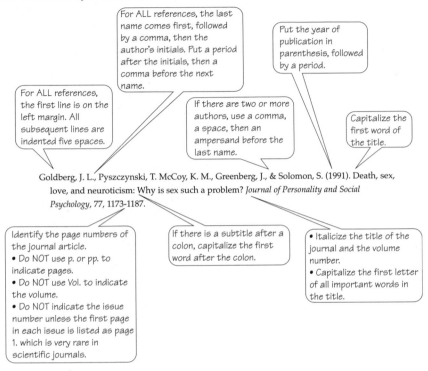

For ALL references, the last name comes first, followed by a comma, then the author's initials. Put a period after the initials, then a comma before the next name.

Put the year of publication in parenthesis, followed by a period.

For ALL references, the first line is on the left margin. All subsequent lines are indented five spaces.

If there are two or more authors, use a comma, a space, then an ampersand before the last name.

Capitalize the first word of the title.

Goldberg, J. L., Pyszczynski, T. McCoy, K. M., Greenberg, J., & Solomon, S. (1991). Death, sex, love, and neuroticism: Why is sex such a problem? *Journal of Personality and Social Psychology, 77,* 1173-1187.

Identify the page numbers of the journal article.
• Do NOT use p. or pp. to indicate pages.
• Do NOT use Vol. to indicate the volume.
• Do NOT indicate the issue number unless the first page in each issue is listed as page 1. which is very rare in scientific journals.

If there is a subtitle after a colon, capitalize the first word after the colon.

• Italicize the title of the journal and the volume number.
• Capitalize the first letter of all important words in the title.

Reference to an Internet-only journal article.

Indicate the exact date of publication in as much detail as possible.

Anderson, P. B., Spruille, B., Venable, R. H., & Strano, D.A. (2005, April 4). The relationships between heavy episodic drinking, sexual assaulting and being sexually assaulted for southern urban university students. *Electronic Journal of Human Sexuality,* 8. Retrieved September 20, 2006, from http://www.ejhs.org/volume8/heavy_drinking.htm

Indicate when you retrieved the article.

Do NOT end the reference with a period because computers consider punctuation marks as part of a web address. An extra period may cause difficulty in accessing the article.

Electronic journals may not have page numbers.

Reference to a traditional journal article accessed online.

Goldberg, J. L., Pyszczynski, T. McCoy, K. M., Greenberg, J., & Solomon, S. (1991). Death,
    sex, love, and neuroticism: Why is sex such a problem? [Electronic Version]. *Journal of*
    Personality and Social Psychology, 77, 1173-1187.

> If the article is based on a traditional, print
> journal, indicate that your version is
> electronic, but the rest of the citation is
> identical to that for a regular journal article.
> Type *Electronic Version* in square brackets.

Reference for a journal article with more than six authors.

> When you cite a source that includes more
> than six authors, type only the first six, then
> add et al. to the end to signify that there are
> other authors.

Halpern, D. F., Smothergill, D. W., Allen, M., Baker, S., Baum, C., Best, D. et al. (1998).
    Scholarship in psychology: A paradigm for the twenty-first century. *American Psychology,*
    53, 1292-1297.

> NOTE: In the text, when there are more than six authors, refer to
> them with only the first author's name followed by et al. (e.g.,
> Halpern et al. 1998).

Reference for which a group is the author.

> NOTE: The group takes the position of the author,
> regardless of whether the citation is online or in a
> traditional journal.

> If a group has authored a paper,
> list the group name as the author.

American Academy of Child and Adolescent Psychiatry. (2004). *Facts for families No. 10: Teen*
    suicide. Retrieved September 21, 2006, from www.aacap.org/publications/factsfam/suicide.
    htm

Reference for a special issue of a journal.

> For a special issue of the
> journal, indicate the editor,
> if there is one, followed by
> the indication, *Ed.* in
> parenthesis.

> Indicate that this is a
> special issue, using
> square brackets.

> Indicate the issue number
> to help the reader find the
> particular issue.

Nodine, B. F. (Ed.). (1990). Psychologists teach writing [Special issue]. *Teaching of Psychology, 17*(1).

References Involving Books

Reference to an entire book.

Petty, R. E., & Cacioppo, J.T. (1986). *Communication and peresuasion: Central and peripheral routes to allitude change.* New York: Springer-Verlag.

> Include the name of the city of publication, followed by a colon and a space, then the publisher's name.

> Italicize book titles.
> Capitalize the first word of the title.
> If there is a subtitle following a colon, capitalize the first word after the colon.

Reference for an edited book.

> Indicate the editor with *Ed.* in parenthesis. If there are multiple editors, use *Eds.*

Sternberg, R. J. (Ed.) (2000). *Guide to publishing in psychology journals.* New York: Cambridge University Press.

Reference to a chapter in a book.

> • Capitalize the first word of the chapter title.
> • If there is a subtitle with a colon, capitalize the first word after the colon.

Kendall, P. C., Silk, J. S., & Chu, B. C. (2000). Introducing your research report: Writing the introduction. In R. J. Sternberg (Ed.) *Guide to publishing in psychology journals* (pp. 41-57). New York: Cambridge University Press.

> Identify the editor(s) of the book, with initials before the last name or names of all editors.

> • Capitalize the first word of the book title.
> • *Italicize the book title.*

> • Give the page numbers of the chapter.
> • Use the abbreviation p. for page or pp. for pages.
> • The chapter title and the page information are NOT italicized.

Reference to a book whose author is also the publisher.

American Psychological Association. (2001). *Publication Manual of the American Psychological Association* (5th ed.). Washington, DC: Author.

> Instead of the publisher's name, just type the word *Author*, with the first letter capitalized.

References in Newsletters

Reference to a newsletter article with an author.

Beins, B. C. (2003, November). APA style: The style we love to hate. *General Psychology Newsletter, 16,* 29-31.

> Indicate the newsletter's year of publication, followed by a comma and the month. If the exact day of the month of publication is available, include it.

Reference to a newsletter article with discontinuous pages.

> Indicate the date in as much detail as listed in the newsletter.

Beins, B. C. (2005, Fall). Professional development through advanced placement psychology. *Psychology Teacher Network, 15(3),* 9, 16.

> • Italicize the publication.
> • Include the volume number.
> • Include the issue number only if the first page of each issue of the newsletter is numbered from page 1.

> If the article appears on discontinuous pages, indicate the pages on which the article appears.

Internet References

Reference to a multiple-page Internet site.

> • If there are multiple web pages on a site with no identifiable author, start with the web site's name.
> • When you cite the URL, give the entry.

Shape up America (n.d.). Body Fat Lab. Retrieved September 1, 2006, from http://www.shapeup.org

> If there is no date for the document, type n.d. to indicate "no date."

> Do not end the web address with a period.

References to Encyclopedia Entries

Reference to an encyclopedia entry.

> If there is no author listed, put the title of the entry, which in this example is *Elisha Gray*, where the author's name usually goes.

Elisha Gray (1974). In *The Encyclopedia Britannica,* (Vol. IV, p. 691). Chicago: Encyclopedia Britannica.

Presentations

Reference to a presentation given at a conference or other meeting.

> • Italicize (i.e., underline) the title of the presentation.
> •Capitalize the first word of the title and the first word of the subtitle.

> Indicate the year and month of the presentation.

McCarthy, M., & Beins, B. C. (2005 January). *Sharing the commitment to learning: Working toward a common goal.* Paper presented at the National Institute on the Teaching of Psychology, St. Petersburg, FL.

> Specify the conference and where it took place.

> Insert a comma between the name of the conference and its location

Reference to a poster presentation given at a conference or other meeting

> • Italicize (i.e., underline) the title of the presentation.
> • Capitalize the first word of the title and the first word of the subtitle.

> Indicate the year and month of the presentation.

Beins, B. C. (2005, October). *Online psychological laboratory: A free resource for experiments and demonstrations.* Poster session at the Northeastern Conference for Teachers of Psychology, New Haven, CT.

> Specify the conference and where it took place.

> Insert a comma between the name of the conference and its location.

Reference to a symposium at a conference or other meeting.

> • Italicize i.e., underline the title of the symposium.
> • Do NOT italicize the title of the talk within the symposium.

> Indicate the year and month.

Weaver, K. A. (2006, August). Building community through professional development. In D. C. Appleby (Chair), *Curricular and extracurricular community-building strategies for psychology departments*. Symposium conducted at the annual convention of the American Psychological Association, New Orleans, LA.

> Specify the conference and where it took place.

> Insert a comma between the name of the conference and its location

15

Final Touches: The Abstract and Formatting Details

The details are not the details. They make the design.

Charles Eames

Blue jeans are not suitable for a wedding, and a tuxedo is not suitable for a picnic. If you are going somewhere, it is probably a good idea to dress for the occasion. Likewise, after you have finished writing your paper, you need to dress it up with the finishing touches. Formatting your paper in APA style dresses it up so it fits the occasion.

In this chapter, you will learn how to assemble your APA-style research paper so that it follows the prescribed format. All APA papers follow the guidelines very closely because readers have certain expectations about what should appear in the paper and where they can find the information they want.

After you write your Introduction, Method, Results, and Discussion sections, you have finished nearly the entire substance of your manuscript. The only writing you have yet to do is the abstract, which is a short summary of your entire paper. Once you complete the abstract, you should take the opportunity to review and revise your writing one final time. You should also check to see that the formatting of your paper conforms with APA style.

As you are already aware, there are more rules of APA style than you probably care to think about. You have already encountered many of them. In this chapter, though, you will learn about some of the more mechanical aspects of creating and formatting your paper in APA style.

THE ABSTRACT

A reader's first exposure to your writing is likely to be the abstract, a summary no longer than 120 words. The abstract is the most recently developed section of published journal articles. APA journals used to print a summary at the end of the article; authors created an abstract, but it was only used for the now-defunct *Psychological Abstracts*, which PsycINFO© replaced. Now, the Summary is gone; the abstract fulfills the same function, but it appears at the beginning of the journal article.

Your abstract should be a very concise description of your research question, your methodology, your results, and your conclusions. The purpose is to give the reader a quick, but good, sense of your project before reading the entire article.

When you write your abstract, it should reflect the most important aspects of your manuscript. It should also be self-contained; that is, a reader should be able to understand everything you say without having to refer to the article itself. This means defining any abbreviations you use, although you don't have to define units of measurements such as minutes, seconds, meters, and so forth. In addition, you should use the present tense of verbs that relate to your conclusions, but past tense for describing what you did and what happened. For instance, you would write:

- The research reveals (present tense) that, on a daily basis, people are likely to be affected by subtle cues in their environment.
- The participants recalled (past tense) as many words as possible in a 5-minute period.

Also, in the abstract, you should use active voice verbs while you avoid first-person pronouns (e.g., *I* or *we*). The abstract is the only section of your paper in which you may not use first-person pronouns; such use is permissible in all other sections. This combination can be difficult because, if you can't use *I* or *we* as the subject of your sentence, the most obvious alternative is to use passive voice verbs. Unfortunately, passive voice verbs create uninteresting prose that may not engage your reader. (See chapter 7 for more information on active and passive voice verbs.)

For manuscripts that deal with empirical (i.e., data-oriented) research, the abstract should be between 100 and 120 words in length; the maximum allowable length is 120 words. There are some specific elements that the abstract should contain.

- the research question;
- the participants and subjects and their characteristics (age, sex, race/ethnicity, number; species if nonhuman);

- the method (e.g., experimental, correlational, factor analytical), including apparatus and materials;
- the research results, including levels of statistical significance;
- conclusions and implications of your results.

In final form, you should type your abstract as a single paragraph. Don't indent the first line; the abstract is a single block of text. An example appears in Figure 15.1.

FORMATTING DETAILS

There are a few places in your manuscript where you need to follow some specific guidelines for formatting. As you have already seen, the

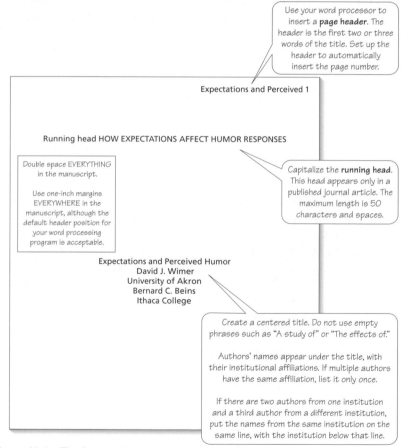

Figure 15.1 The format of the abstract.

format of tables and figures follows pretty well-specified rules. Other sections have their own requirements, too.

Title Page

On the title page, you communicate the title of your paper, which is a pretty obvious component. You also create a page header that appears in the upper-right corner of almost every page of the manuscript (including tables, but NOT figures). You also type a running head that appears only in a published journal article.

You should use your word processing program to insert the page header. The page header consists of the first two or three words of the title of the article, followed by the page number. The words might not make any sense, but they don't have to. The purpose of the page header is to allow an editor to keep track of the manuscript pages that might become separated. This page header and the page number should appear on every page with the exception of figures or other artwork. You can see a sample title page in Figure 15.2. The directions for creating the header appear in Table 15.1.

You should not type in the page header and page number manually on each page. If you insert the header and page number by hand, proper formatting will be lost any time you add or delete material because the page header will move up or down.

Appendixes

Another section that appears on occasion in a manuscript is the Appendix. This section contains material that may be of importance to readers, but more as background than as critical information for understanding the study. An appendix is likely to contain such things as stimuli used in your study, like word lists for a memory study or questionnaires that you created for your study that are not available elsewhere. Regarding questionnaires, you normally do not include them in your manuscript; instead, you give a reference that the reader can consult for details. When you have created a questionnaire yourself, it is not available elsewhere, so you can present it in an appendix.

An appendix, like everything else in your paper, is double spaced. If you have more than one appendix, each one is on its own page or pages. For a single appendix, put the word *Appendix* centered at the top of the page. (The word does not appear in italics.) When there are multiple appendixes, label them by letter (Appendix A, Appendix B, etc.)

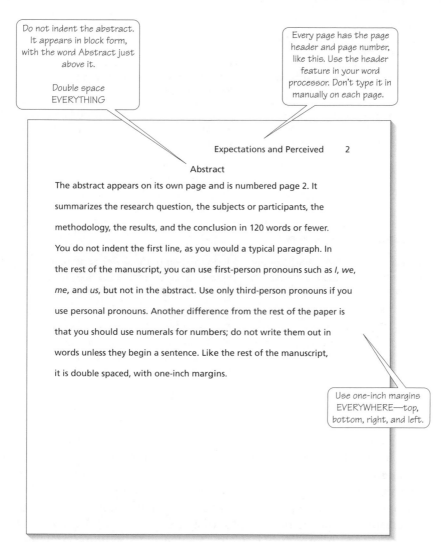

Figure 15.2 Format of the title page.

Footnotes and Notes

In some disciplines, particularly in the humanities, footnotes are common in writing. In APA style, however, footnotes are relatively rare.

One problem with footnotes is that they interrupt the reader's attention to your ideas. The reader has to hold in memory your main point while looking to the bottom of the page for your clarification. In addition, they have to be formatted specifically for a journal article, so they are costly. Generally, if an idea is important enough to include in a footnote, it is important enough to include in the main body of text.

Table 15.1

Directions for Creating the Page Header and Page Number in Word® and WordPerfect®

Creating the page header in Word©	Creating the page header in WordPerfect©
Click on *View* on the menu at the top Select: Header and Footer	• Click on *Insert* on the menu at the top • Select: Header/Footer, Header A, Create
Right justify the header: • <CTRL> R or • Click on Format on the menu at the top • Select → Paragraph → Indents and Spacing: Right Alignment	Right justify the header: • <CTRL> R or <ALT> F7 or • Click on *Format* on the menu at the top • Select → Line → Flush Right
Type the first or three words of the title and then hit the space bar five times (to make space for the page number)	Type the first or three words of the title and then hit the space bar five times (to make space for the page number)
In the Header and Footer bar, click on the hash mark icon, #, which will insert the page number	Click on *Format* on the menu at the top • Select → Page → Insert Page Number • Click on the Insert button, then on the Close button
Click on *Close* in the Header and Footer bar	Move the cursor from the header area to the text

In some cases, footnotes are appropriate or even desirable. For example, in tables, you may include footnotes to the table if information might have to be repeated several times without the footnote. You can also include information such as probability values. You can refer to chapter 12 on presentation of notes on tables. These footnotes go immediately below the bottom rule of a table.

Another footnote appropriate for a table is to indicate copyright permission. You must receive permission from a copyright holder to reproduce a table or a figure; your footnote should state where the table or figure was published, who holds the copyright, and that you have permission to use the table or figure.

If you use footnotes, number them consecutively with superscript arabic numerals (i.e., 1, 2, etc.). The first mention of the footnote appears as follows:

The participants became irritated at being deceived,[1]

If there is any punctuation right after the word, you should almost always type the punctuation mark (e.g., comma, period) before the numeral as shown in the example above. The sole exception involves dashes; in this situation, place the numeral before the dash. When you refer to a footnote in the text, include the reference within parentheses, as follows:

the researchers made the same claim previously (see Footnote 1).

Author's Note

The final type of note is the author's note (or authors' note, for more than one author). This note appears at the end of the article on its own page. The first paragraph of the note gives the names and institutional affiliations of the authors at the time the study was conducted. Type the author's name exactly as it appears on the title page, a comma, then the institution. Separate multiple authors with semicolons and put a period at the end.

In the second paragraph, cite any grant information or other source of financial support. In addition, acknowledge help from others, such as people who helped with data collection, data analysis, and so forth.

The final paragraph offers contact information such as a complete mailing address. Authors also provide email addresses here.

If you include an author's note, type it on a separate page with the label *Author's Note* centered at the top of the page. As always, double space the note. In addition, indent each paragraph as you would any other paragraph.

Order of Manuscript Pages

Your manuscript pages follow a prescribed order. They are numbered here for your information, but you do not number them when you type your manuscript. Not all manuscripts have each element, so you may not include all of them in a single manuscript.

When you type your paper, you begin some sections on a new page: title page, abstract, references, appendixes, author's note, footnotes, and figure captions; in addition, each table and each figure goes on its own page. On the other hand, the Method section starts on the line immediately below the end of the Introduction, the Results section starts right after the Method section, and the Discussion starts right after the Results section.

1. Title page
2. Abstract
3. Introduction
4. Method
5. Results
6. Discussion
7. References
8. Appendixes
9. Author's note
10. Footnotes
11. Tables
12. Figure captions
13. Figures

If your manuscript presents multiple experiments, you may need to repeat elements 4, 5, and 6 for each study. If so, you include a section called *General Discussion* to summarize and integrate all the studies you conducted.

Section Headings

In APA style, there are five different styles for heading sections of the manuscript. Many single-study manuscripts use two of them, Levels 1 and 3. The levels and how you type them appear in Table 15.2, with a schematic example of a two-level manuscript in Figure 15.3.

With a slightly more complicated manuscript that has more subsections, you may need more than two levels of headings. If you require three different levels, use Levels 1, 3, and 4. Figure 15.4 shows this type of arrangement.

Table 15.2
Different Levels of Headings in an APA-style Manuscript

Level	Format
Level 1	Centered with the First Letter of Important Words Capitalized
Level 2	*Centered, in Italics with the First Letter of Important Words Capitalized*
Level 3	*Flush left, in italics, with the First Letter of Important Words Capitalized*
Level 4	*Indented, in italics, with the first letter of the first word capitalized, ending in a period.*
Level 5	CENTERED IN UPPERCASE LETTERS

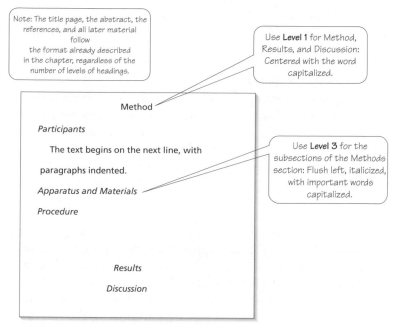

Figure 15.3 Headings for manuscripts with two levels of headings.

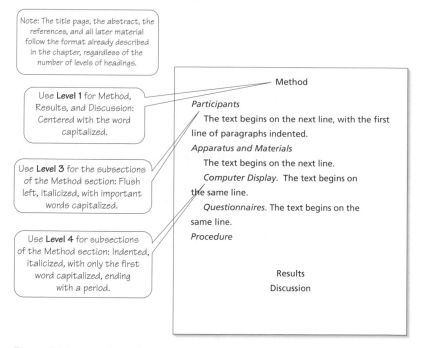

Figure 15.4 Headings for a manuscript with three levels of headings.

If your manuscript involves more than one study, you may need to use three levels of headings. Again, use Levels 1, 3, and 4, as shown in Figure 15.5.

Miscellaneous Formatting Details

There are specific formatting guidelines that appear fairly trivial; they are easy to overlook, though. The rules cited in this chapter involve the common elements of formatting. For the formatting of less common elements, you can refer to the APA *Publication Manual.*

There are specific rules regarding capitalization. Some of them are entirely consistent with the writing style that you probably already use. But some are rather specific to APA style. Examples appear in Table 15.3.

There are other specific points in APA style regarding formatting. They include the use of italics, appropriate use of abbreviations, and creating series within text. The rules and examples are illustrated in Tables 15.4, 15.5, and 15.6, respectively.

One further element of presentation involves quotations. There are two relevant types of quotations for our purposes: direct and indirect. A direct quotation is the kind most people recognize: You use the exact words of another person and enclose those words within quotation marks. Indirect quotations refer to the expression of somebody else's idea, but not the exact words. For either type, you need to cite

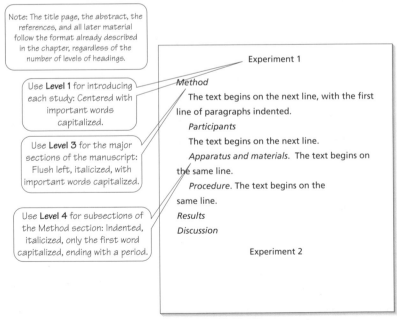

Figure 15.5 Levels of headings for multiexperiment manuscripts.

and give credit to the person. Table 15.7 shows how to format quotations in APA style.

Table 15.3

Guidelines for Capitalization in APA Style

Rule	Example
Capitalize the first word in a sentence	
Capitalize the first word after a colon if it starts a full sentence but not otherwise	• There are many rules: Capitalization [*This is the first word after a colon; it starts a full sentence*] can be confusing. • This table presents guidance on a frequently problematic element of writing: capitalization. [*This word does not start a full sentence, so you do not capitalize it.*]
Capitalize important words in titles of books and journal articles, in figure captions, and titles of tables	• At the bookstore, the writing student bought *The Only Grammar Book You'll Ever Need*.
Capitalize the name of sections of the manuscript when you refer to them in the body of the paper	• The details appear in the Results section.
Capitalize names of departments in a college or university if the proper name is used, but not if the name is used generically	• He joined the Department of Psychology. • He became a psychology major.
Capitalize nouns that are followed by numbers Do not capitalize nouns that: • describe common elements of books and tables, even if they are followed by numbers • precede a variable • are names of effects, conditions, or variables in a study	• He memorized List 3 in Experiment 2. • You can refer to Table 3 in chapter 7 [*a chapter is a common element of a book*] for information on misuse of contractions in writing; specific examples are in column 1 [*a column is a common part of a table*]. • This participant was in the high-anxiety condition. There was no effect of the anxiety variable [anxiety *is the name of the variable; high-anxiety is the name of the specific condition*]
Capitalize variable names that accompany multiplication signs, as with interaction effects Do not capitalize the multiplication sign in an interaction effect	• There was a Sex × Humor interaction. [*Normally, do not capitalize sex or humor because they are variable names, but they appear with a multiplication sign, so they are capitalized in this case.*]
Capitalize the genus, but not the species, of animals	• *Drosophila melanogaster*. [*Note that the genus and species appear in italics.*]

Table 15.4
Guidelines for Italics in APA Style

Rule	Example
Do not use italics to create emphasis; use syntax for emphasis	*Incorrect*: The high-expectation condition was the *only* condition in which an effect emerged. *Better*: The sole condition in which we found an effect was the high-expectation condition. [*Moving the main point to the beginning of the sentence may focus the reader's attention on that point.*]
You may use italics if, by not doing so, a reader might misunderstand the word	The *exhausted* group slowed down. [*If you were studying the effects of fatigue, you could use italics to indicate that this is the name of a specific group, not merely that the participants were tired.*]
Use italics when you are referring to a word as a specific word rather than in its usual meaning	He crossed out the word *before* before he crossed out the word *after*. [*The meaning of the first* before, *in italics, refers to the word, not to the concept of time. If you didn't italicize* before, *the sentence would appear ungrammatical and would confuse the reader. In speech, we use pauses and emphasis to differentiate the meanings.*]
If you are using italics and are going to include a word or phrase that would normally be italicized, such as a book title, switch to Roman type (i.e., do not use italics)	*The speaker relied heavily on Freud's book* Dora: An Analysis of a Case of Hysteria *in the assessment of psychoanalysis.* [*Book titles are normally italicized; in this example, it is in Roman type because the wording around it is in italics.*]
Use italics for: • titles of books and journals • the volume number in a journal you cite • scales on tests • identification of genus, species, and variety of animals	*Psychological Science, Journal of Experimental Psychology: General* *Psychological Science, 17* [*volume 17 of the journal*], 568–571 Scales on the Guilford–Zimmerman Temperament Survey: *G* (*General*), *R* (*Restraint*) *Drosophila melanogaster*
Use italics for statistical tests and for indicating probability, but do not use italics for subscripts in statistical expressions	$t(25) = 1.10, p > .05$ $M_{women} = 3.82$ [*The letter M, representing the mean, is italicized, but the subscript indicating the group is not.*]
Use italics for anchors in a rating scale	The participants rated their sense of humor on a scale of 1 (*poor*) to 7 (*good*)

Table 15.5
Guidelines for Abbreviations in APA Style

Rule	Example
Do not use abbreviations: • if they will distract the reader from your point • if they seldom appear after the first time you introduce them • for variables and conditions if the abbreviation will not be clear to the reader	The IVs and DVs included RTs after lesioning of the LH and VMH. [*Instead, consider writing out some of the abbreviations that might not be obvious to a reader.*]
For the first use of an abbreviation, write out the term in full, followed by the abbreviation in parentheses	The parents' socioeconomic status (SES) accounted for some variability in children's educational attainment.
Abbreviations are acceptable when that is the typical way people write them, including state names	IQ, AIDS; but write out new or relatively rare terms for the first presentation: Emotional Quotient (EQ) NY for New York, AL for Alabama
Use abbreviations derived from Latin (e.g., for example; i.e., that is; &, and) only in parentheses. Use an English variation of the Latin phrase when it appears in the main body of the text. Exceptions: • Use the Latin et al. (meaning *and others*) in references even when the reference is not in parentheses. • Use the ampersand, & (a stylized construction meaning et al.), in the reference list between the final two names in a multi-author study	The high-stress group (i.e., those exposed to the cold-pressor test) showed anxiety. [i.e. *is a Latin abbreviation for* id est, *meaning that is*] The high-stress group, that is, those exposed to the cold-pressor test, showed anxiety.
Do not abbreviate some measures of time because the abbreviations might confuse the reader	• day (not d.) • week (not wk.) • month (not mo.) • year (not yr.)
Use periods with abbreviations for: • initials in people's names	• A. Lincoln, H. M. [*a means of concealing a person's identity, as in the case of H. M., who lost ability to form new memories*]

Continued overleaf.

Table 15.5
Continued.

Rule	Example
• Latin abbreviations	• et al.
• abbreviations in references	• Supp. [for *Supplement*]
Do not use periods for:	
• abbreviations of state or country names	• USA [United States], UK [United Kingdom], OH [Ohio]
• acronyms using capital letters	• APA, APS, CIA, FBI
• common measurements that you abbreviate	• ft [foot], m [meter], cm [centimeter]
Exception: Use a period for abbreviating inch (in.) because otherwise, a reader could confuse it with the preposition *in*	• The line was 5 in. from beginning to end.
To render an abbreviation plural, add the letter *s*. Do NOT use an apostrophe Exceptions:	RTs (reaction times)
• Do not make an abbreviation unit of measurement plural; keep it singular	5 m [for specifying 5 meters; do not use 5 ms)
• Make the abbreviation for the word page plural by adding a second p and a period	pp. 28–59 [*To indicate pages 28 to 59 in a book chapter, use pp. rather than ps*]

Table 15.6
Guidelines for Creating Series in APA Style

Rule	Example
Creating a series of elements in the main body of text involves lowercase letters within parentheses. Note: Use complete parentheses, (a), not just the close-parentheses symbol, a)	Correct: Use 1-inch margins for (a) the top, (b) the bottom, (c) the right, and (d) the left edges of the page. Incorrect: Use 1-inch margins for a) the top, b) the bottom, c) right, and d) left edges of the page.
In a series, use commas to separate the different elements Exception: Use semicolons to separate elements in the series if there are commas within one or more series	Correct: Use 1-inch margins for (a) the top, (b) the bottom, (c) right, and (d) left edges of the page. Correct: The symbols were (a) blue, green, and red; (b) orange and yellow; or (c) black and white.
If your series is a listing of paragraphs, use an arabic (not roman) numeral followed by a period. Do not use parentheses	The participants completed three tasks: 1. They completed a survey. This segment involved ... 2. They identified the reasons for their choices. This task was open-ended ... 3. They decided which task they enjoyed the most. They indicated this by ...

Table 15.7
Guidelines for Using Quotations in APA Style

Rule	Example
Direct quotations	
For quotations, always cite the author's (or authors') name, the year of publication, and the pages on which the quotation appeared. For electronic materials, paragraph numbers can replace page numbers	
Place this information right after the quotation	
• If the quotation is in the middle of a sentence, put the citation within parentheses immediately after the quotation. Do not use any punctuation not required for the structure of the sentence	We know that "poor writing habits are exceedingly difficult to unlearn" (Sommer, 2006, p. 956) once they are ingrained.
• If the quotation ends a sentence, put the citation information within parentheses; put the sentence-ending period after the citation	We know that "poor writing habits are exceedingly difficult to unlearn" (Sommer, 2006, p. 956).
• If the quotation is part of a blocked paragraph, put the citation within parentheses after the final punctuation mark	Various writers have discussed writing styles. Mentors of most graduate students usually train their students in rules of academic style. Writing for the public requires specific training as well. (Sommer, 2006, p. 957)
A quotation is almost always reproduced exactly as it appeared originally, even if there are errors in the original. If there is an error that might confuse a reader, insert [sic], using square brackets, immediately after the error. *Sic* is a word used that writers use to inform readers of the presence of errors. It is Latin for "thus" or "so."	If a writer had incorrectly used there instead of their in a sentence, you would use the incorrect spelling: • The children went to there [sic] homes after school.
Exceptions:	
If a quotation could confuse a reader because the context of the words is not present, you may add clarifying words by inserting them [within square brackets]	A sentence out of context may be missing material needed for understanding it. You can add words to preserve the meaning: • Participants in [the treatment group] were not aware of the manipulation.

Continued overleaf.

Table 15.7
Continued.

Rule	Example
You may shorten a quotation by eliminating unnecessary words and inserting three periods (. . .) to indicate ellipsis. Place a space before and after each period. If a sentence ends immediately before the ellipsis, include the period at the end of that sentence, meaning that you have four periods	
You may add emphasis by italicizing material in a quotation by italicizing the words to be emphasized and indicating in square brackets [italics added]. If material is italicized in the original, indicate this fact by writing in square brackets [italics in original]	If you want to emphasize certain words in a quotation, you can italicize them, indicating that the italics are yours: • The children went to their homes *after school* [italics added].
For quotations of 40 words or fewer, enclose the quotation within "double quotation marks" in the text. For quotations longer than 40 words, create a block paragraph. The block's margins should be indented five spaces on the left and right relative to the main body of text. Do NOT use quotation marks.	
If there is a second quotation within a short quotation, enclose that second quotation within single quotation marks If there is a second quotation within a long quotation, enclose that second quotation within double quotation marks	"The participant said 'I have to leave now' before the experiment had ended."

Direct quotations are relatively rare in psychological writing. The most common use is when another author has made specific points that relate closely to your ideas. Shorter quotations appear within the text like any other material. Longer quotations are set apart from the rest of the text, in a block; they do not make use of quotations marks. When you use quotations, you need to identify the source, including the page number, in the text. Examples of how to format short quotations appear in Figure 15.6, based on research by Rader and Vaughn (2000).

Sometimes you may include a long quotation (i.e., more than 40 words) in your writing. In such a case, you create a separate paragraph in block form and indented five spaces relative to the rest of the text.

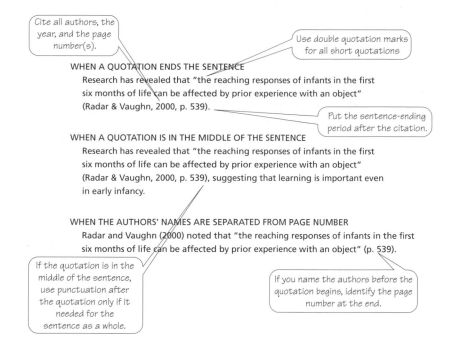

Figure 15.6 Illustration of format of short quotations of 40 words or fewer.

As with all other parts of the manuscript, you use double spacing for this block paragraph. You do not indent the first line of the paragraph, but if the quotation is more than one paragraph, you indent the second and succeeding paragraphs. An example of the style for a long quotation appears in Figure 15.7. If you were writing about perceptions of a just world, you might cite the research by DePalma, Madey, Tillman, and Wheeler (2000), as indicated in the figure.

Indirect quotations present another writer's ideas, but you may change the wording slightly or extensively. As such, you should attribute the work to the other person, but APA style does not mandate including numbers of the pages on which those ideas had appeared, although it is desirable. An indirect quotation does not look any different than the rest of the body of your text.

Finally, there are certain conventions regarding punctuation marks. Some commonly used punctuation marks and guidelines for their use are given in Table 15.8.

Remember that there are other, infrequently used, rules that are part of APA style. You can refer to the *Publication Manual* if you have additional questions.

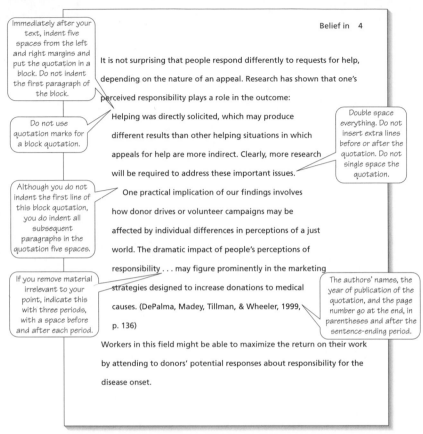

Figure 15.7 Illustration of format of long quotations of 40 words or more.

Table 15.8
Guidelines for Using Common Punctuation Marks

Rule	Example
Comma	
Use a comma between elements in a series, including before the word *and* or *or* that separates the second last and the last element in the series	The flag was red, white, and blue. Note: In some writing styles, one would not insert a comma after white, but in APA style, the comma is appropriate
Use a comma to separate independent clauses. Independent clauses can stand alone as sentences.	He remembered the names, but he forgot the addresses.
Do not use a comma to separate two parts of a compound predicate	He remembered the names but forgot the addresses.

Table 15.8
Continued.

Rule	Example
Use a comma to separate a nonrestrictive clause (i.e., one that is not necessary for the meaning of the sentence and that only provides additional information) from the rest of the sentence	The stimulus, which appeared in the center of the screen, remained visible for 300 msec. Note: The material in the clause beginning with *which* is not necessary for the meaning of the sentence. Such clauses are introduced by the conjunction *which*
Do not use a comma to separate a restrictive clause (i.e., one that is necessary for the meaning of the sentence) for the rest of the sentence	The stimulus that followed the rest period remained visible for 300 msec. Note: The material in the clause beginning with *that* is necessary for the reader to understand the point of the sentence. Such clauses are introduced by the conjunction *that*
Use a comma in citing a specific date	February 27, 1980
Do not use a comma for nonspecific dates	February 1980
Use a comma to separate the year in a citation from other elements	(Rader & Vaughn, 2001)
Use a comma to group large numbers by thousands Exceptions: Do not use commas:	9,876,543
• to separate numbers to the right of the decimal place	1,234.4891
• when reporting temperatures or acoustic measurements	1500°C
• for degrees of freedom	$r(1250) = .03$, $p > .05$
Semicolon Use a semicolon to separate two independent clauses that can stand alone as sentences but that are not separated by a conjunction such as *and*, *or*, or *but*	The participant recalled the words; she also completed the questionnaire.
Use a semicolon to separate components within a series if some components make use of commas	The participant completed the informed consent form, the questionnaire, and the callback form; read the stimulus materials; and recalled the main points from the passage.
Parentheses Use parentheses to indicate publication dates	Smith (2004) found that . . .
Use parentheses for identifying pages on which quotations had appeared	". . . was not apparent" (p. 303).

Continued overleaf.

Table 15.8
Continued.

Rule	Example
Use parentheses to create a series of elements	(a) lines, (b) circles, and (c) squares
Use parentheses the first time you present an abbreviation	We recorded the participant's reaction time (RT).
Do not use parentheses within parentheses. Instead, use square brackets	(The analysis of variance [ANOVA] revealed that . . .) Note: Use the square brackets within parenthetical material
Do not use parentheses to present statistical results. Readers may have trouble processing multiple levels of parentheses	Incorrect: The effect was nonsignificant, (t(25) = 1.02, p > .05)
Hyphens Hyphenate a compound adjective if it could be misunderstood by the reader if you did not use the hyphen	The governor released the details of a public-health issue. Note: Without the hyphen, it is not clear whether the issue involved public health (e.g., the outbreak of a disease) or an issue about the governor's health that had been made public and that he wanted to clarify.
Hyphenate an adjective–noun combination when it precedes a noun it modifies	He was said to have an anal-retentive personality.
Do not hyphenate an adjective–noun combination if it does not precede a noun	His personality was anal retentive.

Part III

Communicating Beyond the Research Paper

16

Creating Poster Presentations

Words and pictures can work together to communicate more powerfully than either alone.

William Albert Allard

Have you ever been trapped at a lecture that seemed to last forever? And you could not find a way to leave without being noticed? Too many students have had that experience in their classes, and too many researchers have had the same feeling at conference presentations. Fortunately, there is a solution to a boring talk that has way too many words. The solution is to create a picture that is worth a thousand words.

Many conferences have poster sessions that capture your attention with lively visual presentations. You can see at a glance what a research project is about. And, if you find it boring, you can just walk away.

The goal in a poster presentation is to create a compelling visual representation of your project. Poster sessions have become a common feature at scientific meetings because a large number of people can display their work and discuss it with others in a face-to-face setting. There may be dozens or even hundreds of posters in an area, depending on the size of a conference. People can walk by the posters and, if a topic catches their eye, talk to the researcher individually.

DIFFERENTIATING VISUAL AND WRITTEN COMMUNICATION

In previous chapters, we have discussed ways to optimize your writing for maximal effect. A poster has a very different orientation than a written paper. In a traditional manuscript, you include important details for the reader to assess. In fact, it is almost the case that you cannot provide too many details in a manuscript. On the other hand, a poster will suffer if you try to include too much information.

The reason for this difference is that a reader can spend as much time on a manuscript as needed. The person can refer to earlier material and check out detail for fuller understanding. A poster session is a more fluid experience. People walk back and forth, look at posters, and approach some posters in order to talk with the presenter. In this forum, there are multiple posters to view and multiple presenters to approach. A poster that has a lot of detail requires a lot of text. Most of the time, people don't want to spend a lot of time reading through minute detail on a poster. Instead, they want to find out about the major points. If they have questions about details, they can talk with the presenter. Consequently, when you create a poster, you should figure out the two or three most important points that you want to convey, then convey them simply.

The details of organizing a poster are still evolving as the technology for creating them changes. Your poster may consist of perhaps a dozen or so individual sheets or it may be a single, large sheet. In either case, visitors to your poster are going to be more receptive if it is easy for them to understand what you are communicating and if it is visually attractive.

REDUCING THE AMOUNT OF INFORMATION

Most posters retain the general format of an APA-style manuscript, although there is no need to pay as close attention to the details of APA style in a poster. You will still need an Introduction, a Method section, a Results section, and some kind of summary. But the exact format relies on your judgment as to what points are most critical to you.

As a rule, people at a poster session tend to walk slowly along the line of posters, glancing at the title of the presentation, then at the layout of information. If the topic is of interest, a person might glance at what seem to be the major points illustrated on the poster. If those points are hard to discern, the person will walk away. What this means is that the most important points of your poster should leap out at a viewer. If your ideas are presented clearly and simply, the person may stop and talk to you about your work.

There are always important points that you cannot include in your poster because of space limitations and because of the need not to overwhelm a potentially interested viewer. You can discuss these details in a face-to-face conversation or in a handout. But if you try to include them all on your poster, the results will be unsatisfactory to you and to the viewer.

An effective poster presents enough information to get the viewer's interest without presenting so much that the person simply walks away.

VISUAL STYLE

Most of the time, people at poster sessions need to view your work from a distance. Thus, your message should be clearly legible from a distance of 3–4 feet away. There are no hard and fast rules about the font size you should use in creating your poster, but it is fairly typical to see 48-point fonts for the title of the poster, 36-point fonts for major section headings, and 18- to 24-point fonts for the main body of the poster.

Generally, presenters are allotted a space as small as 3 × 4 feet (1 × 1.3 meters) or as large as 4 × 6 feet (1.3 × 2 meters). You should always look through the conference material so you know how much space you will have. As you put your poster together, it will seem that there is too little room for everything you want to say. Don't succumb to the temptation to pack in a lot of text in order to make the points you think are important. Limit yourself to the most critical points.

Many people recommend creating a light background with dark lettering. A stark contrast between dark letters and a light background makes viewing easier. On the other hand, a dark background with light lettering may initially attract attention, but viewers can find it tiring to read for long.

If you do not have the capability of producing a large, single-sheet poster, you can still create an attractive poster. The positioning of the various sections of the poster (i.e., Introduction, Method, Results, Discussion) is likely to resemble that in Figures 16.1 and 16.2.

These figures illustrate how you can create a poster with multiple sheets of paper. In Figure 16.1, the title and authors' names are on a standard sheet of paper. In Figure 16.2, the title and authors' names appear on a banner spanning the top of the poster. In the latter version, you would need to type several sheets of paper with partial information, then cut and paste them together so they look like a single long sheet.

For such a display, you can group related information together spatially simply by placing the sheets in proximity to one another. It is also possible to use color to group them. Presenters often use a slightly larger, colored sheet of paper behind the standard white paper to create a colored border to make the pages stand out. The use of two or three different colors can give the viewer a sense of which pages go together.

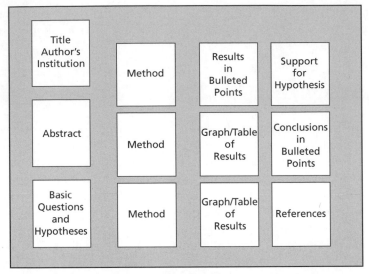

Figure 16.1 Potential layout of a poster using single sheets of paper.

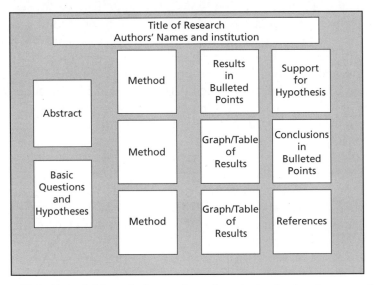

Figure 16.2 Potential layout of a poster using single sheets of paper using a banner title.

Laminating the pages can also enhance your poster's attractiveness and make it easy to carry without damaging it.

In terms of the flow of information on your poster, an up-to-down and left-to-right progression is sensible. People are used to reading in that direction, so when they peruse your poster, they are likely to start at the top left and move down to the bottom, going up to your second column of information, then down again, and so on.

It is common in the first part of the poster that the statement of the basic questions has replaced a traditional Introduction section. If your research was a follow-up to some previous study, you can cite that research. Further, sometimes the references are not in traditional APA style in the introductory part of the poster. That format would take up too much precious space on the poster.

Similarly, the Method section is very much reduced compared with a standard research report. For a poster, all you need to do is to highlight the general nature of the participants, materials, and procedure. One space-saving technique is to include a photograph of any apparatus, which can replace a written description. If a viewer wants more detail, you are there to provide that information; a handout is also helpful for presenting the specifics.

The Results section benefits greatly from graphics. Figures allow a viewer to get the gist of the results easily. A handout can provide an elaboration of the basic sketch that appears on the poster.

Finally, the conclusions can be simple, bulleted points, without much elaboration or context. This simple approach would not work for a full-length research report, but it gives the viewer a good idea of what you concluded.

You should keep in mind that these examples are just suggestions. If you need more space to explain your hypotheses, you should take it and, perhaps, reduce the amount of space you devote to the methodology. The most important point is that you convey the message you want the reader to get. It doesn't matter exactly how you do it, as long as you manage to do it.

YOUR BEHAVIOR: THE ETHIC OF A POSTER SESSION

Attire

A poster session may be your first public and professional activity. You want to make a good impression. As such, some types of clothing are appropriate, but others are not. It isn't unreasonable to consider a poster session as a type of interview. For instance, just as viewers judge the quality of your research, at least in part, from the layout of your poster, they will judge your credibility by the way you look. You should dress as a professional. This means dressing so a person responds to your work rather than to the way you look. You might object to the idea that people will evaluate your work based on how you look, but that is reality.

What constitutes professional attire varies depending on the individual and the venue. At some professional conferences, some presenters wear more formal, business attire while others are more casual. At student conferences, it is more the norm for presenters to dress in "business casual" clothing.

For women, a business suit would never be inappropriate, but it is probably more than you need. Instead, slacks or skirts are usually acceptable. As a rule, a conservative approach to colors is more professional than flashy or trendy colors. Thus, slacks or skirts that are black, brown, khaki, navy blue or other traditional colors will help you make a good impression. A blouse or shirt should coordinate with your slacks or skirt. It is probably best to avoid fabrics such as velour or velvet, denim, or party-like fabrics.

Your shoes should have a professional appearance, so it would not be appropriate to wear extremely casual sandals, high heels or platform shoes. At the same time, you should wear comfortable shoes. Poster sessions last for 1–2 hr. Attractive but painful shoes can detract greatly from your experience.

Men have less latitude than women regarding professional attire. It's generally a business suit, which is acceptable but probably more than you need, or a sport coat with appropriate slacks. Depending on the specific meeting, you may be expected to wear a tie.

Men should wear leather shoes, not athletic shoes.

You may find it interesting that essentially no research has been devoted to what constitutes an effective poster. Many people have proposed guidelines that others have adopted. But the elements of a successful poster are as much a matter of art, tradition, and consensus as anything else.

On the other hand, a team of two researchers has investigated the effect of the clothing of a poster presenter on attention paid to the poster. Keegan and Bannister (2003) discovered that when a presenter's blouse was color coordinated to match the color of her poster, there were more visitors to the poster than when her clothes clashed with the poster.

Covering Your Poster

Poster sessions generally run for 1–2 hr, during which time people expect you to be at your poster. Your research is more interesting to you than to anybody else, so don't be discouraged if quite a few people glance your way and move on without talking to you about your work. In fact, many more people will bypass your poster than will actually stop and talk about it with you. The value of a poster session is that it allows people with similar interests to interact individually; those with other interests can find different posters.

It can be frustrating to watch people walk by, but that is the nature of a poster session. When you are at your poster, if you stand right in front of it, you might block the view of your work, so you should stand slightly to one side.

This doesn't mean that you can't talk to the person whose poster is next to yours or to your friends and co-authors. But it does mean that when an interested viewer approaches, he or she should feel comfortable talking to you. If you are engaged in an animated conversation with a friend, the viewer may not want to interrupt you.

When you are discussing your research, somebody may ask a question that you can't answer. It is acceptable to say you don't know the answer, but you should try to address the issue that was raised.

It also helps to have a handout for people who are interested. The handout could be a small copy of your poster or it could be an APA-style manuscript describing your research. People can talk to you about your work, then study it in greater depth at a later point. Very often there are chairs at poster session on which you can place your handouts so people don't have to ask you for one. Or you could affix a large envelope containing your handouts on the poster board.

Finally, one of the drawbacks to a poster session is that, if you are at your poster, you may not have a lot of time to walk around and view those of others. One remedy is to set up your poster before your session begins, then to walk around the poster area to see what is there; if others have handouts, you can pick them up. Another possibility is to wait until the crowd in the poster session diminishes before you look at other posters. At this point in the poster session, you may have formed a relationship with the person at the poster next to yours; that person can tell any viewers that you will be right back. If you have a co-author on the poster, you can take turns standing at the poster and walking around the display area.

The key to a successful poster presentation is to spend time in advance creating a visually compelling poster with substantial content, being familiar with the work so you can answer questions about it, being comfortable telling people what you know, and adopting a professional demeanor as you interact with viewers.

CREATING YOUR POSTER USING POWERPOINT®

Creating attractive posters using PowerPoint® is fairly easy. There are some basic steps you can use whether your poster will consist of a single, large sheet or multiple, standard sheets.

Once you begin working with PowerPoint®, you will see that most of the mechanical steps associated with creating your poster are relatively straightforward. The most challenging aspects include (a) presenting the content in a clear and compelling way and (b) generating an effective visual layout.

Regarding the visual layout, you might be able to get some guidance from people who have already created posters. Look at their products and take your cues from them. If you have attended previous poster sessions, you might be able to remember what aspects of the posters you found interesting and what aspects you avoided.

You can begin developing your poster by following the steps outlined in Table 16.1. At many points along the way, you will have to make choices. Remember that none of the choices is irrevocable. If you decide you do not like the effect, you can undo it and substitute another.

The steps outlined in Table 16.1 pertain to creating a PowerPoint® poster on a single, large-sheet poster. Table 16.2 gives you guidance on creating any poster, whether on a single sheet or on multiple sheets.

Table 16.1

Initial Steps for Creating a Large, Single-Sheet Poster Presentation Using PowerPoint®

What you want to do	How to do it	The result
Set up the poster	Select *File* on the toolbar and choose *Page Setup* • Choose Slides Sized for → Custom • In the *Width* box, enter the desired poster width • In the *Height* box, enter the desired poster height • Choose *Slide Orientation* → *Landscape*	This lets you specify the size of the poster. Make sure you check the conference information about how much space you will have for your poster. Do not exceed the dimensions of the allotted space
View all or part of your poster	On the toolbar indicating percentage of poster to display, select *Fit* to see how the entire poster looks. Select another percentage for a partial view of the poster. If you select 25%, you will see only one quarter of the poster, but you will be able to work with it more easily	When you select *Fit*, you will be able to see the overall layout, how much space you have used, and how much space you still have. You will not be able to read the text very well When you select a specific percentage of the poster, the larger the percentage, the more of the total poster you will be able to see

Table 16.1
Continued.

What you want to do	How to do it	The result
Display lines to guide poster creation	Select *View* on the toolbar and choose *Grids and Guides* • Under *Grid Settings*, check *Display grid on screen*	This will put lines on the poster so you can align different parts of the poster neatly. The lines that appear here will not appear on your poster
Create the banner for the title	• Create a text box by selecting the Text icon on the Drawing toolbar • Move the cursor to the spot on the poster where you want to place the banner • Drag the mouse to indicate how wide the banner should be • In the toolbar indicating font size, type the font size Depending on the length of the title, you might want to use a font of up to 72 point size. Type the title • In the toolbar indicating font size, type the font size for authors' names and institutional affiliations (usually your school). You might use 48-point font for this	This will let you type text to display wherever you want on the poster. (Note: If the Drawing toolbar is not visible, select View on the toolbar at the time. Click on *Toolbars* and select *Drawing*. When you select it, it should have a check mark next to it)

Table 16.2
Steps for Creating a PowerPoint® Poster Either on a Single, Large Sheet or on Multiple Sheets

What you want to do	How to do it	The result
Format a text box to enter material for your poster	• Create a text box, select the font size you want to use (something around 40-point font) and type the text in it • Left-click in the text box to created the dotted border • Right-click and select *Format AutoShape* • If you want the box to be a certain color, select your color in the box labeled *Fill* • If you want a border around the box, select the color black (a neutral color) in the box for *Line → Color* Under *Line → Style*, you can select line thickness	This will create a text box that is ready for typing. You will have to specify the size of the font you want each time you create a text box

Continued overleaf.

Table 16.2
Continued.

What you want to do	How to do it	The result
Importing graphs from Excel® into your poster	• In Excel®, create your graph • Copy the graph by highlighting it and either pressing CTRL + C or selecting *Edit* from the toolbar, then highlighting *Copy* • Paste the graph into the poster by using CTRL + V or by selecting *Edit* from the toolbar, then highlighting *Paste*	This will move your graph from Excel® exactly as it appears in Excel® Note: By double clicking on the graph, you can change the title, X- and Y-axis labels, and color and pattern of the bars in a bar graph or the type of lines in a line graph
Moving a graph	• Left-click your mouse with the cursor in the graph. A dotted border will surround the graph • Hold the mouse key down and drag the graph to the desired location	This will allow you to place the graph where you want it
Resizing a graph	• Left-click your mouse while the cursor is over one of the open circles on the border of the graph • While holding the mouse button, move the cursor until the graph is the size you would like	This will let you size your graph to fit with the text and other materials surrounding it
Editing a graph in PowerPoint®	• Double click on the graph. The graph will be surrounded by a dotted border, indicating that editing is possible • Move the cursor to the area you want to edit and right-click • Follow the same steps that you would to edit the figure in Excel	These steps allow you to change the lines in a line graph or the bars in a histogram or bar chart. You can also edit the figure title and the labels for the X- and Y-axes. You cannot edit the category labels Note: If you make a change, you can reverse it by selecting *Edit* on the toolbar and highlighting *Undo*. If you reverse the change, you can bring back the change by selecting Edit and highlighting *Redo*. You can also use the Undo arrow ↵ or the Redo arrow ↪

Table 16.2
Continued.

What you want to do	How to do it	The result
Importing a table from Word®	• Highlight the table in Word® • Copy the table using either CTRL + C or select *Edit* on the toolbar at the top and highlight *Copy* • Paste the table into PowerPoint® using either CTRL + V or select *Edit* on the toolbar and highlight *Paste*	This will allow you to reproduce the table exactly as it appears in the Word® document. Note: You can edit the table once it is in PowerPoint® if you want to. See the steps below
Editing a table in PowerPoint®	• Double click on the table. The table will be surrounded by a dotted border, indicating that editing is possible • Move the cursor to the text you want to edit and type the information as you would in a Word® document • To add a row at the end of the table, move the cursor to the last cell on the final line and press the *Tab* key • To add a row anywhere, move the cursor to the row below where you want to put the new row, right-click on the mouse, and select *Insert Rows*	These steps let you change the material in a table simply by retyping it. You can insert new rows but not new columns into the table. Note: If you make a change, you can reverse it by selecting *Edit* on the toolbar and highlighting *Undo*. If you reverse the change, you can bring back the change by selecting *Edit* and highlighting *Redo*. You can also use the Undo arrow ↩ or the Redo arrow ↪

17

Giving Oral Presentations

The human mind is a wonderful thing—it starts working the minute you're born and never stops until you get up to speak in public.
Attributed variously to syndicated columnist Roscoe Drummond, comedian George Jessel, and Mark Twain

According to most studies, people's number one fear is public speaking. Number two is death . . . This means to the average person, if you go to a funeral, you're better off in the casket than doing the eulogy.
Jerry Seinfeld

As the quotations above suggest, if people did not have to speak in public, most wouldn't. Fortunately, there are ways to make it enjoyable. The key is knowing what you want to say and preparing so that your time in front of the audience is more like engaging in a conversation and less like confronting a hostile group. Learning how to prepare and deliver a presentation is a skill that you can develop.

THE DIFFERENCE BETWEEN ORAL AND WRITTEN ENGLISH

Imagine that you are listening to a group of researchers describing their research. Here is what they say:

As psychologists, we know a lot about empathy. We also know that people who are aggressive and antisocial show low levels of empathy, and they have a hard time putting themselves in the place of people around them. Unfortunately, we have a long way to go in understanding the lack of empathy in people with conduct disorders.

Now imagine that the same researchers said the following:

Deficiencies in empathy, defined as understanding and sharing in another's emotional state or context (Eisenberg & Strayer, 1987), have long been considered characteristic of aggressive and antisocial individuals (Cleckly, 1964; Hare, 1978; Hoffman, 1987). Although evidence also suggests that empathy facilitates prosocial behavior and reduces aggressive behavior in both children (Bryant, 1982; Eisenberg & Miller, 1987; Eisenberg -Berg & Lennon, 1980; Feshbach, 1979; Feshback & Feshbach, 1982; Miller & Eisenberg, 1988; Poole, 1992) and adults (Batson, Fultz, & Schoenrade, 1987; Davis, Hull, Young, & Warren, 1987; Mehrabian & Epstein, 1972), few studies of empathy have been conducted directly with individuals demonstrating established histories of antisocial and aggressive conduct. Nor has research on antisocial youth kept pace with important refinements in both the operationalization of empathy and related developmental theory.

Which of the two would you rather listen to? Both passages present the same basic ideas. The first is simple and easy to understand. The second would be nearly incomprehensible as part of an oral presentation, although it would be fine as an opening paragraph in a research report, which is what it is (Cohen & Strayer, 1996).

These two passages demonstrate how you need to adapt your language to the type of presentation you make. If you are writing a paper, you can include a lot of background detail, many references, and complex language. But in an oral presentation, you need to keep your message simple. Keep your sentences short and to the point so you can talk without getting stuck in the middle of a sentence.

You are juggling two competing tendencies. If you include everything you know about the topic, you will present more information than a listener can possibly process. At the same time, if you don't offer important details, the listener will not be able to figure out why you did your research, how you did it, and what it means. Consequently, you have to decide which ideas are worth presenting and which ones you can omit and still get your message across. Table 17.1 highlights a strategy for preparing and organizing your talk.

With a manuscript, a reader can go back and review earlier ideas. In a presentation, the listener has to keep everything you say in memory. As a result, you have to lead your listener on a well-planned path, making connections between ideas logical and apparent.

Table 17.1
Guidelines for Presentation Material

Introduction	• Create an interesting and memorable opening that captures the audience's interest and focuses them on the two or three main points of your research
	• After you capture the audience's interest, identify and describe previous research findings that led to or relates to your research
	• Don't bother identifying individual researchers unless they are particularly important and well known to the audience
	• State your hypotheses and tell how they connect to the research you have already described
	• Restate and briefly summarize the logic that led you to your hypotheses from the prior research
	• Throughout the presentation, create graphics to outline your main points. Keep the number of words to a minimum and use the graphics only to highlight your points. Don't make the audience read; get them to listen to you
	• If you use a laser pointer to highlight material on slides, do so sparingly. Some people do not react well to a point of light bouncing across a screen
Method	• *Participants*: Give the smallest amount of information that captures the nature of your participants adequately for understanding your research. Characterization of gender and ages may suffice unless you are investigating participant characteristics
	• *Materials*: Identify the materials in enough detail for your audience to understand what the participants were exposed to
	• Don't present as much detail as in a written paper, but make sure your audience understands your materials
	• It can be helpful to create graphics to outline the nature of your materials
	• *Procedure*: Outline what the participants did, giving enough detail so your audience can understand what the participants experienced
	• It can be helpful to create graphics to demonstrate to the audience what the participants went through
Results	• Rely on everyday English and simple descriptive statistics to describe the results
	• Use graphics to present the technical aspects of statistical results so the audience can attend to them. You can rely on statements in everyday English to alert the audience to significant and nonsignificant results
	• Create simple tables and figures to highlight results. If a graph or table is too cluttered or complex, the audience might not be able to pick out the important elements
	• If you have multiple results to present, create separate figures and tables for each one

Continued overleaf.

Table 17.1
Continued.

Discussion	• Repeat your results only to highlight them and to refresh your audience's memory
	• Describe the results briefly in everyday English and explain what those results tell you
	• Connect the results to your hypotheses, saying whether the results supported your hypotheses
	• Discuss why you think you obtained the result you did
	• Finish with a strong summary that encapsulates your results and what they mean
Question and answer period	• Don't be afraid to say you don't know the answer to a question
	• If you know part of the answer to a question, tell what you know and say that you don't know the rest
	• Don't hesitate to ask the questioner to explain a question if you don't understand it. If the person restates the question, it might give you additional cues about an appropriate response
	• When somebody from the audience asks a question, repeat the question for the rest of the group. This guarantees that everybody knows the question, and it gives you time to start thinking of an answer
	• Pause and think about the question before you begin to answer it. A few moments of silence may feel very long to you, but the audience will not mind waiting for your response
	• Ask the questioner if your response addressed the issue. It is appropriate to let the person offer his or her thoughts. You can gently ask, "Why might this be important?"
	• If a person in the audience tries to dominate the question and answer period, you can offer to talk to the person individually after the session. It is rude for a person to try to take over the question period, so you are doing your audience a favor in letting others participate
After the presentation	• Thank the audience for their attention
	• Gather all of your materials, including any CDs, flash drives, or laser pointers that you brought with you
	• Be prepared for an emotional letdown after you present. You will be stimulated before and during the talk.After you finish, it may take a little time to begin feeling normal again

ADAPTING APA STYLE TO ORAL PRESENTATIONS

As with poster presentations, in an oral presentation, you can modify your organization to fit your needs. Presenters typically follow the same general structure as they would in writing an APA-style paper, starting with an introduction, describing the methodology, then presenting the results, and concluding with a discussion. Unlike a paper, a presentation needs no abstract.

One of the important decisions to make about a presentation concerns references you might cite. As you can see in the Cohen and Strayer's (1996) passage above, there are numerous references in the opening sentence of their paper. Just about all of them could be left out of an oral presentation. One reason is that none of them is absolutely vital for understanding where the research idea came from. Another reason is that, much of the time, people in the audience will not have heard of any of the researchers. Mentioning researchers unknown to the audience does not do anything to help them understand your point. So it doesn't pay to mention these authors.

There are exceptions to this last point. If you are presenting information to a group of experts in the area, they will be familiar with the research you cite, and they will expect you to discuss more technical detail. As such, it would be appropriate to discuss the researchers whose ideas paved the way for your work. In addition, if your presentation involves describing a series of your own studies on a topic, your audience could benefit from knowing about the sequence of studies. In the end, you need to know your audience; if they are knowledgeable about your topic, they will be able to understand more complex ideas; if the audience consists of nonspecialists, you are better off omitting all of the technical details.

PREPARING FOR YOUR TALK

The first step in organizing your talk is to determine what you want to tell your audience. Identify the two or three main ideas that you want the listeners to get. Then decide what information you need to present to achieve your goal. This process will result in decisions to omit a lot of information that you know. Some key steps in creating your presentation are given in Table 17.2.

As you prepare your talk, allocate specific amounts of time for each segment. If your presentation is 15 min, you could create a breakdown like this:

- Introduction—2 min
- Method—3 min
- Results—4 min
- Discussion—3 min
- Question and answer—3 min

Table 17.2
Creating your Presentation

How to prepare	Why you do it
Identify two or three main points	• Don't overload the listener with too much detail
Decide how to introduce and explain the background and methodology related to your main points	• Keep your presentation focused on the few key points you are addressing • Get a feel for what ideas need to be repeated at various points during your talk
Practice out loud	• Give yourself a feel for what your presentation sounds like and how long it takes • Work out a system in which a friend indicates to you if you are speaking too fast
Set up a system like the one you will be using during your talk	• Get comfortable with the technology so you can concentrate on the content of your presentation rather than on the equipment
Prepare a backup	• Sometimes technology fails. A handout or transparencies can provide a backup for getting your information across

As you can see, you don't have a lot of time for any part of your presentation. You will not be permitted to exceed your allotted time, so creating a coherent structure for your presentation is a good idea.

After determining the two or three key points that listeners should remember, figure out the background that listeners should know if they are to follow your argument. Then include only the major points that led up to your work. Next, describe your methodology. Judicious use of either a PowerPoint® presentation or transparencies on an overhead projector can help you present key elements of your method. Likewise, photographs of your apparatus may reduce the amount you need to say about it.

Similarly, you should scale down the results, presenting only the most important and salient details. If you compare two groups and the difference is significant, you might display t-test results on a screen, but you don't need to mention it when you talk. It is sufficient to note that the difference is significant and which group has the higher mean. You can always fill in the details if somebody asks you a question about them. Finally, you will present your conclusions. It is a good idea to remind the audience of the logic of your research and how your results led to your ultimate conclusion.

People can keep a few ideas in working memory, but if you tell them too much, they will lose the detail. So if they are not familiar with the nature of your research, you should show them only the tip of the iceberg. They won't be able to handle all the information that you want to give them. In general, they won't know you are leaving out a lot, and they won't care. If listeners do care about missing information, they can ask you a question and you can respond.

When you organize your talk, figure out how to communicate with as little technical terminology as possible. It can help to work with a friend who can alert you when you are getting too complex. Sometimes you will have to convey technical information; that is fine, but if you overdo it, you might lose the audience.

Once you organize the talk, prepare notes, then practice it out loud again and again so that you know what you want to say and how you are going to say it and so you have to refer to your notes as little as possible. It isn't possible to be overprepared. Rather, the more you practice your talk, the better your presentation will be.

CREATING GRAPHICS FOR YOUR PRESENTATION

Presentation graphics have evolved from photographic slides, to over-head transparencies, to PowerPoint® presentations. The flexibility of PowerPoint® is such that you can create just about any type of graphic that you desire. Ironically, even though you can generate a slide of any complexity you want, it is probably better to keep your slides simple.

The more information you try to convey on a slide, the harder it is for the audience to key in on the most important information. So keep your visual elements simple and to the point. In addition, in a professional talk, it is wise not to include sounds to introduce a new PowerPoint® slide. After a few slides, the sounds become distracting, then annoying (Daniel, 2004).

GIVING THE PRESENTATION

There are a lot of details associated with a successful presentation. A high level of preparation is one of them. Other important elements appear in Table 17.3.

Your talk is a professional event. This means that you should act like a professional. The audience is expecting you to know something they don't; they are there to gain from your expertise. In addition, they want you to succeed because if you don't succeed, they will be almost as unhappy as you. They will have to sit through a boring or incoherent presentation.

Table 17.3
Preparations at the Conference.

What to do at the conference	Why you do it
Visit the presentation room	• You can get a sense of what the room looks like, where people will be sitting, and what you need to do to be heard • You can also see how to stand so you don't block the screen • Arrange for a friend to sit within your line of sight. Your friend can signal if you are speaking too quickly
Test the equipment	• Sometimes the system you use for practice does not function like the system in the room. You don't want surprises when you plan for your presentation • See what you have to do to get your presentation onto the system in the presentation room and what you need to do to access it right before your talk
Check your attire	• If you have new clothes, make sure tags are removed • Straighten anything that is unprofessional looking • Some conferences have doughnuts for attendees. It is probably not a good idea not to eat powdered doughnuts if you are wearing dark clothes

You are likely to be anxious about your talk. Recognizing that fact can help you deal with it; most speakers get nervous. There are ways to deal with the anxiety. To begin with, make sure you breathe normally. When people are nervous, they sometimes take gulps of air, talk until the air runs out, then they take another gulp. If you find yourself doing this, finish your sentence, take a breath, and pause a moment. It might also help to have water handy. Taking a drink can help relax you.

Remember that the audience is interested in listening to you. Some basic tips can help keep their attention focused on you:

- Don't read from your notes; speak naturally, slowly, and with a relaxed voice.
- Don't do PowerPoint® karaoke; that is, don't simply read from the screen. Use the slides only to offer highlights.
- Don't turn your back on the audience; face them and talk to them.

- Don't move around; stand still with your notes in front of you.

When you are giving your presentation, you might stumble across some of your words. We all do this at times. So if you begin talking and you lose your place, or if you have trouble pronouncing some words, stop and take a breath. If you need to go back to the beginning of your sentence, that is fine. Just do it smoothly. If you need to re-pronounce a word, just do that smoothly, too. You might be very aware of these slips in speech, but your audience will not be. Professional speakers know that listeners don't really pay much attention to interruptions in speech unless the speaker points them out. So don't point them out. If you pay attention to speakers, you will notice that, although their deliveries might be polished, they are not flawless. But most of the time, you don't even notice. During your presentation, your listeners will generally not be aware of small errors in your talk.

After you complete your prepared remarks, expect some questions from the audience. Keep in mind that even experts don't know everything about their topic. As a speaker, you won't be expected to know everything, either. So if you forget something or if you can't answer a question, that's not necessarily a problem. You should prepare so you minimize the need to say you don't know, but it will happen on occasion.

You are likely to be anxious before your presentation. That is completely natural. The more well prepared you are, however, the less your anxiety will matter. You can harness your arousal to enhance your presentation. It might help you relax if you make eye contact with people in your audience, particularly friends who are there. Then, during your presentation, imagine you are talking to a friend.

18

Presenting Your Work
on the Internet

The new information technology, Internet and e-mail, have practically eliminated the physical costs of communications.

Peter Drucker

The Internet is clearly about more than sports scores and email now. It's a place where we can conduct our democracy and get very large amounts of data to very large numbers of people.

Frank James

The columnist Dave Barry seems to understand the Internet. He has said that "If you're willing to be patient, you'll find that you can utilize the vast resources of the Web to waste time in ways that you never before dreamed possible" (Barry, n.d.). Although people do spend a lot of time accessing web sites, not all the time they spend on the Internet is wasted.

The Internet is emerging as a legitimate vehicle for disseminating information in the sciences. The number of Internet journals is increasing, and electronic books (e-books) have started appearing regularly. In addition, psychologists have begun posting their own writing to the Internet.

When psychologists publish their work on the Internet, it often undergoes peer review, in which experts have determined that the work is of high quality. Self-published work is of unknown quality, but you can find reliable information if you know where to look and how to evaluate web sites. (See chapter 3 for guidance on assessing the value of sources.)

Some people have taken word-processed documents and simply uploaded them to the Internet; others have converted their files to portable document format (the so-called *pdf* files). Manuscripts placed on the Internet through either of these approaches are likely to take the traditional APA-style format. But publishing in standard Internet format, using hypertext markup language (HTML), has some advantages that you don't see with either word-processed or pdf files.

NEW CAPABILITIES WITH INTERNET PUBLICATION

Undoubtedly, the most important feature of Internet publishing is that it allows quick dissemination of your work to a world-wide audience. Another feature of Internet publishing involves the use of hyperlinks. Internet users take it for granted that you can click on a link and go to a site that offers information related to a topic. If you post your work to the Internet, you can send your reader to:

- another paper you have written;
- a web site that will further explain the point you are making;
- an image or a figure you have created;
- a citation in your reference list.

When you use hyperlinks, you are making it a little easier for your reader to understand your ideas and the context in which you are presenting them. The downside, of course, is that the reader may face an inordinate amount of information, too much to process at more than a cursory level.

Other elements that you can include in your Internet presentation are audio and video files. So if you are conducting research that makes use of audio or video stimuli, you can save such files on your server and let your readers see or hear them while they are reading your manuscript. Traditionally, journals have been reluctant to publish pictures because images have to be processed and formatted individually, so they are expensive. In addition, pictures take up a lot of journal space. A journal in print format can publish only a limited number of pages per issue or per volume, so space is at a premium.

Internet space is less expensive than paper space. So although publishing a large number of images on paper is not feasible, it is quite reasonable in electronic space. Publishing video and audio is impossible on paper, but very simple electronically.

USING A WORD PROCESSOR TO CREATE MANUSCRIPTS FOR THE INTERNET

Creating a file for the Internet, an HTML file, is very easy. Table 18.1 shows the basic steps using common word processing programs. You can create a basic web page by writing your paper, then easily saving it in web-compatible format.

Table 18.1
Steps for Saving a Word® or WordPerfect® Manuscript for Internet Publishing

Word® version 1	Word® version 2	WordPerfect®
Click on *File* from the menu at the top of the page	Click on *Save As* if it appears on the menu at the top of the page	Click on *File* from the menu at the top of the page
Select *Save As Web Page*	In the box labeled *Save as file type*, select *Web Page*	Click on *Publish to* and select *HTML*

Save the file with a title that has no spaces. Use a dash-like-this or an underscore_like_this if you want to create a title that has multiple words. Or you can just create a title with no break between wordslikethis.

Note: File names on the internet are case sensitive and you can't use spaces.
Note: When you upload your file to a server, make sure you upload the separate folder that has the image files and any other supplementary files you have created.

If you create a manuscript for the Internet, you need to remember a couple of important details. First, the file name must not contain any spaces. In Word® or WordPerfect®, file names can have spaces, but Internet files cannot. Your document will be a web page; names of web pages must consist of an uninterrupted string of characters. When authors want to use multiple words in a file name, they typically separate words with a dash (e.g., *my-file*) or with an underscore (e.g., *my_file*).

A second detail to remember is that file names are case sensitive. Thus, a web browser will treat *My_File.htm* as different from *my_file.htm*. If you are likely to publish a number of documents on the Internet, you would do well to figure out a consistent way of naming your files so you can establish a pattern that is easy for you to remember, for example, using only lowercase letters in file names and separating words with a single dash. It doesn't really matter what convention you choose, but consistency makes life easier in remembering how you name files.

Creating Hyperlinks

If you create a manuscript with a word processing program, it is easy to create hyperlinks in the text. The effect will be to allow the reader to click on a section of text and go either to a different web site or to a different spot in the current document. Tables 18.2 and 18.3 illustrate how to insert hyperlinks for these uses. When is it helpful to create hyperlinks? Any time you think that your reader could benefit from additional information.

Table 18.2
Creating a Hyperlink to an Internet Location Outside your Own Web Document

Word®	WordPerfect®
Highlight the text you want to hyperlink	
Select the Internet icon from the menu at the top of the page OR Select *Insert* from the menu at the top of the page, then click on Hyperlink OR Type *CTRL K*	Select *Tools* and click on *Hyperlink*
In the box labeled *Address* type the URL (i.e., the web address) of the document to which you want to link	In the box labeled *Document/Macro* type the URL (i.e., the web address) of the document
Select *OK*	

Note: You use the same series of steps for linking to any kind of file, including text, audio, and video files.

Table 18.3
Creating a Hyperlink to a Location Within Your Own Web Document

Word®	WordPerfect®
Highlight the first word of the text where in the document the hyperlink will take you. The word you highlight will become the bookmark OR Move the cursor next to the first word of the text where the hyperlink will take you. Select *Insert* on the menu at the top of the page	
Click on *Bookmark* and type in a name for the bookmark	Click on *Tools*, then select *Bookmark* Click on the button *Create* In the box labeled *Bookmark Name* type a name for the bookmark
Note: The first word of the text that is hyperlinked can serve as a good name for the bookmark, but you can create any label you want	
Select *Insert* on the menu at the top of the page and click on *Bookmark* Highlight the appropriate bookmark in the box	Select *Tools* on the menu and click on *Hyperlink* In the box labeled *Bookmark*, type in the name of the bookmark you created
Click *OK*	Click *OK*

Another common use of hyperlinks in online journals is for citing references. If you discuss previous research, you need to cite the article in your References section. Authors frequently create a hyperlink when they mention an article in the text so that when the reader clicks on the link, the web browser goes to the appropriate citation in the reference list.

Inserting Images

If you have pictures or graphs you want to insert into your manuscript, you can accomplish this easily. All you have to do is to display the image on your computer monitor, copy it, then paste it into the document where you want it.

When you save a document with images, those images are saved in a folder separate from your original document. When you upload your documents to a server, you must upload not only the manuscript but also the folder with the images.

If you have graphs that you want to insert, you can present a thumbnail, that is, a version that presents the graph in a size that gives a sense of the results but that is small enough to fit within the text. If you create a hyperlink from the thumbnail to the full-sized version, the reader can click on the small version to get the full-size picture.

ADVANTAGES OF INTERNET PUBLISHING SOFTWARE

Although the most convenient way to create an Internet manuscript may be by using the common word processing programs, there are some advantages to using Internet publishing software programs such as Front Page® or Dreamweaver®. These programs are easy to understand and use, and they offer features that make formatting quite easy.

With some practice, you should be able to put together a competent Internet manuscript with the Internet publishing software, but it will take a little time for you to learn about the special features of the programs. One of the advantages of this software is that you can include elements known as *metatags*. The most important of these tags is the title metatag, which tells your web browser to insert a title at the very top of the display. Other types of tags can provide information about the author of the web page, its title, its contents, and descriptors of its content.

The Internet publishing software is also useful because it provides more flexibility in formatting your work. Some of the features that are easy to implement with this software appear in Table 18.4. They include such details as sizing and placement of tables, figures, and text. But there are many more useful features that you can learn as you

Table 18.4

Useful Features of Internet Publishing Software that are not as Easy or are Impossible with Word Processors

Feature	Why the feature is useful
Creating a title metatag	This tells your web browser to put the title of your document at the top of the window containing your document
Opening hyperlinks in separate pages	You can send the reader to a new web site without closing the window with your work on it. This feature makes it easier for the reader to get back to your web document
Manipulating images	You can size images as you desire. In addition, you can wrap text around the images, putting the image on the left margin, for example, and putting text above it, to the side, and below
Using background color and "wallpaper"	You can add color and patterns to the background of your web page. It can make them more attractive and, perhaps, easier to read with the right color combinations
Using tables to format your web page	You can create tables that help you format your web document and organize the content. You can hide the lines of the table. Many web pages use tables in their layout
Sizing fonts in your document	Word processing programs let you size text easily, but with internet publishing software, it is easier to make changes and to see their effect immediately
Creating email links	You can easily create a hyperlink that lets a reader email you

develop your skills. You can also select background colors or wallpaper patterns to make your web manuscript easier to read or to make it look more appealing. In word processing, these tasks are either difficult or impossible because the primary purpose of that software is not to create Internet documents.

If all you intend to do is to post your manuscript on the Internet, a word processing program provides a very easy tool for doing so. Internet publishing software has an incredible array of features, and it allows you to generate some interesting and useful effects, but for putting a standard APA-format paper on the web, word processing will work pretty well. And if you are writing the paper to begin with, it really doesn't take all that much extra work to publish it on the Internet with some of the helpful features such as hyperlinks.

PUBLISHING YOUR POSTER ON THE WEB

If you create a single-sheet poster using PowerPoint®, you can also publish it on the Internet. All you need to do to save it in a format compatible with the Internet is to choose the *Save As* function, then save it using the file type *Single File Web Page*. Some browsers may not accept this type of file, so you should try it to see in what conditions it works.

UPLOADING YOUR MANUSCRIPT TO THE INTERNET

This chapter highlights the basics of creating a manuscript that you can publish on the Internet. Word processors are adequate for creating a basic Internet document. You can probably accomplish just about anything you need to in a research report. But there will be limitations regarding the flexibility of formatting provided by such software.

Regardless of how you create the manuscript, though, you need to get it onto a server that allows Internet users to access it. How to place your information on a server is beyond the scope of this book, but colleges and universities typically let students and faculty develop web sites. Commercial organizations also sell space on servers.

Regardless of which approach you choose, software will be available to move your files from your computer to a server. After that, your work will be part of the Internet.

19

Submitting Your Plan to an Ethics Committee

Organizations engaged in research need to focus on the special pressures that researchers confront in science, engineering, and the social sciences, and on the special ethical values that undergird their activities.

Ethics Resource Center (2004)

Most researchers don't feed their subjects radioactive oatmeal, withhold treatment for fatal diseases, imprison them, or turn them into stutterers on purpose. But all of these have been part of research in the past (Beins, 2004). Owing to lapses in ethical judgments by researchers, legislators have passed laws that protect people from this kind of research.

So after you have created your study and are ready to start testing participants, you can't begin right away. You first have to get approval from a committee that is responsible for seeing that you don't engage in behaviors such as feeding children radioactive food. Your research isn't likely to be quite so problematic, but it is the job of a review committee to make sure that you haven't overlooked the potential for harming your participants.

ETHICAL STANDARDS IN RESEARCH

Researchers bear a responsibility to those who participate in their research, whether the subjects are people or animals. (Strictly speaking, psychologists refer to human and nonhuman animals, but because the ethical regulations for these two classes of animals differ so greatly, we will refer to people and animals, respectively.) The responsibility regarding humans is to make sure that the chance of physical or psychological harm is minimized. Animals must be treated humanely and, if discomfort is necessary, it must be as small as possible.

People have differing views on some aspects of the ethics of research. For example, some people have made arguments that it is unethical to deceive people in research and that it should be outlawed (Ortmann & Hertwig, 1997), although others have noted that deception is not necessarily problematic (Korn, 1998; Lawson, 1995). Similarly, some people argue against nearly all animal research, but as a society, we have decided to permit such research, subject to certain provisions. Because there are legitimate disagreements regarding ethical issues in research, the federal government has established regulations for animal care and use.

If you are planning research, you will need approval from an appropriate organization before you can carry out your study. If you intend to study people, you will have to write a proposal and submit it to your institution's Institutional Review Board (IRB). The IRB has a legal mandate to review every research project involving people. A similar committee, the Institutional Animal Care and Use Committee (IACUC), reviews research with animals. It is beyond the scope of this chapter to discuss the complexities of the research requirements, but they are available online from the federal government for human research (Penslar, n.d.) and for animal research (Licensing and Registration, 2004).

According to federal guidelines, the IRB has five major tasks that have an impact on your IRB proposal:

1. identify the risks associated with the research, as distinguished from the risks of therapies the subjects would receive even if not participating in research.
2. determine that the risks will be minimized to the extent possible.
3. identify the probable benefits to be derived from the research.
4. determine that the risks are reasonable in relation to the benefits to subjects, if any, and the importance of the knowledge to be gained.
5. assure that potential subjects will be provided with an accurate and fair description of the risks or discomforts and the anticipated benefits (Penslar, n.d.).

In addition, IRBs need to consider whether the researchers have taken appropriate steps to protect the privacy of subjects and to make sure that the data remain anonymous and confidential.

Fortunately, most laboratory-based psychological research poses no physical risk and a vanishingly small likelihood of psychological risk. So it is usually pretty easy to make a case as to why the research you are planning is acceptable. But you do have to make the case because the law mandates that the IRB understand and approve your plan.

Institutions may have their own regulations in addition to federal rules. At some schools, for example, students can only undertake research under the guidance of a faculty member. Likewise, some schools may require that researchers complete training before submitting a proposal. You should check on your institution's requirements.

WRITING A PROPOSAL FOR AN INSTITUTIONAL REVIEW BOARD FOR RESEARCH WITH HUMAN SUBJECTS

The IRB (commonly called the Human Subjects Committee by many researchers) at your institution probably has a stipulated form that you must complete. But most institutions ask for essentially the same information. It is important for you to follow their guidelines very closely. IRBs are not known for being very flexible; sometimes they have reputations for erecting barriers. So give them the exact information they request.

Throughout this section, we will present excerpts from a proposal that an IRB approved at Ithaca College. The project involves informing participants that others had rated a set of jokes as either funny or not funny (or told nothing at all). In reality, all jokes were the same and the project was designed to investigate whether expectations could influence joke ratings.

Abstract

Your abstract is a relatively brief statement of what you intend to study, what your participants will actually do, and what materials you will use in your research. Your statement of the purpose of your study is also important because, if a study has more than a minimal level of risk, the IRB is supposed to decide whether the study's benefits will outweigh the risk. The purpose of this abstract differs from that of an abstract described in chapter 15 that begins a research paper. The abstract in your IRB proposal describes a study you intend to carry out and focuses on your methodology.

> **Abstract.** After completing an informed consent form (see Appendix A), participants will take three min to complete a child's 12-piece puzzle as a group or individually. They will then rate a set of 20 jokes played on an audio tape. Most of these jokes have been approved for use in previous research. The original jokes appear in Appendix B; two new jokes that were recorded on tape are similar in tone to the previous ones; one is sexually suggestive.

The participants will learn that the jokes have been rated as either positive or as negative in previous research. We are investigating whether this knowledge will influence their ratings of and mirth reactions to the jokes. The participants will be observed by two experimenters, one of whom will appear to be a participant. The debriefing will clarify this for the participants.

The jokes were chosen by a group of seven students who felt that these jokes are representative of humor that college students would generally appreciate. These jokes are generally the same ones that the All College Review Board for Human Subjects Research has approved. Some of them contain sexual themes or may be otherwise offensive, but both the recruitment statement and informed consent forms forewarn participants that the jokes may be in bad taste or offensive and they should either refrain from signing up for the study or could withdraw from the study at any time or for any reason.

What the Participants Will Actually Do

The IRB will want to know the procedures you are going to use. As a rule, it is better to give more detail than less because if the IRB has questions it cannot answer from your proposal, there may be a delay in the approval process; the members of the IRB may request additional information from you.

Description of Subject Participation

You should include a complete description of what participants will be doing, presenting the important details in your summary.

Subjects will be tested individually or in groups of 4 participants. The first task will be to complete a 12-piece child's puzzle either individually (when a single person participates) or as a group. They will then listen to 20 recorded jokes and then will rate the jokes as to humor value on a scale of 1 (*low humor value*) to 7 (*high humor value*). The observers will record mirth reactions.

After hearing and rating the jokes, the subjects will be told of the purpose of the study. They will learn that one of the participants was actually an observer who watched their reactions. The participants will further learn that this method of observation was used in order to keep them from feeling uncomfortable with the idea that a group of researchers was observing them.

Risks and How You Will Deal With Them

Most psychological studies are relatively free of major risk, but you have to convince the IRB that yours is no exception. Risk could be physical, psychological, social, or economic, according to the government. The last two types of risk are virtually nonexistent in psychological research. The federal government has defined *risk* as the probability of harm that could result from participation in the research. If a person is no more likely to be harmed in your study than in everyday life, the research will fall into a category of *minimal risk*.

If you are asking your participants to engage in some behavior that could lead to injury, you need to identify that behavior and how you are going to minimize that risk. If they suffer some physical harm, you have to say how you will minimize the effects of the injury. Studies of therapeutic effectiveness may involve physical harm, particularly if drugs are involved, but in the vast majority of psychological studies, the likelihood of physical harm is negligible.

If risk exists in your research, it is most likely to be psychological. People may engage in tasks that frustrate, depress, or bore them. Or their self-esteem may suffer if they are given false information about their performance. In your description of psychological risk, you must identify potential problems and tell why any negative effects will be minor and transient. Most of the time, there really will not be any significant risks. But it is important to engage in critical thought to anticipate what might happen.

You may want to include a statement that, if a participant seems to be reacting negatively to his or her performance on a task, you will debrief the participant, explaining that the task is difficult and that you expect that many people will struggle with it. This should not be an empty promise; if such a situation arose, you would have to deal with it appropriately. But in over 30 years of laboratory research with students, we have never encountered a participant who appeared to be harmed, in even a very temporary way, by any of our manipulations.

Risks of Participation: There are no major risks associated with this project. The jokes that we will use could reasonably be told with virtually any college-aged students, without noticeable risk of embarrassment. In any case, because some of the jokes may be sexually suggestive or potentially offensive otherwise, we will indicate this in the recruitment statement and on the informed consent form; in this way, students who may be offended will know that some stimuli may be troublesome. In debriefing, we will provide them with information about the nature of the study and answer any questions they might have. We believe, on the basis of previous studies, that the risks are quite minor.

Risk–Benefit Analysis

As part of your proposal to the IRB, you have to explain the benefits of your research. Most laboratory research (like any individual research project) has minimal benefit in and of itself. The value is through the knowledge accumulated across a large body of research. Behavioral questions are too complex for us to be able to find complete answers in a single project. Still, there will be some benefit from a well-designed study.

The benefit to the participants is that they will learn how psychological research is carried out. They may also gain some insight into themselves, even if that is not the ostensible purpose of the study. They may also feel positively about themselves because they have helped contribute to the generation of new knowledge that may ultimately be important in understanding people's behaviors and thoughts. Discussing the benefits to society from your research may help the IRB with its decision, but the welfare of the people who participate in your study is the prime consideration of the IRB.

Benefits of the Study

Describe the benefits from participation in your study.

> The results of this study will benefit the participants in that they will learn how psychological research is done. They will also be exposed to jokes that may be enjoyable in and of themselves. The data from the study will provide us with information about changes in mood and the effect on evaluation of jokes.

Informed Consent

The IRB will insist that your participants be informed in advance of what they will be doing and what risks they will face. You need to present this information to participants as thoroughly as possible. You also need to let them know that they do not need to participate and that they can withdraw from the study at any point if they so desire. You should also tell the IRB how you will maintain confidentiality and, if appropriate, anonymity in your data. All of these issues will appear at some point on your informed consent form. A sample informed consent form appears in Figure 19.1.

Informed Consent
Humor Appreciation

1. *Purpose of the study.* This is a study about humor appreciation. We are conducting this project to find out about your appreciation of jokes. You will complete a child's 12-piece puzzle and then listen to a series of jokes and rate each one according to its humor value.

2. *Benefits of the study.*
   a) You will benefit from this study by learning a little about how people respond to humor. After you complete the ratings, we will tell you about the purpose of the study. In addition, you may be eligible for extra credit if one of your instructors has indicated that this is possible.
   b) The scientific community will benefit in two ways. First, the student who is testing you will learn more about how to do good research. Second, after the study, we will know a little more about people's reactions to humor.

3. *What you will be asked to do.* You will work on a puzzle for a few minutes, then you will rate a group of jokes as to how funny you think they are.

4. *What you can expect to happen as a result of your participation in this study.* This study is fairly short (about 30 min or less), so we won't be taking too much of your time. If you want to leave, you are free to do so at any time. If you have any questions, just ask us and we will try to help. Some of the jokes have sexual content or may be otherwise offensive; if you think you might be offended, you should decline to participate in this study.

5. *If you would like more information about this study.* If you have questions during the study, please ask the experimenter who will try to answer them to your satisfaction. After the study, you can contact Prof. Barney Beins (274-3304) in the Psychology Department.

6. *Withdrawal from the study.* You are free to terminate your participation in this study and leave at any time, for any reason. If you decide to withdraw, simply give your rating form to the experimenter and leave the room. If you have any questions or concerns, you can ask the experimenter or contact Prof. Beins.

7. *Confidentiality of your data.* Your name will not be written on the data sheets. Thus, after you leave, there will be no way for anybody to find out your ratings of the jokes. Your participation in this study will remain confidential.

I have read the above and I understand its contents. I agree to participate in the study. I acknowledge that I am 18 years of age or older.

Signature: Date:

Printed name:

Figure 19.1   Example of an informed consent form.

Sometimes researchers use deception to keep participants from knowing the true nature of the study. If there is active deception, you need to clarify that in your proposal to the IRB. Dealing with passive deception is a little trickier. Obviously, you cannot tell your participants everything about the topic you are studying, and they would not want you to. So the question is whether leaving out some information about the study deceives them as to their participation in the study. You cannot omit risk issues, but you don't tell them everything about the study either. If you are leaving out critical information when you tell participants about the study, you should justify to the IRB why it is important to omit it and why it does not pose risk issues.

WRITING A PROPOSAL FOR THE INSTITUTIONAL ANIMAL CARE AND USE COMMITTEE (IACUC) FOR ANIMAL RESEARCH

Regulations dealing with research with nonhuman animals require that investigators submit detailed proposals to the IACUC. The standards of treatment for animals used in research will differ greatly from those for people, but the underlying concept for both is that the researcher must minimize pain and distress to the greatest extent possible.

Regulations for care and treatment differ across species, so you should familiarize yourself with the guidelines for the species that you intend to use. Mammals are accorded greatest protection, but there are regulations for nonmammalian vertebrates as well. The issue is somewhat complex, though, because the definition of *animal* varies. In some definitions rats and mice bred specifically for research are not considered animals, although in others they are (Essentials for animal research, 1995).

The government has identified seven aspects of research and animal care procedures involving animal research. Your IACUC has to consider each of them:

1. Procedures with animals will avoid or minimize discomfort, distress, and pain to the animals, consistent with sound research design.
2. Procedures that may cause more than momentary or slight pain or distress to the animals will be performed with appropriate sedation, analgesia, or anesthesia, unless the procedure is justified for scientific reasons in writing by the investigator.
3. Animals that would otherwise experience severe or chronic pain or

distress that cannot be relieved will be painlessly killed at the end of the procedure or, if appropriate, during the procedure.

4. The living conditions of animals will be appropriate for their species and contribute to their health and comfort. The housing, feeding, and nonmedical care of the animals will be directed by a veterinarian or other scientist trained and experienced in the proper care, handling, and use of the species being maintained or studied.

5. Medical care for animals will be available and provided as necessary by a qualified veterinarian.

6. Personnel conducting procedures on the species being maintained or studied will be appropriately qualified and trained in those procedures.

7. Methods of euthanasia used will be consistent with the recommendations of the American Veterinary Medical Association (AVMA) Panel on Euthanasia, unless a deviation is justified for scientific reasons in writing by the investigator (Public Health Service Policy, 2002).

When you prepare a proposal for the IACUC, you should include a project description (suitable for nonscientists), a statement of the purpose of the project, a rationale for the use of animals and the number of animals used, an explanation of why a nonliving model is not appropriate, certification that this project does not duplicate previous studies, a description of how the animals will be used and cared for and what means are taken to insure a minimum of discomfort and suffering of the animals, and how the animals will be disposed of at the end of the study (Assurance of compliance, 2006).

Appendix A

Example of APA-Style Manuscript With Common Errors

When you write an APA-style paper, there are many details to remember. In this appendix, the sample manuscript illustrates the use of APA style and common errors that writers make.

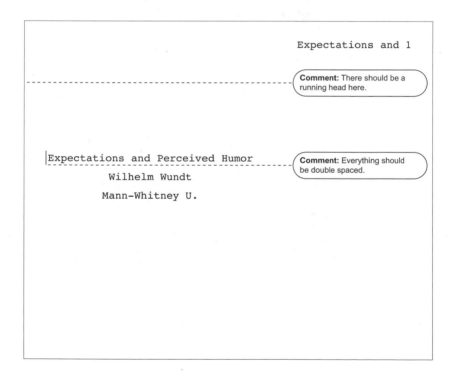

Expectations and 1

Comment: There should be a running head here.

Expectations and Perceived Humor

Comment: Everything should be double spaced.

Wilhelm Wundt

Mann-Whitney U.

---

1   This sample manuscript is based on Wimer, D.J., & Beins, B. C. (in press). Expectations and perceived humor. *Humor: International Journal of Humor Studies.* Used with permission of Mouton de Gruyter.

Expectations and 2

Abstract

In two experiments, participants read and rated a set of jokes for their humor value. In each experiment, participants were told that the jokes had been rated previously. In different conditions, participants believed that the jokes had been rated low or rated high by others. The results showed that when participants thought the jokes had been rated as very funny, his/her own ratings tended to be high. When participants thought the jokes had been rated as not very funny, their own ratings were low. In a control condition where participants did not learn that others had rated the jokes, their ratings were between those of the other groups. I concluded that, because jokes do not have an intrinsic humor level, people rely on cues from others to help them decide how funny they are.

Comment: Do not use bold type for any section headings.

Comment: APA—Do not indent the abstract.

Comment: Avoid passive voice verbs. There are several passive verbs in this abstract.

Comment: APA—Avoid this construction.

Comment: Use where for locations. A better construction here would be *in which*.

Comment: APA style permits use of the first person *singular pronoun*, *I*, but not in the abstract. You can use it in other sections of the paper.

Comment: Ambiguous referent— does *they* refer to the people being funny or the jokes being funny.

Expectations and 3

Expectations and Perceived Humor

Wilhelm Wundt

Mann-Whitney U.

> **Comment:** On the first page of text, only use the title, not the author's name or the institution.

Introduction

> Comment: APA—The introduction needs no heading because, *by virtue of its placement*, it introduces the rest of the article.
>
> Also, don't insert an extra space between lines.

One difficulty in studying humor is that no reliable metric exists for measuring humor appreciation. Various individual and social characteristics are likely to affect one's evaluation of humorous material. The humor value of a joke depends on many factors, including the context in which one encounters the joke.

> **Comment:** APA—There is only one author here. If you use a pronoun, use *my*.

In our study, participants' reactions to jokes were examined based on

> **Comment:** Passive voice.

information I provided about the jokes. We examined whether people's ratings of the humor value of a set of jokes would change if they learned that others had found the jokes more or less funny. It was suggested by Gavansky (1986) that

> **Comment:** Passive voice.

there is a difference between the internal and affective psycho-emotional responses and the cognitive, rational estimation of

> **Comment:** This is gobbledygook.

humor as detected through the use of a research-generated self-report inventory. Joke ratings presumably involve the cognitive component; as such, they might be susceptible to changes in evaluation based on information.

Expectations and 4

    In addition, the effect of group participation was investigated. Several

> **Comment:** Passive voice.

researchers have documented the effect of group size on responses to humorous material. Generally, the effect of groups is on observable, mirth responses (e.g.,

> **Comment:** Use an ampersand (&) within parentheses instead of the word *and* when citing a source with more than one author.

Levy and Fenley, 1979); further, Nosanchuk and Lightstone (1974) note that private and

> **Comment:** Use past tense for verbs that describe research already done.

public responses to humorous material are different. Even an imaginary audience can affect mirth responses, as with canned laughter (Martin and Gray, 1966). That is, a person's outward responses to humor differ depending on whether they are alone

> **Comment:** The noun associated with this pronoun is singular. The pronoun should match the number of the noun.

or in a group. At the same time, being in a group may not relate to cognitive evaluation, although being in a group may provide clues about how funny a joke "really" is.

> **Comment:** APA—Do not insert extra space between sections.

Method

> **Comment:** APA—This should be in italics.

Participants

> **Comment:** APA—Do not begin a sentence with a numeral. If you do start a sentence with a number, write it out.

    90 undergraduates participated in Experiment 1, and 120 undergraduates participated in experiment 2. They volunteered in order to receive extra credit in psychology classes.

> **Comment:** APA—There should be more detail describing participants.

Materials

> **Comment:** APA—This should be in italics.

Expectations and 5

In both experiments, 21 jokes appeared in a small booklet. The theme of the jokes varied, but were judged by a group ofstudents to be typical of those that other college students would appreciate. The jokes came from disparate sources, such as Isaac *Asimov's Treasury of Humor* (Asimov, 1967) and various internet sites and other printed matter.

> **Comment:** APA—This should be in italics.

Procedure

Upon arrival and after completing informed consent, participants, who took part in the study in groups, were instructed to rate a series of jokes on a scale of 1 (not funny) to 7 (very funny). The

> **Comment:** *Were instructed* is a passive voice construction, which you should avoid. Besides you can eliminate this phrase altogether—it is not needed. Say "the participants rated..."

> **Comment:** APA—Italicize the anchors in a Likert-type scale.

participants also learned that the jokes had previously been rated. Although everyone actually rated the same set of jokes, participants were informed that all the jokes they would see had previously received ratings of (1) horribly unfunny, (2) not funny, (3) very funny, (4) hysterically funny (Experiment 1), or not funny or very funny (Experiment 2). There was also a control condition in Experiment 1 that heard nothing specific about supposed previous ratings.

> **Comment:** Passive voice.

> **Comment:** APA—Use (a),(b), and so forth for series. Also, use the so-called Oxford comma, the comma separating the penultimate and ultimate items in the series (i.e., the second last and the last items), in this case, after *very funny*.

The two experiments differed in that, in Experiment 1, we tested participants in groups but did not vary the group size systematically. In experiment 2, we systematically varied group sizes. Participants rated

> Comment: APA—This is one of many plural pronouns. The singular *I* would be better. Don't use the editorial *we*.

> **Comment:** Capitalize the e in *experiment*.

the jokes alone, in groups of 3 or 4, or in groups of 7 or 8.

> **Comment:** The numerical values appear written out in words.

Results and Discussion

In experiment 1, after learning about previous ratings, the jokes were rated differently, F=8.591, p=.000. When participants did not have expectations about the jokes, they rated them in the middle.

> **Comment:** Misplaced modifier: the jokes did not learn about previous ratings; the participants did.

> **Comment:** Passive voice.

> **Comment:** Throughout the results, statistical tests and p-values should be italicized.

> **Comment:** APA—You need to indicate degrees of freedom.

While it is possible that participants were responding to demand characteristics, I do not believe this is true because the two extreme groups, Hysterically Funny and Horribly Unfunny, received the same ratings as the neutral group. Thus, our participants were quite capable of ignoring information that was clearly discrepant with reality. In fact, the jokes were neither horrible nor wonderful. The data shows that the ratings in the neutral group fell slightly more positively than the middle point on a 7-point scale. When being debriefed, the manipulation wasn't obvious to the participants.

> **Comment:** *While* is a conjunction involving time. Do not use it when you mean *although* or *whereas*.

> **Comment:** *Data* is plural, so this should be *data show*.

> **Comment:** This is a misplaced modifier—the manipulation was not debriefed, the participants were.

> **Comment:** Avoid contractions in formal writing.

In experiment 2, I eliminated the two extreme categories (Hysterically Funny and Horribly Unfunny) and repeated the study with a systematic examination of the effects of group size. Previous research has suggested that being part of a group affects humor responses. If rating the jokes involves a cognitive evaluation, however, we might not expect to see

> **Comment:** APA—Group names should appear in lower case.

> **Comment:** Avoid the editorial *we.*

Expectations and 7

an effect of group size on ratings,
although outward expression of mirth
might be susceptible to group effects
(|for example|, Levy |and| Fenley, 1979).

> Comment: Use Latin—et al.—within parentheses. Use English—for example—outside of parentheses.

The second study produced the same
effect of information on putative
funniness of the jokes |F=9.878,| |p=000|.|

> Comment: APA—**Within parentheses**, use an ampersand (&) instead of the word *and* in the list of authors. If the authors are mentioned **outside of parentheses**, use the word **and**.

Jokes that were supposed to be funny were
rated as such; jokes that were not
supposed to be funny were not. Table 1
presents these results.

> Comment: APA—Degrees of freedom?

> Comment: Some researchers do not like to see *p*-value of .000; they prefer, *p*<.001. In any case, it would be inappropriate to say *p*=0 (with no decimal places).

There |wasn't| an effect of group
size on joke ratings, F|=0.426, p=.654|. There
was also no interaction between group size
and information, F|=1.714, p=.185|. These
results suggest that |since| groups affect
only displays of mirth, they do not have
an effect on cognitive evaluation of jokes.|

> Comment: Avoid contractions in formal writing.

> Comment: APA—Degrees of freedom? Also, use italics for statistic and the probability value.

> Comment: APA—Degrees of freedom?

> Comment: APA—*Since* is a temporal conjunction. The word *because* would be better.

Expectations and 8

Table 1. Mean ratings of jokes as a function of testing format and participants' expectations of the jokes.

> **Comment:** APA—Don't include vertical rules in your table.
>
> The table belongs on a separate page after the references.
>
> Also, the word Table should be in Roman, not italic letters, and the title of the table belongs on the next line.

Expectation	Very Unfunny	Very Funny	
Testing Format			
Individual	3.48	3.65	(3.56)
Group of 3 or 4	3.30	4.18	(3.72)
Group of 7 or 8	3.39	3.92	(3.66)
	(3.39)	(3.88)	

When people listen to jokes, they are likely to find them funny if they are skewed by the presentation and transmission of manipulated information. This is probably why professional comedians are able to get laughs from their audiences. *When there is a group*, it is likely that people are going to laugh because others do.

> **Comment:** Unclear referent—what does *they* refer to?

> **Comment:** More gobbledygook. Just say that what you tell people affects the way they behave.

> **Comment:** APA—Do not use italics for mere emphasis. For emphasis, use syntax.

Finally, these results provide one indication of how humor appreciation is multifaceted, one component being cognitive assessment. An interesting follow up would be to assess Martin & Gray's (1996) finding on how group effects and cognitive processes affect mirth responses in a controlled experimental setting.

> **Comment:** Use English—*and*—outside of parentheses; use Latin—the ampersand (&)—within parentheses.

Expectations and 9

References

Gavanski,I (1986). Differential
Sensitivity of Humor Ratings and Mirth
Responses to Cognitive and Affective
Components of the Humor Response.
*Journal of Personality and Social
Psychology,* 51(1), 209–214.

Levy, S.G., & Fenley, W.F. (1979) Audience
Size and Likelihood and Intensity of
Response During a Humorous Movie.
*Bulletin of the Psychonomic Society,
13(6),* 409–412.

Martin, G.N., & Gray, C.D. (1996). The
Effects of Audience Laughter on Men's
and Women's Responses to Humor. *The
Journal of Social Psychology, 136(2),*
221–231.

Nosanchuk, T.A., & Lightstone, J.(1974).
Canned Laughter and Public and Private
Conformity. *Journal of Personality and
Social Psychology, 29(1),* 153–156.

Source: D.J. Wimer & B.C. Beins (in press).
Expectations and perceived humor. *Humor:
International Journal of Humor Studies.*
Copyright Mouton de Gruyter. Adapted with
permission.

Comment: APA—References start on a separate page.

Capitalize only first word of titles of articles.

Comment: Include the issue number only if pagination in every issue starts at Page 1.

Appendix B

Corrected APA-Style Manuscript

The manuscript in this appendix shows how you create and format a manuscript in correct APA style. We have corrected the errors in the previous appendix, so the version here conforms to APA guidelines. This example includes two experiments. In most papers, you would include separate sections for the two studies, but for the purposes of this example, we combined them so the manuscript has the format you would use for a paper that reports a single study.

```
                                       Expectations and 1

        Running head: EXPECTATIONS AND PERCEIVED HUMOR


             Expectations and Perceived Humor

                      Wilhelm Wundt

                 Mann-Whitney University
```

Abstract

In two experiments, participants read and rated a set
of jokes for their humor value. In each experiment,
participants heard that others had previously rated
the jokes. In different conditions, participants
believed that the jokes had been rated low or
rated high by others. The results showed that when
participants thought others had rated the jokes as
very funny, their own ratings tended to be high. When
participants thought that others had rated the jokes
as not very funny, their own ratings were low. In a
control condition in which participants did not learn
that others had rated the jokes, their ratings were
between those of the other groups. The results suggest
that, because jokes do not have an intrinsic humor
level, people rely on cues from others to help them
decide how funny the jokes are.

Expectations and Perceived Humor

One difficulty in studying humor is that no reliable metric exists for measuring humor appreciation. Various individual and social characteristics are likely to affect one's evaluation of humorous material. The humor value of a joke depends on many factors, including the context in which the joke is encountered.

In the present study, I examined participants' reactions to jokes based on information I provided about the jokes. The research examined whether people's ratings of the humor value of a set of jokes would change if they learned that others had found the jokes more or less funny. Gavansky (1986) suggested that there is a difference between the internal and affective, emotional responses and the cognitive ratings of humor. Because joke ratings presumably involve the cognitive component, they might be susceptible to changes in evaluation based on information.

In addition, the research focused on the effect of group participation. Several researchers have documented the effect of group size on responses to humorous material. Generally, the effect of groups is on observable, mirth responses (e.g., Levy & Fenley, 1979); further, Nosanchuk and Lightstone (1974) noted that private and public responses to humorous material are different. Even an imaginary audience can affect mirth responses, as with canned laughter (Martin & Gray, 1996). That is, people's outward responses to humor differ depending on whether they are alone or in a group. At the same time, being in a group may not relate to cognitive evaluation, although being in a group may provide clues about how funny a joke "really" is.

Method

Participants

Ninety undergraduates participated in experiment 1, and 120 undergraduates participated in experiment 2. They volunteered in order to receive extra credit in psychology classes. The participants in the first study included 61 women and 29 men whose ages ranged from 17 to 23 years ($\underline{M}$ = 18.9, $\underline{s}$ = 1.2). The sample in the second study consisted of 83 women and 37 men whose ages ranged from 18 to 23 (M = 19.1, s = 1.1). They volunteered in order to receive extra credit in psychology classes.

Materials

In both experiments, 21 jokes appeared in a small booklet. The themes of the jokes varied, but were judged by a group of students to be typical of those that other college students would appreciate. The jokes came from disparate sources, such as *Isaac Asimov's Treasury of Humor* (Asimov, 1967) and various internet sites and other printed matter.

Procedure

Upon arrival and after completing informed consent, participants, who took part in the study in groups, rated a series of jokes on a scale of 1 (*not funny*) to 7 (*very funny*). The participants also learned that others had previously rated the jokes. Although everyone actually rated the same set of jokes, participants learned from the experimenter that all the jokes they would see had previously received ratings of (a) horribly unfunny, (b) not funny, (c) very funny, or (d) hysterically funny (Experiment 1), or not funny or very funny (Experiment 2). There was also a control condition in Experiment 1 that heard nothing specific about supposed previous ratings.

The two experiments differed in that, in Experiment 1, participants were in groups but I did not vary the group size systematically. In Experiment 2, I systematically varied group sizes. Participants rated the jokes alone, in groups of three or four, or in groups of seven or eight.

Expectations and 5

Results and Discussion

In Experiment 1, after learning about previous ratings, participants rated the jokes differently, $F(4, 85) = 8.591$, $p = .000$. When participants did not have expectations about the jokes, they rated them in the middle. The mean ratings were as follows: hysterically funny, 3.8; very funny, 4.9; control, 4.0; very unfunny, 3.1; and horribly unfunny, 3.6.

Although it is possible that participants were responding to demand characteristics, I do not believe this is true because the two extreme groups, Hysterically Funny and Horribly Unfunny, received the same ratings as the neutral group. Thus, our participants were quite capable of ignoring information that was clearly discrepant with reality. In fact, the jokes were neither horrible nor wonderful. The data show that the ratings in the neutral group fell slightly more positively than the middle point on a 7-point scale. When being debriefed, the participants reported that manipulation was not obvious to them.

In Experiment 2, I eliminated the two extreme categories (hysterically funny and horribly unfunny) and repeated the study with a systematic examination of the effects of group size. Previous research has suggested that being part of a group affects humor responses. If rating the jokes involves a cognitive evaluation, however, one might not expect to see an effect of group size on ratings, although outward expression of mirth might be susceptible to group effects (e.g., Levy & Fenley, 1979).

The second study produced the same effect of information on putative funniness of the jokes, $F(2, 114) = 9.878$, $p < .001$. Participants rated jokes that were supposed to be funny as such; jokes that were not supposed to be funny received lower ratings. Table 1 presents these results.

There was no effect of group size on joke ratings, $F(2,$ 114) $= 0.426$, $p = .654$. There was also no interaction between group size and information, $F(2, 114) = 1.714$, $p = .185$. These results suggest that, because group size affects only displays of mirth, they do not have an effect on cognitive evaluation of jokes.

People listening to jokes are likely to find the jokes funny if they receive information that predisposes them to view the humor as funny. This phenomenon is probably why professional comedians are able to get laughs from their audiences. When there is a group, it is likely that people are going to laugh because others do.

Finally, these results provide one indication of how humor appreciation is multifaceted, one component being cognitive assessment. An interesting follow up would be to assess Martin and Gray's (1996) finding on how group effects and cognitive processes affect affective, mirth responses in a controlled experimental setting.

Expectations and 7

References

Gavanski, I. (1986). Differential sensitivity of humor ratings and mirth responses to cognitive and affective components of the humor response. *Journal of Personality and Social Psychology*, 51, 209-214.

Levy, S. G., & Fenley, W. F. (1979). Audience size and likelihood and intensity of response during a humorous movie. *Bulletin of the Psychonomic Society*, 13, 409-412.

Martin, G. N., & Gray, C. D. (1996). The effects of audience laughter on men's and women's responses to humor. *The Journal of Social Psychology*, 136, 221-231.

Nosanchuk, T. A., & Lightstone, J. (1974). Canned laughter and public and private conformity. *Journal of Personality and Social Psychology*, 29, 153-156.

Table 1

Mean ratings of jokes as a function of testing format and participants' expectations of the jokes.

Expectation Testing Format	Very Unfunny	Very Funny	
Individual	3.48	3.65	(3.56)
Group of 3 or 4	3.30	4.18	(3.72)
Group of 7 or 8	3.39	3.92	(3.66)
	(3.39)	(3.88)	

References

American Psychological Association. (1997). *Publication Manual of the American Psychological Association*. Washington DC: Author.

American Psychological Association. (2001). *Getting in: A step-by-step plan for gaining admission to graduate school in psychology*. Washington DC: Author.

Amodio, D. M., Harmon-Jones, E., Devine, P. G., Curtin, J. J., Hartley, S. L., & Covert, A. E. (2004). Neural signals for the detection of unintentional race-bias. *Psychological Science, 15*, 88–93.

Asimov, I. (1967). *Isaac Asimov's Treasury of Humor*. Boston: Houghton-Mifflin.

Assurance of compliance with public health service (PHS) policy on humane care and use of laboratory animals. (2006). Retrieved November 21, 2006, from http://www.ithaca.edu/attorney/policies/vol2/Volume_2-222.htm

Baron, J., Bazerman, M. H., & Shonk, K. (2006). Enlarging the societal pie through wise legislation. *Perspectives on Psychological Science, 1*, 123–132.

Barry, D. (n.d.). The Internet explained. Retrieved January 29, 2007, from http://www.geocities.com/CollegePark/6174/db-Internet.htm

Becker, E. (1963). *The denial of death*. New York: Free Press.

Beins, B. C. (1993). Writing assignments in statistics classes encourage students to learn interpretation. *Teaching of Psychology, 20*, 161–164.

Beins, B. C. (2004). *Research methods: A tool for life*. Boston: Allyn & Bacon.

Beins, B. C. (2006). The scholarship of teaching and pedagogy. In W. Buskist and S. F. Davis (Eds.), *Handbook of the teaching of psychology* (pp. 11–15). Malden, MA: Blackwell.

Beins, B. C., Agnitti, J., Baldwin, V., Lapham, H., Yarmosky, S., Bubel, A., MacNaughton, K., & Pashka, N. (2005, October). How expectations affect perceptions of offensive humor. Poster presented at the annual convention of the New England Psychological Association, New Haven, CT.

Beran, M. J., Smith, J. D., Redford, J. S., & Washburn, D. A. (2006). Rhesus macaques (*Macaca mulatta*) monitor uncertainty during numerosity judgments. *Journal of Experimental Psychology: Animal Behavior Processes, 32*, 111–119.

Best, J. (2001). *Damned lies and statistics: Untangling numbers from the media, politicians, and activists*. Berkeley: University of California Press.

Best, J. (2004). *More damned lies and statistics: How numbers confuse public issues*. Berkeley: University of California Press.

Blum, T. (1984). Racial inequality and salience: An examination of Blau's theory of social structure. *Social Forces, 62*, 607–617.

Boag, S. (2006). Freudian repression, the common view, and pathological science. *Review of General Psychology, 10*, 74–86.

Brewer, B. W., Scherzer, C. B., Van Raalte, J. L., Petitpas, A. J., & Andersen, M. B.

(2001). The elements of (APA) style: A survey of psychology journal editors. *American Psychologist, 56,* 266–267.

Brannon, L. and Feist, J. (2006). *Health psychology: An introduction to behavior and health* (6th ed.). Belmont, CA: Wadsworth.

Brewin, C. (2003). *Posttraumatic stress disorder: Malady or myth?* New Haven: Yale University Press.

Britt, T. W. (2005). The effects of identity-relevance and task difficulty on task motivation, stress, and performance. *Motivation and Emotion, 29,* 198–202.

Bruchac, M. (1999, December). Thoughts on Indian names, images, and respect. Retrieved September 4, 2006, from http://freepages.genealogy.rootsweb.com/~massasoit/bruchac.htm

Cheating far more pervasive today than ever before say forum presenters, (2004, March 20). *Ethics Today Online, 2*(7). Retrieved January 29, 2007, from http://www.ethics.org/

Children's Defense Fund. (1994). *The state of America's children yearbook—1994.* Washington DC: Author.

Cohen, D., & Strayer, J. (1996). Empathy in conduct-disordered and comparison youth. *Developmental Psychology, 32,* 988–998.

College Board. (2004). *Writing: A ticket to work. . . or a ticket out. A survey of business leaders.* New York: Author. Retrieved from http://www.writingcommission.org/prod_downloads/writingcom/writing-ticket-to-work.pdf

Cronin, K. L., Fazio, V. C., & Beins, B. C. (1998, April). Mood does not affect the funniness of jokes but jokes affect your mood. Presented at the Thirteenth Annual University of Scranton Psychology Conference, Scranton, PA.

Daniel, D. (2004, January). How to use technology to ruin a perfectly good lecture. Presentation at the annual National Institute on the Teaching of Psychology, St. Petersburg Beach, FL.

DePalma, M. T., Madey, S. F., Tillman, T. C., & Wheeler, J. (2000). Perceived patient responsibility and belief in a just world affect helping. *Basic and Applied Social Psychology, 21,* 131–137.

Devine, P. G. (1989). Stereotypes and prejudice: Their automatic and controlled components. *Journal of Personality and Social Psychology, 56,* 5–18.

de Vogel, V., Y de Ruiter, C. (2005). The HCR-20 in personality disordered female offenders: A comparison with a matched sample of males. *Clinical Psychology & Psychotherapy. Special Issue: Forensic Psychology, 12,* 226–240.

Dutton, D. (1999, February 5). Language crimes: a lesson in how not to write, courtesy of the professoriate. *The Wall Street Journal.* Retrieved February 19, 2007, from http://denisdutton.com/language_crimes.htm

Essentials for animal research: a primer for research personnel. (1995). Retrieved November 21, 2006, from http://www.nal.usda.gov/awic/pubs/noawicpubs/essentia.htm

Eysenck, H. J. (1971). Personality and sexual adjustment. *British Journal of Psychiatry, 118,* 593–608.

Eysenck, H. J. (1991). Personality, stress, and disease: An interactionist perspective. *Psychological Inquiry, 2,* 221–232.

Eysenck, H. J., & Eysenck, S. B. G. (1967). *Personality structure and measurement.* London: Routledge & Kegan Paul.

Fairburn, C. B., Welch, S. L., Norman, P. A., O'Connor, B. A., & Doll, H. A. (1996). Bias and bulimia nervosa: How typical are clinical cases? *American Journal of Psychiatry, 153,* 386–391.

Felton, M., & Lyon, D. O. (1966). The post-reinforcement pause. *Journal of the Experimental Analysis of Behavior, 9,* 131–134.

France, C. M. & Uhlin, B. D. (2006). Narrative as an outcome domain in psychosis. *Psychology & Psychotherapy: Theory, Research & Practice, 79,* 53–67.

Friedman, H. S., & Booth-Kewley, S. (1987). The disease-prone personality: A meta-analytic view of the construct. *American Psychologist, 42,* 539–555.

Gallo, L. C., Troxel, W. M., Matthews, K. A., & Kuller, L. H. (2003). Marital status and quality in middle-aged women: Associations with levels and trajectories of cardiovascular risk factors. *Health Psychology, 22,* 453–463. Retrieved February 13, 2007, from http://www.apa.org/journals/releases/hea225453.pdf

García, A. E. & Ostrosky-Solís, F. (2006). From morality to moral emotions. *International Journal of Psychology, 41,* 348–354.

Goldenberg, J. L., Pyszczynski, T. McCoy, K. M., Greenberg, J., & Solomon, S. (1999). Death, sex, love, and neuroticism: Why is sex such a problem? *Journal of Personality and Social Psychology, 77,* 1173–1187.

Grandey, A. A., Fisk, G. M., & Steiner, D. D. (2005). Must "service with a smile" be stressful? The moderating role of personal control for American and French employees. *Journal of Applied Psychology, 90,* 893–904.

Gross, T., & Miller, D. (2006, May 17). Fresh Air [Radio broadcast]. Philadelphia, PA: National Public Radio.

Haggerty, R. J. (1980). Life stress, illness and social supports. *Developmental Medicine and Childhood Neurology, 22,* 391–400.

Halpern, D. F., Smothergill, D. W., Allen, M., Baker, S., Baum, C., Best, D. et al. (1998). Scholarship in psychology: A paradigm for the twenty-first century. *American Psychologist, 53,* 1292–1297.

Hatch, R. A. (n.d.). How to write a college paper {not}. Retrieved February 15, 2007, from http://web.clas.ufl.edu/users/rhatch/pages/02-TeachingResources/readingwriting/05-write-not_txt.htm

Holland, A. (2007). Eureka! The importance of good science writing. Retrieved March 14, 2007, from http://www.writersblock.ca/winter2002/essay.htm

Huesmann, L. R., Moise-Titus, J., Podolski, C. L., & Eron, L. (2003). Longitudinal relations between children's exposure to TV violence and their aggressive and violent behavior in young adulthood: 1977–1982. *Developmental Psychology, 39,* 201–221. Retrieved February 13, 2007, from http://www.apa.org/journals/releases/dev392201.pdf

Huff, D. (1954). *How to lie with statistics.* New York: W. W. Norton.

Hyde, J. S. (2005). The gender similarities hypothesis. *American Psychologist, 60,* 581–592. Retrieved February 13, 2007, from http://www.apa.org/journals/releases/amp606581.pdf

Hymes, R. W., Leinart, M., Rowe, S., & Rogers, W. (1993). Acquaintance rape: The effect of race of defendant and race of victim on White juror decisions. *Journal of Social Psychology, 133,* 627–634.

Jackson, B., Kubzansky, L. D., & Wright, R. J. (2006). Linking the perceived unfairness to physical health: The perceived unfairness model. *Review of General Psychology, 10,* 21–40.

Jacobs, M. A., Spilken, A., & Norman, M. (1969). Relation of life change, maladaptive aggression, and upper respiratory infection in male college students. *Psychosomatic Medicine, 31,* 31–43.

Jafari-Sabet, M. (2006). NMDA receptor blockers prevents the facilitatory effects of post-training intra-dorsal hippocampal NMDA and physostigmine on memory retention of passive avoidance learning in rats. *Behavioral Brain Research, 169,* 120–127.

Jayson, Sharon. A right time to fool around. Study: infidelity can be biological. *USA Today* January 4, 2006: 7d.

Josselson, R., & Lieblich, A. (1996). Fettering the mind in the name of "science." *American Psychologist, 51,* 651–652.

Kaiser, C. R., Vick, S. B., & Major, B. (2006). Prejudice expectations moderate preconscious attention to cues that are threatening to social identity. *Psychological Science, 17,* 332–338.

Keegan, D. A., & Bannister, S. L. (2003). Effect of colour coordination of attire with poster presentation on poster popularity. *Canadian Medical Association Journal, 169,* 1291–1292.

Kendall, P. C., Silk, J. S., & Chu, B. C. (2000). Introducing your research report: Writing the introduction (pp. 41–57). In R. J. Sternberg, *Guide to publishing in psychology journals,* New York: Cambridge.

Kemeny, M. E., & Laudenslager, M. L. (1999). Introduction beyond stress: The role of individual difference factors in psychoneuroimmunology. *Brain, Behavior, and Immunity, 13,* 73–75.

Killeen, P. R. (2005). An alternative to null-hypothesis significance tests. *Psychological Science, 16,* 345–353.

Klinesmith, J., Kasser, T., & McAndrew, F. T. (2006). Guns, testosterone, and aggression: An experimental test of a mediational hypothesis. *Psychological Science, 17,* 568–571.

Korn, J. H. (1998). The reality of deception. *American Psychologist, 53,* 805.

Kruger, J., & Dunning, D. (1999). Unskilled and unaware of it: How difficulties in recognizing one's own incompetence lead to inflated self-assessments. *Journal of Personality and Social Psychology, 77,* 121–134.

LaGreca, A. M., Silverman, W. K., Vernberg, E. M., & Prinstein, M. J. (1996). Symptoms of posttraumatic stress in children after Hurricane Andrew: A prospective study. *Journal of Counseling and Clinical Psychology, 54,* 712–723.

Lawson, C. (1995). Research participation as a contract. *Ethics and Behavior, 5,* 205–215.

Licensing and registration under the animal welfare act: Guidelines for dealers, exhibitors, transporters, and researchers. (2004). Retrieved November 19, 2006, from http://www.aphis.usda.gov/lpa/pubs/awlicreg.html

Lynch, M., & Haney, C. (2000). Discrimination and instructional comprehension: Guided discretion, racial bias, and the death penalty. *Law and Human Behavior, 24,* 337–358.

Martin, J., & McGaffick, S. (2001, February). The effects of mood induction on humor appreciation. Poster presented at the University of Scranton Psychology Conference, Scranton, PA.

Mathie, V. A., Buskist, W., Carlson, J. F., Davis, S. F., Johnson, D. E., & Smith, R. A. (2004). Expanding the boundaries of scholarship in psychology through teaching, research, service, and administration. *Teaching of Psychology, 31,* 233–241.

Matters, G., & Burnett, P. C. (2003). Psychological predictors of the propensity to omit short-response items on a high-stakes achievement test. *Educational and Psychological Measurement, 63,* 239–256.

Milgram, S. (2003). The perils of obedience. In L. Behrens and L. J. Rosen (Eds.), *Writing and reading across the curriculum* (8th ed.) (pp. 316–328). New York: Longman. (Reprinted from 1974. Obedience to authority. *Harper's Magazine*)

Moscovice, L. R., & Snowdon, C. T. (2006). The role of social context and individual experience in novel task acquisition in cottontop tamarins, *Saguinus oedipus. Animal Behaviour, 71,* 933–943.

National Institute of Mental Health (NIMH). (2005). *Facts about NIMH.* Retrieved August 28, 2006, from http://www.nimh.nih.gov/about/nimh.cfm

Nordgren, L. F., van der Pligt, J., & van Harreveld, F. (2006). Visceral drives in retrospect. *Psychological Science, 17,* 635–640.

O'Connor, J. (2002). Literacy in context for GSCE student's book. Cambridge: Cambridge University Press.

Ortmann, A., & Hertwig, R. (1997). Is deception acceptable? *American Psychologist, 52,* 746–747.

Pashka, N. J., Agnitti, J. Y., Bubel, A., MacNaughton, K. B., & Beins, B. C. (2005, April).

Humor in groups: Appreciated but not remembered. Presented at the Eastern Colleges Science Conference, New Britain, CT.

Penslar, R. L. (n.d.). Office for Human Research Protections (OHRP): IRB Guidebook. Retrieved November 19, 2006, from http://www.hhs.gov/ohrp/irb/irb_guidebook.htm

Petty, R. E. & Cacioppo, J. T. (1986). *Communication and persuasion: Central and peripheral routes to attitude change.* New York: Springer-Verlag.

Piferi, R. L., Jobe, R. L., & Jones, W. H. (2006). Giving to others during national tragedy: The effects of altruistic and egoistic motivations on long-term giving. *Journal of Social and Personal Relationships, 2,* 171–184.

Plous, S. (1996). Attitudes toward the use of animals in psychological research and education. *American Psychologist, 51,* 918–927.

Public Broadcasting Service (PBS). (1995–2006). *About PBS: Welcome.* Retrieved August 28, 2006, from http://www.pbs.org/aboutpbs/

Public health service policy on humane care and use of laboratory animals. (2002). Retrieved November 21, 2006, from http://grants.nih.gov/grants/olaw/references/phspol.htm

Rader, N., & Vaughn, L. A. (2000). Infant reaching to a hidden affordance: Evidence for intentionality. *Infant Behavior & Development, 23,* 531–541.

Rank, O. (1936). *Will therapy.* New York: Norton.

Ray, O. (2004). How the mind hurts and heals the body. *American Psychologist, 59,* 29–40.

Reder, L. M., Oates, J. M., Thornton, E. R., Quinlan, J. J., Kaufer, A., & Sauer, J. (2006). Drug-induced amnesia hurts recognition, but only for memories that can be unitized. *Psychological Science, 17,* 562–567.

Rescorla, R. A. (2006). Deepened extinction from compound stimulus presentation. *Journal of Experimental Psychology: Animal Behavior Processes, 32,* 135–144.

Roberts, R. D., Zeidner, M., & Matthews, G. (2001). Does emotional intelligence meet traditional standards for an intelligence? Some new data and conclusions. *Emotion, 1,* 196–231.

Rosen, G. M. (2004). *Posttraumatic stress disorder: Issues and controversies.* Chichester, UK: John Wiley & Sons.

Rosenthal, R., & Fode, K. L. (1963). The effect of experimenter bias on the performance of the albino rat. *Behavioral Science, 8,* 183–189.

Rosnow, R. L., & Rosenthal, R. (1993). *Beginning behavioral research: A conceptual primer.* New York: Macmillan.

Russano, M. B., Meissner, C. A., Narchet, F. M., & Kassin, S. M. (2005). Investigating true and false confessions within a novel experimental paradigm. *Psychological Science, 16,* 481–486.

Salovey, P. (2000). Results that get results: Telling a good story. In R. J. Sternberg (Ed.), *Guide to publishing in psychology journals* (pp. 121–132). New York: Cambridge University Press.

Salovey, P., & Grewal, D. (2005). The science of emotional intelligence, *Current Directions in Psychological Science, 14,* 281–285.

Scheibe, C. L. (2004). A deeper sense of literacy: Curriculum-driven approaches to media literacy in the K-12 classroom. *American Behavioral Scientist, 48,* 60–68.

Schutte, N. S., Malouff, J. M., Hall, L. E., Haggerty, D. J., Cooper, J. T., Golden, C. J., & Dornheim, L. (1998). Development and validation of a measure of emotional intelligence. *Personality and Individual Differences, 25,* 167–177.

Senecal, C., Vallerand, R. J., Guay, F. (2001). Antecedents and outcomes of work-family conflict: Toward a motivational model. *Personality and Social Psychology Bulletin, 27,* 176–186.

Shatzman, K. B., & McQueen, J. M. (2006). Prosodic knowledge affects the recognition of newly acquired words. *Psychological Science, 17,* 372–377.

Smith, R. A. (2006, August). Teaching of Psychology editor's report. Presented at the business meeting of the Society for Teaching of Psychology at the annual convention of the American Psychological Association, New Orleans, LA.

Sommer, R. (2006). Dual dissemination: Writing for colleagues and the public. *American Psychologist, 61*, 955–958.

Sommers, S. R., & Ellsworth, P. C. (2000). Race in the courtroom: Perceptions of guilt and dispositional attributions. *Personality and Social Psychology Bulletin, 26*, 1367–1379.

Sommers, S. R., & Ellsworth, P. C. (2001). White juror bias: An investigation of prejudice against black defendants in the American courtroom. *Psychology, Public Policy, and Law, 7*, 201–229.

Stephenson, H., Pena-Shaff, J., Quirk, P. (2006). Predictors of college student suicidal ideation: Gender differences. *College Student Journal, 40*, 109–117.

Stephenson, J. H., Belesis, M. P., & Balliet, W. E. (2005). Variability in college student suicide: Age, gender, and race. *Journal of College Student Psychotherapy, 19*, 5–33.

Summary report of journal operations. (2005). *American Psychologist, 61*, 559–560.

Thomas, G. V., & Blackman, D. (1992). The future of animal studies in psychology. *American Psychologist, 47*, 1679.

Tufte, E. R. (1983). *The visual display of quantitative information.* Cheshire, CT: Graphics Press.

Uhlmann, E. L., & Cohen, G. L. (2005). Constructed criteria: Redefining merit to justify discrimination. *Psychological Science, 16*, 474–480.

University of Kent at Canterbury. (2006). Plagiarism: Important information for psychology students. Retrieved December 3, 2006, from the Department of Psychology Web site: http://www.kent.ac.uk/psychology/studying/studyskills/plagiarism.htm

Vorauer, J. D., & Sakamoto, Y. (2006). I thought we could be friends, but. . .: Systematic miscommunication and defensive distancing as obstacles to cross-group friendship formation. *Psychological Science, 17*, 326–331.

Wang, Q. (2006). Earliest recollections of self and others in European American and Taiwanese young adults. *Psychological Science, 17*, 708–714.

Wang, S., & Baillargeon, R. (2005). Inducing infants to detect a physical violation in a single trial. *Psychological Science, 16*, 542–549.

Warren, J. M. (1965). The comparative psychology of learning. *Annual Review of Psychology, 16*, 95–118.

Weary, G., Vaughn, L. A., Steward, B. D., & Edwards, J. A. (2006). Adjusting for the correspondence bias: Effects of causal uncertainty, cognitive busyness, and causal strength of situational information. *Journal of Experimental Social Psychology, 42*, 87–94.

Weise, E. (2006, August 22). Men, women: Maybe we are different . . . ; New book argues that the female brain is wired to nurture. *USA Today*, p. 9d.

Whipple, G. M. (1910). The teaching of psychology in normal schools. *Psychological Monographs, 12*(4, Whole No. 51), 2–40.

Wilkinson, L. (1999). Statistical methods in psychology journals: Guidelines and explanations. *American Psychologist, 54*, 594–604.

Wimer, D.J., & Beins, B. C. (In press). Expectations and perceived humor. *Humor: International Journal of Humor Studies.*

Winer, B. J., Brown, D. R., & Michels, K. M. (1991). *Statistical principles in experimental design* (3rd ed.). New York: McGraw Hill.

Zeidner, M., Shani-Zinovich, I., Matthews, G., & Roberts, R. D. (2005). Assessing emotional intelligence in gifted and non-gifted high school students: Outcomes depend on the measure. *Intellitelligence, 33*, 369–391.

Subject Index

Author Index